SEGREGATION AND APARTHEID IN TWENTIETH-CENTURY SOUTH AFRICA

Edited by William Beinart and Saul Dubow

 Routledge
Taylor & Francis Group

LONDON AND NEW YORK

First published 1995
by Routledge
11 New Fetter Lane, London EC4P 4EE

Simultaneously published in the USA and Canada
by Routledge
29 West 35th Street, New York, NY 10001

Transferred to Digital Printing 2003

Routledge is an imprint of the Taylor & Francis Group

Typeset in Palatino by
Florencetype Ltd, Stoodleigh, Devon

Printed and bound in Great Britain by
Selwood Printing Ltd, West Sussex

British Library Cataloguing in Publication Data
A catalogue record for this book is available from the British Library

Library of Congress Cataloguing in Publication Data
Segregation and apartheid in twentieth-century South Africa / edited
by William Beinart and Saul Dubow.
p. cm. — (Rewriting histories)
Includes bibliographical references.
1. Apartheid—South Africa.   2. South Africa—Race relations.
3. South Africa—History—1909–1961.   4. South Africa—
History—1960– I. Beinart, William. II. Dubow, Saul.
III. Series.
DT1757.S44 1995
323.1'68'0904—dc20 94-36134

ISBN 0–415–10356–8 (hbk) ISBN 0–415–10357–6 (pbk)

CONTENTS

use summaries of each

v

CONTENTS

SERIES EDITOR'S PREFACE

Rewriting history, or revisionism, has always followed closely in the wake of history writing. In their efforts to re-evaluate the past, professional as well as amateur scholars have followed many approaches, most commonly as empiricists, uncovering new information to challenge earlier accounts. Historians have also revised previous versions by adopting new perspectives, usually fortified by new research, which overturn received views.

Even though rewriting is constantly taking place, historians' attitudes towards using new interpretations have been anything but settled. For most, the validity of revisionism lies in providing a stronger, more convincing account that better captures the objective truth of the matter. Although such historians might agree that we never finally arrive at the 'truth', they believe it exists and over time may be better approximated. At the other extreme stand scholars who believe that each generation or even each cultural group or subgroup necessarily regards the past differently, each creating for itself a more usable history. Although these latter scholars do not reject the possibility of demonstrating empirically that some contentions are better than others, they focus upon generating new views based upon different life experiences. Different truths exist for different groups. Surely such an understanding, by emphasizing subjectivity, further encourages rewriting history. Between these two groups are those historians who wish to borrow from both sides. This third group, while accepting that every congeries of individuals sees matters differently, still wishes somewhat contradictorily to fashion a broader history that incorporates both of these particular visions. Revisionists who stress empiricism fall into the first of the three camps, while others spread out across the board.

Today the rewriting of history seems to have accelerated to a blinding speed as a consequence of the evolution of revisionism. A variety of approaches has emerged. A major factor in this process has been the enormous increase in the number of researchers. This explosion has reinforced and enabled the retesting of many assertions. Significant ideological shifts have also played a major part in the growth of revisionism. First, the crisis of Marxism, culminating in the events in Eastern Europe in 1989, has given rise to doubts about explicitly Marxist accounts. Such doubts have spilled over into the entire field of social history which has been a dominant subfield of the discipline for several decades. Focusing on society and its class divisions implied that these are the most important elements in historical analysis. Because Marxism was built on the same claim, the whole basis of social history has been questioned, despite the very many studies that directly had little to do with Marxism. Disillusionment with social history simultaneously opened the door to cultural and linguistic approaches largely developed in anthropology and literature. Multi-culturalism and feminism further generated revisionism. By claiming that scholars had, wittingly or not, operated from a white European/American male point of view, newer researchers argued that other approaches had been neglected or misunderstood. Not surprisingly, these last historians are the most likely to envision each subgroup rewriting its own usable history, while other scholars incline towards revisionism as part of the search for some stable truth.

Rewriting Histories will make these new approaches available to the student population. Often new scholarly debates take place in the scattered issues of journals which are sometimes difficult to find. Furthermore, in these first interactions, historians tend to address one another, leaving out the evidence that would make their arguments more accessible to the uninitiated. This series of books will collect in one place a strong group of the major articles in selected fields, adding notes and introductions conducive to improved understanding. Editors will select articles containing substantial historical data, so that students – at least those who approach the subject as an objective phenomenon – can advance not only their comprehension of debated points but also their grasp of substantive aspects of the subject.

The study of segregation and apartheid provides a long history of revisions of common understandings. Scholarly opinion had held that forms of white domination related particularly to the racism of the Afrikaner population. More recently, historians pointed to British culpability and economic motivations. While historians have not abandoned these last two factors, this volume emphasizes both the role of ideas and the ability of black South Africans to resist control. Also included are essays documenting the ironies and contradictory effects of segregation and apartheid. Recognizable in the transformation of this subject are trends present in other historical fields. Of particular interest is the emphasis here on agency, in this case of blacks. More generally, this approach might be added to those responsible for changing the entire field of history.

Jack R. Censer

ACKNOWLEDGEMENTS

All extracts and articles published in this volume, with the exception of the piece by Martin Legassick, have already been published. We would like to thank the following copyright holders for permission to reproduce their work:

Maynard Swanson, '"The Sanitation Syndrome": Bubonic Plague and Urban Native Policy in the Cape Colony, 1900–1909', *Journal of African History* 18 (1977) (Cambridge University Press).

Harold Wolpe, 'Capitalism and Cheap-Labour Power in South Africa: From Segregation to Apartheid', *Economy and Society* 1 (1972) (Routledge).

S. Marks, 'Natal, the Zulu Royal Family and the Ideology of Segregation', *Journal of Southern African Studies* 4 (1978).

B. Bozzoli, 'Marxism, Feminism and Southern African Studies', *Journal of Southern African Studies* 9 (1983).

S. Dubow, 'The Elaboration of Segregationist Ideology', in *Racial Segregation and the Origins of Apartheid in South Africa c. 1919–1936* (Macmillan, 1989).

W. Beinart, 'Chieftaincy and the Concept of Articulation: South Africa c. 1900–1950', *Canadian Journal of African Historical Studies* 19 (1985).

D. Posel, 'The Meaning of Apartheid Before 1948: Conflicting Interests and Forces within the Afrikaner Nationalist Alliance', *Journal of Southern African Studies* 14 (1987).

H. Giliomee, 'The Growth of Afrikaner Identity', in H. Adam and H. Giliomee, *Ethnic Power Mobilized: Can South Africa Change?*

(Yale University Press, 1979).

C. Murray, 'Displaced Urbanization: South Africa's Rural Slums', *African Affairs* 86 (1987).

J. Peires (anon.), 'Ethnicity and Pseudo-Ethnicity in the Ciskei', in L. Vail (ed.), *The Creation of Tribalism in Southern Africa* (James Currey, 1989).

All papers except Murray's Peires's and Posel's have been extracted, shortened and/or adapted for this volume. The present volume is intended primarily for students of modern South African history. Those with scholarly interests in particular articles are advised to consult the originals.

TABLES AND MAPS

TABLES

MAPS

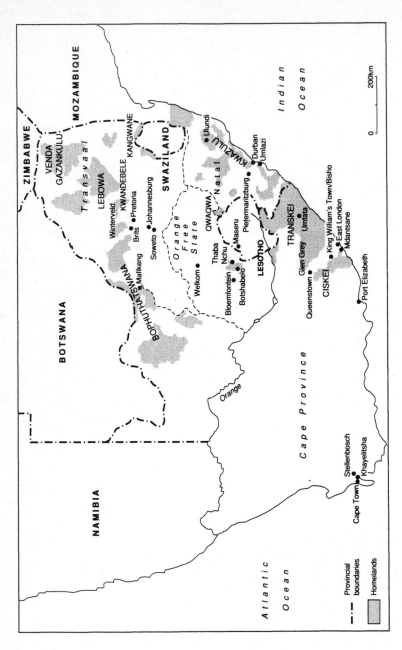

Map 0.1 South Africa c. 1980

INTRODUCTION:

The historiography of segregation and apartheid[1]

William Beinart and Saul Dubow

THE MEANING AND CONTEXT OF SEGREGATION

Segregation was the name coined in early twentieth-century South Africa for the set of government policies and social practices which sought to regulate the relationship between white and black, colonizers and colonized. Many elements of segregation had precursors in the period of Dutch rule between 1652 and 1806, as well as in the nineteenth-century Boer republics and British colonies.[2] But it was only in the twentieth century that the ideology of segregation was refined and the reach of the system fully extended. This followed a lengthy historical process which saw the final conquest of African chiefdoms in the 1890s and the consolidation of the boundaries of the South African state in the aftermath of the 1899–1902 South African War. Modern segregation represented a response to the industrialization of the subcontinent, initiated by the discovery and exploitation of diamonds and gold from the 1860s. It arose out of the modernizing dynamics of a newly industrializing society and was therefore not, as some have suggested, a mere carryover into the twentieth century of older traditions of slavery, agrarian paternalism or frontier conflict.

South Africa differed from most colonial territories in Africa in that it attracted a high proportion of European settlers. The southern tip of the continent was not the first port of call for European mariners. Their presence was felt earlier in West Africa which had been the centre of trade in tropical commodities and slaves from the sixteenth century. But in West Africa, so an early Portuguese sailor wrote, 'God has placed a striking angel with a flaming sword of deadly fevers, who prevents us from penetrating . . . to

1

the springs of this garden'.[3] Diseases such as malaria, blackwater fever and trypanasomiasis, so inimical to white settlement there, proved far less of an obstacle in the more temperate south. And the hinterland of Cape Town, the first node of settlement, was populated by small and dispersed communities of Khoisan ('Bushman' and 'Hottentot') peoples who were far less equipped to offer effective armed resistance than the large kingdoms of West Africa.

Southern Africa also differed from most New World colonies in the Americas and Australasia in that the bulk of the indigenous population suffered no major demographic setback. True, the hunter-gatherer San and pastoral Khoikhoi suffered severely from new diseases, especially smallpox. But the black African communities who dominated the eastern half of the subcontinent had already been exposed to many of the diseases which the settlers brought with them. They were more numerous than the Khoisan and their mixed economic system of pastoralism and cultivation gave them a far more certain food supply and political capacity. Contrary to the expectations of some nineteenth-century European observers who believed that the indigenous peoples of the subcontinent would 'die out' in the face of European settlement, this was patently not the case in southern Africa where the apparent 'vigour' of Africans helped to fuel colonial fears arising from their demographic superiority.[4] Whereas colonial labour supplies in the New World were largely drawn from imported slaves and immigrants, in South Africa it was largely indigenous African people who laboured on the settler farms, in the rich gold mines, and later in the factories.

By 1910, after two and a half centuries of immigration and expansion, a little over 20 per cent of the population within the newly unified country was classified as white or European. This percentage was probably greater than in any other African context and remained relatively stable until the 1960s. Yet, even at the height of their power, whites were a minority of the country's population. After 1960, they became a declining minority in the face of rapid black population growth. Segregation thus developed in a context in which Europeans had conquered the indigenous population but could only partially displace it. The fact that white settlers and indigenous Africans were not the only established communities added to the complex form that segregation took: in the Cape a group known as 'coloureds' (descendants of the Khoisan, imported slaves and settlers) came to occupy an intermediate social position between black Africans and whites. The importation of Indian indentured workers into Natal from the 1860s gave rise to another legally defined racial group whose status in the social hierarchy was likewise ambiguous.

Social divisions in this colonial society increasingly took on a rigid racial character. After Union in 1910, white power was used to forge one of the most extreme forms of racial discrimination in the twentieth-century world. This system, which matured from segregation to apartheid in the second half of the century, has long been at the heart of political debates in the country. It has also become a central issue for historians and social scientists. Whereas the strength and size of the settler population in the United States, Canada or Australia meant that race relations were for many years relegated to the peripheries of national historiography, race was an abiding concern even in the most inward-looking settler histories of South Africa. Only certain Afrikaner historians felt able to produce a version of the country's history that concentrated very largely on themselves.[5]

As the political tension between white and black intensified, so competing explanations of segregation and apartheid proliferated. The extracts presented here are drawn from literature published over the last twenty years of debate. Essays have not been selected because they represent 'the best' or most recent thinking in South African historiography. Nor do they fully reflect the experiences of black South Africans and their political struggles against white control. Our intention is more restricted. The choice has been circumscribed by an attempt to follow some of the most interesting contributions to the debate on the causes and content of racial segregation. We also include material which tries to explain how apartheid (Afrikaans for 'apartness') was developed and applied by the Afrikaner National Party, after it came to power under D.F. Malan in 1948. The distinction between segregation (from about 1900 to 1948) and apartheid (from 1948 to 1990) is generally followed in the extracts.

Segregation in South Africa encompassed many different social relationships. It is often discussed as a series of legislative Acts which removed and restricted the rights of 'non-whites' in every possible sphere. Among the most important of these measures were the 1911 Mines and Works Act (segregation in employment), the 1913 Natives Land Act (segregation in the countryside and prohibitions on African land purchase), the 1923 Natives (Urban Areas) Act (urban residential segregation), the 1936 Representation of Natives Act (abolition of the remnant African franchise) and the 1936 Native Trust and Land Act (an elaboration of the 1913 Land Act). One of the distinctive aspects of South Africa was the range and extent of its discriminatory legislation. Many facilities and services – from education and health, to transport and recreation – were progressively restricted and divided on a racial basis, more tightly than under the 'Jim Crow' laws in the United States.[6] Even sexual relationships between individuals of different colour were officially proscribed.

Segregation was, however, more than a panoply of restrictive legislation: it refers as well to a composite ideology and set of practices seeking to legitimize social difference and economic inequality in every aspect of life. Many of the spatial and social elements of segregation, such as the division of churches on the basis of colour, were initially governed by convention rather than law. Similarly, the exclusion of blacks from skilled work, and especially from the exercise of supervisory functions over whites, was determined by custom as well as legislative bars. The system of large-scale oscillating labour migration (cited by a number of scholars as one of the core institutions of segregation and apartheid) is another case in point. Black labourers' freedom of movement was certainly curtailed by pass laws. But the evolution and functioning of the migrant labour system depended too on a range of social and cultural assumptions, not all of which were legislatively enshrined.

EXPLAINING SEGREGATION

Explanations of segregation, like many recent historical debates, have veered between the materialist and the ideological, the structuralist and the individualist. On the one hand, scholars have tried to explore the thinking and ideas behind various phases of racial legislation and segregatory practice, questioning why colour became such a critical faultline of social division. On the other, they have examined the ways in which rigid forms of racial discrimination have helped to facilitate capitalist growth and provide whites with material and political benefits. The different forms of explanation are not mutually exclusive, nor has

4

there necessarily been agreement within shared paradigms. In the 1970s and early 1980s, when a powerful left and materialist critique of existing historiography was developed, approaches polarized and debates became more intense. Many academics took seriously Marx's dictum that their task was not just to interpret the world but to change it; from this it seemed to follow that a scholar's political affiliation and commitment were revealed by his or her interpretation of history. Since then, South African historiography has become more eclectic and varied – and perhaps less passionate.

For many years, historical explanation of racial separation was dominated by the assumption that its main agents were the Dutch-speaking descendants of the earlier settlers, the Boers or Afrikaners. Though their origins were diverse (including French and German immigrants and also some admixture with slaves), a broad Afrikaner identity was gradually constructed from the late nineteenth century. Political unity proved elusive but, by the 1920s, an elaborate ethnic and linguistically based nationalist movement reached into every aspect of Afrikaner social existence. English-speaking historians suggested Afrikaners had absorbed rigid racial attitudes in the era of slavery (to 1834). Boer frontier graziers were seen to have had a harsh and conflictual relationship with the Africans they encountered, culminating in a long series of wars throughout the late eighteenth and nineteenth centuries. When a minority of Afrikaners trekked to the interior in the 1830s and 1840s, the states they established excluded non-whites from citizenship.

The idea of a continuity of Afrikaner racism become bound up with the argument that the frontier had shaped South Africa – just as it had shaped the national character of the United States. Pre-Enlightenment values, it was suggested, had been carried over into the political and industrial structures of the twentieth century – 'new frontiers for old', as C.W. de Kiewiet, the doyen of early liberal scholarship, crisply expressed it.[7] Evidence of such attitudes was sought in the social and religious tenets of Calvinism and in the values of stubborn independence and exclusivity that these were supposed to have engendered. Afrikaner nationalist historians themselves stressed the continuity of the people (*volk*) and its identity in the battle against acquisitive British imperialism, on the one hand, and swamping by the 'uncivilized' black hordes, on the other.

5

This explanation appeared all the more convincing at the height of Afrikaner Nationalist rule from 1924 to 1933 and again after 1948, when racial legislation was relentlessly driven through parliament. Some English-speaking historians argued that a society ordered on racial lines was not a foregone conclusion. An alternative had briefly seemed possible in the nineteenth-century Cape when a mid-Victorian British parliament, together with local allies, developed a form of colonial self-government which was potentially non-racial in character. Blacks were admitted to a qualified franchise on the same basis as whites and a group of largely English-speaking colonials – liberals, missionaries and merchants – attempted to defend this arrangement, albeit (as Trapido has pointed out) not purely from humanitarian motives.[8] A major theme in liberal historiography from the 1930s onwards, therefore, is the idea that the tragedy of race relations in South Africa reflects the capitulation of English-speakers' flexible views to the harshly doctrinaire approach of Afrikaner nationalism.

While many English-speakers did initially oppose apartheid after 1948, there is a different British legacy to explore in the history of colonization in Natal. David Welsh took up the suggestion that the establishment of African reserves and the survival of African chieftaincy as central elements of segregation originated not in the Boer republics, but in Natal, the most British of colonies.[9] The system of control developed by Theophilus Shepstone, for many years Secretary of Native Affairs, devolved substantial local control to African chiefs who were seen as the best guarantors of a stable social order. Natal's version of segregation, it was subsequently argued by Shula Marks, reflected distinctively British colonial racial ideas. Rather like the practice of indirect rule elsewhere in colonial Africa, its form resulted from the relative weakness of the colonial state and its dependence on the taxation of African peasants. Segregation in Natal therefore represented an attempt by colonial authorities both to gain access to African labour and to control the 'still pulsating remains of powerful African kingdoms'.[10]

One of the most striking analyses of the British imperial role in creating a segregated social order was Maynard Swanson's work, reprinted here, on bubonic plague. When the plague reached Cape Town in 1901, the government and medical authorities decided to remove thousands of Africans from the city centre in the belief that this would facilitate plague control. In 1902,

6

legislation was passed providing for more systematic long-term urban residential segregation by the creation of peri-urban African locations. Swanson's analysis constituted a significant academic breakthrough. First, he located urban segregation firmly within the world of the British empire at the turn of the century, rather than as part of a Boer or specifically South African legacy. Second, he argued for the power of ideas in shaping political initiatives. Third, Swanson began to suggest how popular everyday racial imagery and ideas about pollution and infection could intersect with more formal medical theory to produce segregationist policies.

The wave of radical scholarship that swept southern African studies in the 1970s confirmed suggestions about the imperial role in segregation. An important contributor to this literature was Martin Legassick, whose doctoral thesis on the frontier region of the northern Cape argued that race relations there were rather more fluid in the eighteenth and nineteenth centuries than had hitherto been assumed. The corollary of this point was that the origins of more rigid racial attitudes should be sought elsewhere.[11] Legassick's attention subsequently turned to the reconstruction era in the aftermath of the South African War. In a series of influential but unpublished papers (one of which is reproduced for the first time in this volume), he argued that English-speaking policy-makers – especially the British High Commissioner, Lord Milner, and his officials – played an instrumental role in elaborating segregationist ideology. Their approach was distilled in the *South African Native Affairs Commission* (1903–5), a document produced by British and English-speaking experts which in many ways systematized thinking about segregationist 'native policy' for the future. In Legassick's view, imperialism, capitalism and segregation were inextricably linked.

Early radical interpretations challenged the notion that twentieth-century segregation represented a survival of prior racial beliefs. Racial ideas could not in themselves explain the complex and subtle changes in policy and legislation in the early twentieth century. This 'revisionist' scholarship extended economic interpretations of imperialism and analysed the motivations for segregation primarily in economic terms. Racial beliefs were understood to be a product or rationalization of economic imperatives. Research focused on the mining industry, the motor of South Africa's economic growth, whose overwhelming need was seen to be

7

cheap labour. If policy-makers were not actually in thrall to the mining magnates of Kimberley and Johannesburg, the state and employers nevertheless colluded in a system which allowed the exploitation of black workers. On the white-owned farms, segregation policy aimed at turning relatively independent black tenants and sharecroppers into labour tenants and labourers.

More than any other work, Harold Wolpe's discussion of the cheap labour and reserve-subsidy thesis, reprinted here, became central to the radical analysis of segregation. Wolpe argued that cheap labour in the South African context was best procured through the system of migrant labour and that key elements of segregation policy reinforced this arrangement. The migrant labour system ensured that the mines predominantly used the labour of adult males whose families remained in rural areas. Capitalists were able to pay African workers meagre 'bachelor' wages because the costs of both the physical and social reproduction of the labour force was borne by their families who remained primarily responsible for maintaining subsistence agriculture in the reserves. If this system was to survive, reserves for African people had to be entrenched – a central feature of the 1913 Land Act. Wolpe did not argue that this was necessarily the main explicit intention of the Act, but that its 'possibly unintended' consequences were to underpin the migrant labour system.

The most important early challenge to this explanation, summarized in the extract by Beinart, came from historians working on the history of African societies and the origins of migrant labour. Both Marxist and liberal interpretations had focused on the state and the power structures of white society. In many of these analyses Africans were cast as passive objects of policy and victims of segregation; while it was taken for granted that they were opposed to their fate, they were hardly conceived of as historical actors and agents in their own right. Seen from the vantage point of late nineteenth-century chiefdoms, however, the origins of migrancy were revealed as rather more complex. In the early phases of labour migrancy (in some cases preceding formal colonial control) chiefs sometimes sent out workers and tried to benefit from their earnings by encouraging the acquisition of firearms to defend the independence of their kingdoms. Subsequently, the pressures on rural men to earn wages multiplied. But many African communities wanted to retain their hold over the men who went out to work and tried to devise methods of ensuring their return.[12] As long as land was available in communal tenure systems this also remained an attractive option for migrant men themselves. Migrancy could therefore be seen as having arisen as much out of the dynamics of African societies as the demands of the mines.

Belinda Bozzoli took the explanation which focused on African priorities a step further by examining the gendered nature of migrancy. In the article reprinted here, Bozzoli argues that migrancy on a large scale was only possible because the mines and African societies shared certain interests in the system. The legacy of patriarchal control in African societies, and the division of labour between men and women, enabled African men to keep women at home, thereby underpinning the survival of rural society. Bozzoli perhaps pays insufficient attention to the priorities of rural women themselves; though the demands upon them were undoubtedly great, their participation in rural protests against state intervention suggests they too wished to defend their 'own' world. Nevertheless, these reinterpretations of the origins and persistence of migrant labour led to an important reassessment of the balance of power between African societies, on the one hand, and the state and capitalism, on the other. They also raised further questions about the relationship of rural Africans to segregation.

A weakness common to liberal as well as early radical critiques of segregation was that both approaches assumed that Africans were available for incorporation into colonial society – whether as Christian modernizers seeking a relatively privileged position or as aspirant urban workers. Some certainly were. But in the early decades of the century, many were not. In the 1920s, for example, mass movements emerged in the South African countryside which challenged white rule by linking urban strands of protest with more traditionalist rural expressions of resistance.[13] The new spirit of 'Africanism' drew on black American ideas and images, including the radical separatism of Marcus Garvey. As the aspirations of the mission-educated Christian élite to be incorporated within colonial society were thwarted, so some examined alternative strategies such as alliances with chiefs and specifically African forms of Christianity.

Building on these insights, the extracts by William Beinart and Shula Marks suggest that segregation was not simply imposed from above.[14] The shape it took was considerably influenced by the intiatives and responses of people in the often forgotten rural areas where over 80 per cent of Africans continued to live until the 1930s. Attempts by the rurally based African population to defend their old ways of life were not segregationist in the sense that whites understood the term. But these could be compatible with elements of segregation in certain respects – as an expression of their own separate African identity, as a means to retain some control over their residual land, or as an expression of popular support for chiefs.

Shifting back to the urban perspective, it may be observed that most interpretations of segregation have emphasized the perceived threat to white society posed by rapid African urbanization. Whites saw a permanent black urban proletariat, living in poverty, as a crucible for trade unionism or as representing a dangerous threat to social order. In some early Marxist accounts capitalists were portrayed as collaborating to prevent the emergence of a class alliance between exploited African and white workers.[15] This outcome was said to be achieved by deliberately restricting skilled and supervisory jobs for whites as well as by granting them special political concessions. Although the cost of certain categories of labour was increased as a result, this was outweighed by the benefits of keeping white labour as a buffer between African workers and white capitalists. Marxist scholars overemphasized the potential of interracial alliances of workers to challenge capitalism and racism at the same time.[16] It should be borne in mind that their argument was also with those liberal writers who seemed to assign responsibility for the imposition of industrial and urban segregation to the racial attitudes of white workers and poor whites, rather than employers.

The broader ramifications of white fears about urbanization and proletarianization have been drawn out by Saul Dubow, whose particular concern is with the role of intellectual and social thought. He argues that segregation has been interpreted too narrowly as an economic strategy producing cheap labour. Instead, Dubow analyses it as a more generalized and defensive response to the forces unleashed by industrialization – a means to defuse potential class conflict and maintain overall white hegemony. In this account, segregation is viewed as an umbrella ideology which was capable of serving a range of white interest groups, and even some black ones. The flexible nature of segregationist ideology addressed a variety of constituencies: white farmers

10

were promised a ready supply of labour; the mines were assured that the system of migrant labour on which they had come to depend would remain intact; and white workers were given to believe that segregation would protect them from competition in the job market.

Drawing on earlier literature, in particular the unpublished work of Martin Legassick, Paul Rich and Saul Dubow began to explore in some detail the ideological elements that went into the making of segregation.[17] In contrast to the view that segregationist philosophy was the legacy of the nineteenth-century Boer republics, they found that some of the most influential protagonists of segregation in the 1910s and 1920s consciously conceived of themselves as liberal-minded South Africans. These English-speaking liberal paternalists tried to plot a course between the apparently 'assimilationist' approach associated with mid-nineteenth-century missionaries – which they felt was tolerable neither to whites, nor to many blacks – and the 'repressive' policies of the Afrikaners.

Although segregation was a primarily a modernizing ideology, it also reflected widespread fears about the modern age. These centred on social Darwinist and eugenic anxieties about racial 'deterioration' or 'degeneration' in the amorphous context of industrial cities. Segregation encompassed a conservative and backward-looking horror of the levelling and atomizing consequences of capitalism. As a policy it therefore appealed to conservatives who were inclined to romanticize the countryside as a source of social order, tradition and deference. The developing anthropological notion of cultural relativism was readily adopted by segregationist ideologues who proclaimed the need to preserve the distinct identity of different cultures and the internal coherence of African societies. In the age of apartheid, Christian-Nationalist thinkers greatly embellished this idea of the primacy of separate cultural identity among both Afrikaners and Africans. They presented cultural differences in a highly idealized and distorted fashion and went further than segregationist thinkers in equating such differences with national, ethnic and racial identities.

The nuances and contradictions of interracial contact have long been a central preoccupation for writers of South African fiction, though less so for academic researchers whose concerns have tended to be more theoretical. Discussion of changing informal

11

relationships, and their impact on formal ideologies and state policy is, however, beginning to extend our understanding of segregation. In this respect the work of social historians has been of particular importance. South African farms, in many ways bastions of *baasskap* (domination), have been revealed as the site of complex paternalistic relationships between white landowners and black tenants.[18] The intricate nature of paternalism has also been explored in the context of domestic service where, typically, black women have raised the children of white employers while remaining separated from their own families in segregated 'locations' or the distant countryside.[19] Suggestive work has also been conducted on outbreaks of mass social hysteria or 'moral panics' associated with instances of heightened racial tensions.[20] Together, such approaches are helping to construct a fuller appreciation of the everyday language and practice of social relations under conditions of segregation.

THE RISE AND DEMISE OF APARTHEID

In analysing the transition from segregation to apartheid some writers stress elements of continuity. They point out that much of the core apartheid legislation amounted to a mere elaboration of earlier segregationist measures. For others, apartheid represented so great an intensification of segregationist ideology and practices that it could be considered as qualitatively different. Afrikaner nationalism and apartheid has even been likened to fascism.[21] But, although some Afrikaners were profoundly influenced by fascist ideas and supported Germany during the Second World War, the analogy breaks down in crucial respects.[22] Nevertheless, it is true to say that apartheid purported to be a rigorous and totalizing ideology in a way that segregation had never been.

The rhetoric of apartheid bore considerable similarities to white supremacist statements of the segregation era, but the central appeal to Afrikaner ethnic exclusivity was a distinctive aspect of apartheid. The context in which apartheid was introduced was also markedly different from the earlier segregationist period. In the era of European colonialism, segregation in South Africa did not appear exceptional. By contrast, in the democratizing postwar world and at the time of decolonization, apartheid began to stand out internationally as an immoral

12

system in a way that its predecessor had not. By the 1960s, with the banning of the African National Congress and the Pan-Africanist Congress and the systematic jailing of the African nationalist leadership – most notably Nelson Mandela – South Africa came to be regarded as a pariah state. Internationally, apartheid came to embody the evils of racist exploitation, while the South African liberation struggle served to symbolize, along with the civil rights movement in the United States, the aspirations of all those who strove for common human dignity and freedom.

The transition from segregation to apartheid is addressed by Wolpe, who sees the maintenance of the migrant labour system as the centrepiece of apartheid. According to this view, the government hoped to extend the economic and political advantages of a cheap and controlled migrant labour force to the growing manufacturing sector. In order to do so effectively it had to restore the crumbling economies of the African reserves. But this was insufficient in itself as the reserve economy could no longer provide a base for the bulk of African people. Tighter 'influx' controls and decentralized industries were therefore designed to inhibit the development of a black urban working class. Labour-hungry commercial farmers, who formed a vital part of the government's political constituency, also stood to gain from apartheid labour allocation policies.

Economic explanations were developed by other radical social scientists in the early 1970s at the height of the apartheid era. In international terms, South Africa enjoyed relatively rapid growth rates through most of the 1960s (except in the immediate aftermath of the Sharpeville uprising at the beginning of the decade). To writers like Frederick Johnstone, this seemed to offer conclusive evidence that, far from the claims of liberal economists who argued that apartheid would automatically be eroded through economic growth and the rationality of the market, the apartheid system and capitalist development were in fact mutually sustaining.[23] At the very least apartheid and economic growth did not appear contradictory.

Drawing on the work of Barrington Moore and other theorists of modernization, Stanley Trapido pointed out that democratic systems did not necessarily follow from industrialization and growth. Extensive state intervention (and even totalitarianism) often characterized successful late industrialization.[24] The debate about the relationship between apartheid and economic growth

13

was intensified by its relevance to opposition political strategies such as sanctions. Those supporting boycotts and disinvestment emphasized that economic growth was unlikely in itself to bring change. They questioned the motives of those who argued for continued trade, investment or 'constructive engagement' in the hope that growth would erode apartheid. For supporters of sanctions this seemed an excuse for 'business as usual'.

Radical scholars' understanding of the economic success of apartheid has since been modified and academic positions have softened. One of the central issues has been the position of manufacturing industry which, by the 1940s, had outstripped mining, though not agriculture, as an employer. Liberals had long pointed to the shortage of a stable supply of skilled labour as an indication that state intervention in the labour market led to great inefficiencies and that apartheid actually retarded economic growth.[25] Cheap migrant labour might have been beneficial to the mining industry which sold its products internationally and had to depress labour costs in order to maintain profits, but the system inhibited the growth of a local market for manufactured commodities. Although capitalism might have lived easily with apartheid in the 1960s, these weaknesses were more acutely revealed when manufacturing growth slowed between 1975 and 1980 and subsequently stagnated. Terence Moll has recently argued that, while growth during the apartheid era was strong, it was not as spectacular in international terms as had earlier been suggested because comparisons tended to be made with Europe rather than other developing countries.[26]

More recent radical writing has also diverged from the argument that apartheid primarily involved an extension of migrant labour. Doug Hindson and Deborah Posel have detected a more pragmatic policy to divide urban African 'insiders' from rural migrant 'outsiders' by means of complex legislative and bureaucratic processes. They view apartheid as an attempt at 'labour differentiation': the control of African urbanization and redistribution of labour between different sectors of the economy, rather than a wholesale extension of migrant labour.[27] Posel in particular distinguishes between the intentions and the practical consequences of government policy. Apartheid, she argues, was never fully able to control black population movements. Building on earlier interpretations of segregation, Posel suggests further that modifications in policy were often a response to

14

African resistance as much as to ideological canons or capitalist interests.

Arguments about the nature of apartheid have also switched back to the question of ideology. Deborah Posel's article in this volume argues that apartheid was not a unitary ideology embodying a preconceived 'grand plan'. Nor was the apartheid state a monolithic entity. In the pre-1948 period, the Afrikaner nationalist movement represented an alliance of conflicting interests. Likewise, in the decade after the Nationalists came to power, its hold was rather more fragile than was apparent in the interlude between the Sharpeville uprising of 1960 and the Soweto revolt of 1976. Like analysts of segregation, Posel maintains that apartheid policy spoke with different voices to the differing constituencies out of which its support was carved. Thus, the conception of apartheid as articulated by Afrikaner businessmen differed in significant respects from that of idealistic theoreticians and intellectuals who were inclined to do without African labour in order to achieve the goal of 'total segregation'.[28]

Hermann Giliomee's contribution also directs attention away from debates about the specificities of economic rationality and labour control. Giliomee takes his cue from the powerful strand in Afrikaner writing which reveals a preoccupation with their own nationhood and identity rather than their policy towards blacks. He acknowledges that apartheid has involved the use of ethnic power for economic gain and, indeed, one of the most interesting elements of Giliomee's work is his understanding of the changing social composition of Afrikanerdom.[29] Particular attention is drawn, for example, to the ways in which Afrikaner nationalist ambitions in the 1930s and 1940s mobilized around the need to resolve the problem of 'poor whiteism'. But Giliomee does not consider that class interests are as salient as ethnic imperatives. He insists that 'cultural and psychosocial fears' are critical in understanding the development of ethnic mobilization. Rather than conceiving of apartheid either as a sacrosanct ideology, or as a deliberate ploy to secure material advantages, Giliomee sees apartheid first and foremost as a vehicle for nurturing the unity of the *volk*. Anticipating the events of the late 1980s, he suggested that if apartheid were to become inimical to the ethnic interests of Afrikanerdom, it could be substantially modified or even jettisoned.

The era of 'high apartheid', roughly from 1960 to 1976, was a

15

period in which the government engaged in a massive process of social engineering. Relatively rapid economic growth for much of this period provided the apartheid state with the opportunity to put its ideas into practice. The most striking policy development in this respect was the attempt to turn the existing reserves into self-governing ethnic statelets or 'homelands'. Debates about the homelands have been central to critiques of apartheid. The very word 'homeland' has been rejected because it seemed to lend legitimacy to the state's policy of balkanization and exclusion. Opposition forces preferred instead to retain the word 'Bantustan', which suggests the artificiality of configuring geographical regions so as to correspond to supposed 'tribal' divisions.

The Afrikaner leader most closely identified with the development of the homelands was Hendrik Verwoerd, Prime Minister from 1958 to 1966 and before that Minister of Native Affairs. Verwoerd envisaged the creation of the Bantustans as a form of political decentralization or internal decolonization. He calculated that this would defuse the rising tide of African nationalism and parallel the decolonization policies pursued by Britain and France in Africa from the late 1950s. In theory, the new separate nations would be able to house the bulk of black people and provide the basis for national self-determination. Emphasis was placed on the virtues of 'separate development' rather than the racially exclusivist aspects of apartheid. This initiative involved a new system of local and regional government in which chiefs were elevated to positions of unprecedented authority. The Bantu Authorities Act of 1951 and the 1959 Promotion of Bantu Self-Government Act paved the way for nominal Bantustan independence, granted first to the Transkei in 1976.

In order to secure the fantasy of independent homelands, a vast administrative apparatus was established to regulate the rights of Africans to live and work in 'white' cities and towns. For many years, academic critics tended to focus on the 'success' of this policy, reflected, for example, in the massive number of pass law arrests. From 1960 to 1980, the proportion of the total African population in what were classified as the main 'white' urban areas actually declined from 29.6 to 26.7 per cent (though this still represented an absolute increase of over two million people). The population of the homelands grew from 4.2 million in 1960 (39 per cent of all Africans) to over eleven million in 1980 (52.7 per cent).

Pioneering social reporting by the Catholic priest Cosmos Desmond followed by careful demographic work and a nation-wide survey by the Surplus People Project revealed a little more clearly what was entailed in this process.[30] The policy of forced population removals (which continued until the mid-1980s) was carried out on a vast scale. One of the consequences of this programme was that urban-type settlements were diverted away from the major metropolitan areas. Many were established within or near homelands where they became apartheid's human 'dumping grounds'. Colin Murray's article describes and analyses this process in areas of the Orange Free State and the Transvaal. Previously rural zones, they rapidly became the sites of huge African settlements which were urban in respect of their population density and lack of agricultural opportunity, but rural in their isolation and lack of services and employment.

In the process of creating and justifying homelands, the restoration of chieftaincy and the invocation of 'tribalism' played a vital role. The government wished Africans to be Zulu or Xhosa, Pedi or Tswana, and so on. Apartheid therefore involved creating clear legal distinctions not just between black, coloured, Asian and white, but also within African society. For many years both liberal and radical scholars eschewed discussion of 'ethnic' or 'tribal' differences among blacks, fearing that this would lend legitimacy to the state's plans for the balkanization of South Africa. As a result – and compared to that of many other African countries – the South African historiography of ethnicity has until recently been rather weak.

Although 'tribalism' in the apartheid era was undoubtedly imposed from above, several studies suggest that it could nevertheless resonate with strands in African politics. Beinart points to significant legacies in popular rural consciousness about the value of 'traditional society' and chieftaincy which initially afforded Bantustan politicians some degree of political purchase.[31] Material interests were also of significance because large sums of money were channelled through the homeland governments: the politics of patronage and the opportunities offered to individuals in the newly created institutions of government or in business proved highly alluring.

By no means all attempts to develop ethnic identity were successful and there remains within the literature a strong strain that sees the 'creation of tribalism' as a mechanistic and corrupt

17

affair. Jeff Peires's article (originally published anonymously because of its political sensitivity) amply illustrates this point with reference to the Ciskei. One of the more unlikely of the independent homelands, based on a spurious geographical division of Xhosa-speakers between itself and Transkei, Ciskei's nominated leaders lacked popular support in an area with a strong tradition of African nationalist politics. Attempts by the Ciskeian government to appropriate the symbols and historical sites of the old Xhosa chiefdoms largely failed and, after being granted independence in 1981, it increasingly resorted to naked repression (with the active assistance of the South African state).

Nevertheless, even if the idea of Ciskeian nationhood failed to take root at a popular level, this does not mean that ethnicity can simply be wished away. Murray's comments on the tense politics of ethnicity on the peripheries of the Bophuthatswana homeland is a case in point. Above all, the growth of Chief Buthelezi's Inkatha movement and the attractiveness of ethnic consciousness to many Zulu-speakers has demanded reconsideration of the explosive potential of local nationalisms and fragmented identities.[32] Buthelezi initially presented himself as a leading opponent of apartheid and refused to take independent status for KwaZulu. But from the early 1980s he increasingly distanced himself from the mass nationalist opposition movements. Buthelezi looked instead to a more conservative black constituency and sought to secure a strong form of autonomy for a Zulu-dominated region. Whatever his popular support, the power of Inkatha's local warlords and its capacity to mobilize large groups of men placed chiefs and ethnicity firmly on the political and academic agenda.

Many recent analyses accept that apartheid was not a static system of racial division. Government commitment to white supremacy was sustained but the precise form of racial ideology and policy shifted significantly through the years. From the mid-1970s a number of interrelated processes began to force more rapid reform. Soon after P.W. Botha came to power in 1978 he warned whites to 'adapt or die'. The government sought to strengthen its links with the business community and black trade unions were legalized. Attempts were made to stabilize parts of the urban black population and to encourage the development of a black urban middle class. Botha introduced constitutional reforms in an effort to grant a limited political voice to the coloured and Asian communities and thereby to win their support.

The reform era (1978–84) has been extensively analysed as a period when many basic tenets of apartheid were defended while the more extreme manifestations of social deprivation began to be addressed. The Afrikaner-controlled government made important symbolic concessions in the direction of deracialization, but it refused to relinquish political power. Undoubtedly, the changing international context contributed to reform. Up to the mid-1970s white rule was cushioned by the circle of settler and colonial states around it. In 1974, when a coup in Portugal – prompted not least by the costs of its colonial wars – displaced the Caetano dictatorship, decolonization in Angola and Mozambique followed rapidly. From the mid-1970s the war in Zimbabwe intensified and despite South African assistance, settler rule succumbed in 1979. International sanctions, though unevenly applied, began to bite.

In general, scholars have concentrated on domestic rather than external causes of reform. Consideration of these forces has to some degree contributed to a narrowing of the analytical divide between radicals and liberals, though some important differences remained, for example, over the desirability of external economic sanctions in the 1980s. Economic setbacks after the oil crisis of the mid-1970s played an important role in dissolving the certainties of apartheid. Merle Lipton's sectoral analysis of the South African economy – a sophisticated development of liberal positions – led her to argue that new economic demands in themselves, and a greater realization by business and commercial interests of the costs of apartheid, were major instigators of change.[33] The necessity of change was also stressed by a rising class of technocrats who readily absorbed Thatcherite and Reaganite ideology and developed their own variant of free-market anti-communism. Reformers eagerly adopted this combination of liberal economic policy and conservative social philosophy. But it soon became apparent that free-market approaches to labour, land and ownership could have explosive implications in a racially constituted economy like South Africa.

Radical scholars in the 1980s moved beyond the discussion of purely economic imperatives to reform and paid increasing attention to the crisis of political legitimacy following the renaissance of mass black opposition. The political scientist Sam Nolutshungu attempted to integrate these interrelated explanatory elements, examining changes in white society as well as the

19

resistance

powerful new forces unleashed by the black consciouness movement, industrial militancy and the independent trade unions.[34]
Economic growth over previous decades had also strengthened
the position of urban black 'insiders', entrepreneurs and professionals. After the Soweto rebellion of 1976 it became increasingly
difficult for the state to contain protest and insurrection. The
deference which whites expected in the high apartheid years –
and to some degree received – gradually gave way to a distinct
culture of opposition, shaped in particular by the emergence
of the black consciousness movement and the inspiring leadership of figures like Steve Biko. The reform era could thus be
seen in most radical analyses as in large measure a response
to black protest and the threat this posed to white political
hegemony.

Further cycles of popular anger were provoked by the many
acts of brutal oppression which accompanied Botha's reforms. It
was not least the violent reaction by the urban youth against
those who looked to benefit from reform that eventually forced
further compromise. The state mostly failed in its quest to find
black urban allies who would take their place alongside homeland leaders. F.W. de Klerk's dramatic release of Nelson Mandela
from prison in February 1990, together with the unbanning of the
ANC and other liberation movements, amounted to a recognition
of the political stalemate. Nevertheless, it took more than four
years of tortured negotiations and heightened levels of violence
before a non-racial election could be held in April 1994 and
power formally transferred.

Despite allegations of ballot-rigging in some regions, the overall results of South Africa's first democratic election broadly
reflected the spread of popular feeling. Contrary to expectations,
the dramatic process engendered a remarkable sense of euphoria
throughout South African society and its cathartic influence led
to a significant decrease in levels of violence. The majority of
African people supported the African National Congress, which
won over 60 per cent of the total votes cast; most whites
remained loyal to a reformed National Party which polled 20 per
cent of votes overall. Coloured people in the Western Cape voted
in sufficient numbers for the Nationalists to ensure their victory
in that region. Inkatha secured about 10 per cent overall although
the scale of their victory in KwaZulu/Natal region has led to suspicions of systematic electoral malpractice. Far right groupings,

the liberal Democratic Party and the radical Pan-Africanists were all marginalized.

The demise of white rule is unlikely to signal the end of racial division, ethnic identity or economic inequality in South Africa. Although African people voted overwhelmingly for a party which sought to unite them and the country under a common non-racial nationalism, voting followed the lines of colour to a significant degree and Inkatha survived as a specifically Zulu force. The academic debate on these issues must remain central to historical writing on the country because the troubled conflicts which it addresses are by no means resolved; discussion helps to frame appropriate questions about political and ethical decision-making in the future as well as the past. Historical analysis of South Africa can also contribute to comparative understanding of colonial societies and racial division.

As a new majoritarian system of rule takes root, and nine regions replace the four provinces and ten homelands, both the locus of political power and the nature of social identities will be modified. New emphases in the explanation of segregation and apartheid are also likely to emerge. As this volume illustrates, the recent historiography of segregation and apartheid incorporates a variety of intellectual traditions. While there is by no means intellectual consensus, it may be possible to develop an overview that is sensitive to a number of approaches. It is clear that segregation and apartheid primarily served white interests. However, monocausal explanations elevating the Afrikaner heritage or the imperatives of a cheap labour supply are clearly inadequate in themselves, although both are of critical importance in clarifying the particular form taken by segregation and racial ideology in South Africa. To understand segregation and apartheid more fully, a wider range of historical and ideological reference points are required. These include the impact of modernity, the influence of social Darwinism and the metaphors, symbols and everyday assumptions that help to sustain notions of racial difference and political entitlement.

As important, any analysis of segregation must recognize that African societies in the region were conquered but never entirely dominated. Many fought to defend themselves from full incorporation into colonial and capitalist society. The balance of power in South African society, the nature of African responses, and the salience of ethnicity among blacks as well as whites must be

21

taken into account if the longevity and starkness of racial domination in South Africa is to be captured analytically.

NOTES

1 We are grateful to Professor Shula Marks for her careful reading of a draft version of this introduction.
2 For detail on this period, see R. Elphick and H. Giliomee (eds), *The Shaping of South African Society, 1652–1840* (Longman, 1989). General histories of South Africa include: P. Maylam, *A History of the African People of South Africa* (Cape Town, 1986); *The Reader's Digest Illustrated History of South Africa* (Cape Town, 1989); L. Thompson, *A History of South Africa* (New Haven, CT, 1990). B. Bozzoli and P. Delius (eds), *History from South Africa* (New York, 1990), vol. 46/47 of the *Radical History Review* includes interesting historiographical surveys. See also W. Beinart, *Twentieth-Century South Africa* (Oxford, 1994).
3 A. Crosby, *Ecological Imperialism* (Cambridge, 1986), 139.
4 G.M. Theal, *The Yellow and Dark-Skinned People of Africa South of the Zambesi* (London, 1910), 175, 174, 340–52.
5 For example, C.F.J. Muller, *500 Years: A History of South Africa* (Pretoria, 1969).
6 For stimulating works looking comparatively at segregation in the United States and South Africa: S. Greenberg, *Race and State in Capitalist Development* (New Haven, CT, 1980); G.M. Fredrickson, *White Supremacy: A Comparative Study on American and South African History* (New York, 1981); J. Cell, *The Highest Stage of White Supremacy: The Origins of Segregation in South Africa and the American South* (Cambridge, 1982).
7 C.W. de Kiewiet, *A History of South Africa, Social and Economic* (London, 1941), ch. 3; M. Legassick, 'The Frontier Tradition in South African Historiography', in S. Marks and A. Atmore (eds), *Economy and Society in Pre-Industrial South Africa* (London, 1980).
8 S.Trapido, '"The Friends of the Natives": Merchants, Peasants and the Political and Ideological Structure of Liberalism in the Cape, 1854–1910', in Marks and Atmore (eds) *Pre-Industrial South Africa*.
9 D. Welsh, *The Roots of Segregation* (Cape Town, 1971).
10 S. Marks, *The Ambiguities of Dependence in South Africa* (Baltimore, MD, 1986), 5. See also Marks, *Reluctant Rebellion* (Oxford, 1970) and Chapter 4 in this volume.
11 Legassick, 'The Frontier Tradition'.
12 See P. Delius, 'Migrant Labour and the Pedi, 1840–80', in Marks and Atmore (eds), *Economy and Society*; and P. Harries, 'Kinship, Ideology and the Nature of Pre-Colonial Labour Migration', in S. Marks and R. Rathbone (eds), *Industrialization and Social Change in South Africa: African Class Formation, Culture and Consciousness 1870–1930* (London, 1982).
13 H. Bradford, *A Taste of Freedom* (New Haven, CT, 1987); W. Beinart

and C. Bundy, *Hidden Struggles in Rural South Africa* (London, 1987).

14 For a more extended analysis, see Marks, *Ambiguities of Dependence;* W. Beinart, *The Political Economy of Pondoland 1860–1930* (Cambridge, 1982); Beinart and Bundy, *Hidden Struggles.*

15 R.H. Davies, *Capital, State and White Labour in South Africa, 1900–1960* (Brighton, 1979); H. Wolpe, 'Industrialism and Race in South Africa', in S. Zubaida (ed.), *Race and Racialism* (London, 1970).

16 For a fascinating fictional representation of this position, see Peter Abrahams, *Mine Boy* (London, 1946).

17 P. Rich, *White Power and the Liberal Conscience* (Johannesburg, 1984); Cell, *The Highest Stage of White Supremacy;* S. Dubow, *Racial Segregation and the Origins of Apartheid in South Africa, 1919–36* (London, 1989).

18 See C. van Onselen, 'Race and Class in the South African Country-side: Cultural Osmosis and Social Relations in the Sharecropping Economy of the South-Western Transvaal, 1900–1950', *American Historical Review*, 95, 1 (1990), 99–123; C. Murray, *Black Mountain* (Edinburgh, 1992); T.J. Keegan, *Rural Transformations in Industrializing South Africa* (Johannesburg, 1986).

19 J. Cock, *Maids and Madams* (Johannesburg, 1980); C. van Onselen, *Studies in the Social and Economic History of the Witwatersrand 1886–1914*, 2 vols (London, 1982).

20 N. Etherington, 'Natal's Black Rape Scare of the 1870s', *Journal of Southern African Studies*, 15, 1 (1988), 36–53, J. Krikler, 'Social Neurosis and Hysterical Pre-Cognition: A Case-Study and Reflection', *South African Historical Journal*, 28 (1993), 63–97.

21 B. Bunting, *The Rise of the South African Reich* (Harmondsworth, 1969).

22 P. Furlong, *Between Crown and Swastika* (Middletown, CT, 1991).

23 F.A. Johnstone, 'White Prosperity and White Supremacy in South Africa Today', *African Affairs*, vol. 69, issue 275 (1970), 124–40.

24 S. Trapido, 'South Africa in a Comparative Study of Industrialisation', *Journal of Development Studies*, 7, 3 (1971), 309–20.

25 R. Horwitz, *Expand or Explode: Apartheid's Threat to South African Industry* (Cape Town, 1957); M. Lipton, *Capitalism and Apartheid: South Africa 1910–1986* (Aldershot, 1985).

26 T. Moll, 'Did the South African Economy "Fail"?', *Journal of Southern African Studies*, 17, 2 (1991), 271–91.

27 D. Hindson, *Pass Controls and the Urban African Proletariat in South Africa* (Johannesburg, 1987); D. Posel, *The Making of Apartheid 1948–1961* (Oxford, 1991).

28 This argument was developed at the same time by John Lazar, whose work on the development of apartheid has only recently been published. See his 'Verwoerd Versus the "Visionaries": The South African Bureau of Racial Affairs (SABRA) and Apartheid, 1948–1961', in P. Bonner *et al.* (eds), *Apartheid's Genesis 1935–1962* (Johannesburg, 1993).

29 See also Heribert Adam, *Modernizing Racial Domination: The Dynamics of South African Policy* (Berkeley, CA, 1971).

30 C. Desmond, *The Discarded People: An Account of African Resettlement in South Africa* (Harmondsworth, 1971); L. Platzky and C. Walker, *The Surplus People: Forced Removals in South Africa* (Johannesburg, 1985).
31 See also Beinart and Bundy, *Hidden Struggles*; Marks, *Ambiguities of Dependence*; L. Vail (ed.), *The Creation of Tribalism in South Africa* (London, 1989).
32 G. Maré and G. Hamilton, *An Appetite for Power: Buthelezi's Inkatha and South Africa* (Johannesburg, 1987).
33 Lipton, *Capitalism and Apartheid*.
34 Sam C. Nolutshungu, *Changing South Africa* (Manchester, 1982). See also John S. Saul and Stephen Gelb, *The Crisis in South Africa*, rev. edn (London, 1986); Stanley B. Greenberg, *Legitimating the Illegitimate* (Berkeley, CA, 1987).

1

THE SANITATION SYNDROME:

Bubonic plague and urban native policy in the Cape Colony, 1900–09[1]

Maynard W. Swanson

Maynard Swanson, a historian based at Miami University, wrote this highly original article on the 'sanitation syndrome' in 1977. Drawing on a wide comparative international and Africanist historical literature, Swanson was concerned to show that public fears of epidemic disease were utilized by authorities in the early twentieth century to justify residential racial segregation in two of the Cape Colony's chief cities, Cape Town and Port Elizabeth. White colonial officials in these cities were deeply concerned about chaotic social and sanitary conditions in the urban areas, identifying Africans, 'coloureds' and 'Malays' as a threat to public health. Influenced by the rise of social Darwinist thought in Europe, they used fashionable biological and bodily imagery to justify class and racial separation in the social context and to rationalize white race prejudice. Underlying these fears was the imperative to manage a newly industrializing society and to maintain social control in the burgeoning cities. In this closely argued extract, Swanson therefore demonstrates how political and material interests interacted with ideological concerns in the construction of segregationist policy. He indicates, too, that the origins of modern segregation have to be sought in the context of the planning initiatives of the English-speaking (and so-called 'liberal') Cape Colony.

* * *

The public health is the foundation on which repose the happiness of the people and the power of a country. The care of the public health is the first duty of a statesman.

Benjamin Disraeli
In debate on Public Health Act, 1875

The thesis of this article is that medical officials and other public authorities in South Africa at the turn of this century were imbued with the imagery of infectious disease as a societal metaphor, and that this metaphor powerfully interacted with British and South African racial attitudes to influence the policies and shape the institutions of segregation. In previous articles this writer has suggested that urban public health administration was of considerable importance in accounting for the 'racial ecology' of South Africa and of colonial societies generally.[2] Overcrowding, slums, public health and safety, often seen in the light of class and ethnic differences in industrial societies, were in the colonial context perceived largely in terms of colour differences. Conversely, urban race relations came to be widely conceived and dealt with in the imagery of infection and epidemic disease. This 'sanitation syndrome' can be traced as a major strand in the creation of urban apartheid. As disease and epidemiology became a widespread societal metaphor during the late nineteenth and early twentieth centuries, other historical changes taking place in South Africa as elsewhere were leading to the evolution of segregationist ideology. In this context the accident of epidemic plague became a dramatic and compelling opportunity for those who were promoting segregationist solutions to social problems.

In a recent bibliographical essay, 'Disease and Medicine in African History', K. David Patterson has suggested that 'studies of colonial medical efforts could tell us much about the attitudes, objectives, and priorities of European rulers',[3] but he does not discuss urban development. Some writers have touched upon the medical theme but almost no systematic urban history has been written from this perspective. The sanitation syndrome in the Cape Colony finds parallels in the broader context of new trends in social and cultural history outside Africa. In his presidential address to the American Historical Association in 1957, William L. Langer pointed out the possibilities of applying the insights of psychology to history and urged consideration of epidemic catastrophe as a trauma of historical significance.[4] Similar themes are developed by Gareth Stedman Jones in his superb study *Outcast London*. Jones shows how London became after the 1850s a focal point for the deepening fears and anxieties of the Victorian élite about the endemic poverty and potential violence of the 'casual labourer'. These twin phenomena were viewed in the image of contagion as a threat to Victorian expectations of progress and social order. Theorists eventually concluded that urbanism had developed a pathology which endangered society in Darwinist terms. Their prescriptions for social policy were influenced by epidemiology and sanitary science, but were also developed as an exercise in moral philosophy. The early approaches employed sanitary legislation to attack overcrowding and slums, which were identified as the 'rookeries' or haunts of a criminal class and the 'hot beds' of social decay, 'cholera, crime, and chartism'. The general failure of urban renewal policies to eliminate the social problem led to later proposals – which were never realized in law – for reclaiming the 'respectable' working classes for progressive society while segregating the 'residuum' of 'unregenerate poor'. The latter would be removed, by compulsion if necessary, to labour colonies outside the imperial metropolis. There social discipline might be instilled and the 'imperial race' be saved from contamination.[5]

That the responses to outcast London were not identical in origin or conception nor directly linked with the question of racial segregation in South Africa should not obscure their interest as analogues to the subject of the present article. Moreover, it is reasonable to expect that the European background formed a major source of inspiration for the white response to social problems in Africa. In South Africa, especially in Natal and Transvaal, fear of epidemic cholera, smallpox and plague both roused and rationalized efforts to segregate Indians and Africans in municipal locations from the 1870s onward. The municipality of Durban, for example, attempted in the 1870s to establish an Indian location to remove the 'breeding haunts and nursery grounds of disease, misery and discomfort' with which Indian settlement was believed to menace the town. In the early 1890s Durban leaders tried again to impose municipal locations upon Indians in order to achieve, in the words of its Mayor, 'the isolation with better hopes of cure of this our social leprosy'.[6] In short, the metaphoric equation of 'coolies' with urban poverty and disease became a steady refrain of white opinion and a

27

preoccupation of police and health officers in the South African colonies long before 1900.

The sanitation syndrome was a force in its own right, but it also provided a rationale for economic jealousy – the unemployment fears of white artisans and the trading rivalry of white shopkeepers – as well as the political fear of electoral 'swamping' when white Natal moved towards self-government in 1893. Thus plague warnings helped foment and justify the famous 'Asiatic invasion' incident at Durban in 1897, when mass demonstrations opposed the landing of M.K. Gandhi and two shiploads of Indians.[7] Likewise the Transvaal Law 5 of 1885 denied to 'Asiatics' the electoral franchise and withheld property or residential rights except in 'such . . . locations as the government for purposes of sanitation shall assign them'. This measure was defended before the Anglo-Boer War by the Transvaal State Secretary, W. Leyds, ostensibly on grounds of public health, and it was applied with vigour after the war by the British administrator, Sir Godfrey Lagden, who argued that 'the lower castes . . . are as a rule filthy in habit and a menace to the public health'.[8]

Indians were a special target because they were at first the more obviously intrusive urban group, but Africans were increasingly included in this reaction. Natal again provides an example. The African presence in Durban and Pietermaritzburg, especially as unemployed or casual labour – and thereby not readily subject to the control of master and servant relations – was by the 1880s labelled as 'the social pest . . . spreading like an epidemic . . . undermining all sense of security'.[9] Sir Theophilus Shepstone, father-figure of Natal's rural segregation, lent his support to urban pass laws because, as he said, 'our towns become the pest spots of our body social and political; all such mischiefs [unruliness, crime and vagrancy] radiate from centres which offer the conditions most favourable for their incubation'.[10] Despite the occasional alarms, however, urban segregation was sporadic and ineffectual in the nineteenth century. A much more determined approach developed in the aftermath of the Anglo-Boer War, when in terms of scale and urgency a new era dawned.[11] The imagery of infection now broadly embraced the rapidly emerging urban African populations. In this situation a crisis of bubonic plague, spreading to major centres of population, precipitated action which permanently altered the racial ecology of South Africa.

I

The third great pandemic of bubonic plague in recorded history began in South China in the second half of the nineteenth century. Reaching Canton and Hong Kong in 1894, it was carried by ocean shipping around the globe by the First World War.[12] It reached South Africa in 1900 during the Anglo-Boer War. There the seaports of Cape Town, Port Elizabeth, East London and Durban lay open to infection, burdened by wartime commerce, swollen with refugees from the interior and large numbers of migrant African labourers.

Cape Town was the first to be affected. Forage for the British army imported from Argentina, India or Australia carried the plague bacillus in the rats and fleas that accompanied it. By December 1900, rats were seen dying in great numbers at the docks but the military officers in charge did not report this to the public health authorities. Early in February 1901 the first human cases of plague appeared in the city among Cape coloured and African dockworkers. Warned at last, but practically too late, the municipal and colonial Medical Officers of Health (MOH) anxiously informed their governments that, as Cape Town's Mayor put it, 'the dreaded Bubonic Plague – the scourge of India – had at length made its appearance in our midst'.[13] His tone expressed the thrill of fear which galvanized the city. Many citizens knew the baleful imagery of Europe's historic 'Black Death'. The others readily caught the mood and message it conveyed.

Cape Town's rulers had reason for concern – even alarm – over the condition of their city at the turn of the century. It was an old, slum-ridden town composed of a colonial society in which, in general, whites existed in favoured circumstances surrounded and served by 'coloured', Malay, 'Asiatic' and 'Kafir' or 'native servants'. Since the onset of the war, rapidly increasing numbers of black rural migrants from the eastern Cape and Transkei had been left on their own to 'pig it'[14] where and how they could. Thus, of 64,500 inhabitants in 1900, 30,500 were whites, including about 7,000 poverty-stricken refugees. Of the rest some 7,000 – the number growing rapidly – were Africans.[15]

Faced with the plague crisis, the first and most powerful anxieties of the medical officers and the emergency Plague Administration focused on the presence of the Africans ('Kafirs'), whom they associated directly and inherently with the social and sanitary conditions that harboured the plague. 'Rest the blame where it may', Cape Town's Medical Officer, Barnard Fuller, wrote later, 'these uncontrolled Kafir hordes were at the root of the aggravation of Capetown slumdom brought to light when the plague broke out ... [Because of them] it was absolutely impossible to keep the slums of the city in satisfactory condition.' For years Fuller had warned of the danger of epidemic disease, such as typhus, arising from 'scattered nests of filth' where 'Kafirs' lived. Thus the plague itself did not create anxieties full-blown, but it focused them sensationally. The MOH of Cape Town directed the special attention of his sanitary inspectors to the systematic searching and cleaning-out of 'Kafir haunts' throughout the city.[16]

Far more drastic action was forthcoming: the Plague Administration sought no less than the mass removal of Cape Town's African population, even though the number of Africans contracting the plague was less than either whites or coloureds. For a year beforehand proposals had been under somewhat leisured consideration for an African reserve or residential 'location' beyond the borders of Cape Town and its suburbs. In September 1900 the Prime Minister, Sir Gordon Sprigg, had appointed a commission to recommend action. The commission, chaired by Walter E. Stanford, Superintendent of Native Affairs, and composed of Dr John Gregory, Acting Colonial MOH, Capt. J.A. Jenner, Chief of Police, and Dr Barnard Fuller, had found 'frightful' living conditions, profiteering slumlords and hearty support among 'leading men' (African clergy) for a special government location away from the city.[17] Suddenly in February 1901 this idea became a priority. It was the merest step of logic to proceed from the isolation of plague victims to the creation of a permanent location for the black labouring class.

One of the first actions of the Cape government, therefore, was to rush a native location into being under the Public Health Act at the sewage farm called Uitvlugt, several miles from town on the Cape Flats. There was no other law affecting municipalities which provided the authority to remove Africans forcibly if necessary.[18] This Act had been inspired by a devastating small-pox epidemic at Cape Town, May 1882 to March 1883, when over four thousand people died in ten months. The casualties had been mostly Cape coloureds and Malays; Africans had not yet appeared at Cape Town in significant numbers. The deaths vastly outnumbered those in the plague of 1901. The difference in response was a measure not only of the development of government powers and public health administration, but of the readiness by the 1900s of Cape authorities to turn to territorial segregation in dealing with the black presence in urban areas. In the midst of the plague during March 1901, some six or seven thousand Africans were moved to Uitvlugt (later known as Ndabeni), and settled in six hundred lean-tos, twenty-four huts, five hastily constructed wood-and-iron barracks, a twenty-bed hospital and various outbuildings. Many officials and white citizens considered the move a major success, pointing the way to future policy and practice.[19] The plague was arrested among Africans and because of that, it was believed, in the city. By September 1901 the plague had receded in Cape Town, with 807 cases and 389 deaths of which sixty-nine were whites, 244 coloureds and seventy-six Africans.[20] True, Cape Town employers experienced a labour shortage, but it was thought this might be alleviated if the location were set up as a labour bureau, funnelling Africans through a pass system to employers who applied for them.

At last, it seemed, a vexed question was settled. The Cape government had stepped in to relieve the city of its burden of uncivilized, low-paid, slum-bound, disease-ridden black labourers. But that, of course, was not really so. A vast issue emerging gradually for years past had merely moved another notch towards definition.

II

The underlying question was one of overall social control: how to organize society to provide for the mutual access of black labourers and white employers in the coming industrial age without having to pay the heavy social costs of urbanization or losing the dominance of white over black. This question arose in the 1890s as increasing numbers of Africans congregated in the vicinity of large industrial enterprises.[21] White farmers raised the classic complaints of stock theft, 'loafing', drunkenness and disorder against these unregulated settlements. Their major motive was the traditional demand for ample, subservient rural labour – forced if necessary. The traditionally rural orientation of 'native policy' was, however, no longer going to be adequate.

Legislation was introduced in 1899 to provide a special jurisdiction where industrial employers could house and control their
workers in private locations. The new 'Native Labour Locations
Bill' (Act 30 of 1899) proposed to exempt these industrial workers from the penalty tax formerly imposed on 'lazy natives' to
shunt labour towards the farmers. Workers would pay instead a
ten shilling hut tax on location houses. 'Undesirable elements'
would be excluded by a pass system tied to work contracts. 'We
must earmark the native', said the Prime Minister, W.P.
Schreiner. 'A badge or ticket ... [would enable] employers to
protect themselves against loafers ... and the public to protect
itself against stock thefts.' Schreiner, a renowned moderate in
Cape politics whose increasing concern for African problems
gave him a liberal reputation in postwar years, seemed concerned to avoid imputations of illiberality: 'The badge', he
assured his hearers, 'would not in any way interfere with [the
native's] liberty.'[22]

Although the Bill did not deal directly with urban areas, the
'special problem' of Cape Town was recognized in debate.
Schreiner made the connection specific. 'We had in the neigh-
bourhood of Cape Town', he believed, 'some 10,000 raw natives.
(Hear, Hear.)'

> They lived all over the place. . . . And they were learning all
> sorts of bad habits through living in touch with European
> or Coloured surroundings. We could not get rid of them:
> They were necessary for work. What we wanted was to get
> them practically in the position of being compounded. . . .
> (Hear, Hear.) Keep the natives out of harm's way; let them
> do their work, receive their wages; and at the end of their
> term of service let them go back to the place whence they
> came – to the native territories, where they should really
> make their home. (Hear, Hear.) The present Bill would at
> least make provision in this direction. The great difficulty
> was the enforcement of compounding, a thing they should
> not be afraid of, because it was really the solution of the
> whole question.

Schreiner concluded with a plea for the strictest kind of liquor
prohibition – in that era the touchstone of liberal prescriptions for
social policy.

His fellow moderate, James Rose Innes, was even more

strongly identified as a liberal friend to African interests. He hailed the Bill as 'the first move' in regulating how Africans were to be brought into contact with civilization, and referred to Kimberley's mining compounds as 'the only feasible and practical manner in which that question had been properly grappled'. As for Schreiner's proposed 'earmarking', Innes had always been opposed to a pass law but now accepted it in the case of industrial labour because he believed the alternative was worse: corruption of the Africans. It fell to Herbert Travers Tamplin, who normally voted with Innes, to chide his colleagues: 'He regretted to see a strong tendency on the part of the government to go in for Transvaal phraseology and practices. This badge of servitude, for instance, ... was not a healthy sign.' But Tamplin, too, wanted locations in large centres like Cape Town.

Innes, indeed, took the case of Cape Town as his clinching argument. It was 'overrun with hordes of natives – uncivilized barbarians. ... [This] Bill contained the germ of principle which offered a remedy', Innes said, but in order to apply that remedy the law must get hold of the independent, urbanized Africans as well. To do this, parliament must confront the 'inconvenience' of the Native Voters Act under which African property holders possessed civil rights that exempted them from a pass law. This independent class would hinder enforcement of urban locations. It interfered with control because it 'erected a barrier against dealing with natives as a whole'.[23]

This is an important point, for it shows that in the minds of these Cape leaders urban social policy was to be founded on a racial category – 'natives as a whole', rather than a non-racial pluralism. In this conception class and race converged. In effect, these guardians of the Cape liberal tradition seem to have been prepared from the outset to undermine for the sake of social and humanitarian concerns an already tenuous future for African liberties – the chance to enter a common society through the urban nexus. Their anxieties focused on the preservation of civilized society, which they believed was threatened with disorder and decay apparent to them in the festering 'hordes' of 'raw natives' at Cape Town and other urban centres. Their prescription included the major elements of urban policy as it emerged in the generations to come: that Africans should be considered as one category; that urban blacks should remain migrant labour segregated from white society lest they corrupt and be corrupted;

and that the means to this end must be compulsory removal or
expulsion to compounds and locations. The plague then cata-
lysed this mixture with the fear of a medical disaster.

III

With the plague emergency the definitive step of quarantine and
segregation was taken. Yet the public health laws of 1883 and
1897 provided no permanent solution, for the authority given by
them depended upon the existence of 'urgent necessity' during
an epidemic of infectious disease.[24] The Native Labour Locations
Act of 1899 was for private industrial locations only. The next
step was, therefore, a search for new legal powers.

As the plague receded, administration relaxed and Africans
drifted back into town in large numbers. As Innes had predicted
in 1899, even the plague removal had been qualified by numerous
exemptions for black freeholders and leaseholders, domestic
servants and stevedores barracked near the docks. By December
1901, increasing complaints of disorder and vagrancy, and fears
of reverting to pre-plague conditions, were voiced by the local
authorities of Cape Town and its satellite municipalities.[25] As for
Uitvlugt itself the brave start of 1901 soon ran into heavy weather.
Deficits mounted to £1,500 a month. Yet the government was
determined to make locations pay for themselves. Revenue was
vital for the location schemes. But Africans, defended by white
critics of the policy, some of whom as slumlords had interests of
their own at stake, resented on principle having to pay rent where
they were compelled to live. The doubtful legality of continued
proceedings under the Public Health Act was advertised to the
blacks and resistance developed. Riots at Uitvlugt created a sen-
sation over location policy and something had to be done.[26]

Municipalities and government tossed the ball of obligation
back and forth: who should have responsibility for urban
Africans? Under what laws and regulations? Towns wanted the
government to establish and operate locations. The colony's
Native Affairs Department (NAD) resisted, arguing that with
the recession of the plague they could not do so, nor did they
wish to, and that towns should use the 1899 Locations Law to
establish private locations under their own control, since they
were the beneficiaries of the labour thus acquired. Early in 1902
the Colonial Undersecretary for local government and public

health went so far as to advise the town clerk of Sea Point (a residential suburb of Cape Town) that there was 'nothing to prevent your Council from applying to have the whole of their Municipal area declared a Location ... and then setting aside a portion of ground on which it should be compulsory for all natives to reside'. We may imagine the hilarity and exasperation with which Sea Point's town councillors entertained the thought of proclaiming their entire municipality a 'native location'.[27]

Soon a new 'Native Reserve Locations Bill', for protecting and regulating the supply of Native Labour' appeared in the Cape parliament. It called for government powers to establish locations near urban areas; to compel residence in them; to exact rents under threat of criminal penalties; to control any and all public services such as sanitation, schools and trade in them; and to prohibit the sale of liquor. But the government's NAD sought to limit severely the Bill's compulsory powers and criminal penalties[28] and wished municipalities to make their own regulations to force Africans into locations.

Dr A. John Gregory, Medical Officer of Health for the Cape Colony, was asked to advise in the preparation of the Bill. Gregory was a man of intelligence, administrative ability and, as is common in medical men, authoritarian spirit. A certain bigotry was revealed by his petulant opposition to changing the name of Uitvlugt Location to 'Ndabeni' because it was 'not a good working name for Europeans'. He took a hard line against the position of the NAD. The latter, he asserted, were so reluctant to coerce Africans that they were trying to water down the legislation's essential provisions. He had no doubt whatever that force was an absolutely necessary element in any effective urban native policy. Without it, 'the Native ... would leave the Location in favour of the attractions which residence in the Town offer[s] him'. Gregory went further, calling for total control through a comprehensive pass system applying to whole districts beyond municipalities and their locations. If the NAD was 'squeamish' about this, let the powers at least go to municipalities, and if they in turn failed to exercise them, the Governor himself should put them into effect.[29]

Gregory's concern went far beyond health and sanitary matters alone. He believed Africans should be segregated on principle, and saw the police, not civil or medical administrators, as the appropriate agency. No permits of exemption from the new law should be allowed without the agreement of the police. Gregory's police mentality showed that the sanitation syndrome implied much more than amelioration: 'The Police are the proper authority [to permit exemption from locations] ... especially as the mere question of the sanitary condition[s] ... is of less importance than some of the other points. ... Indeed if only the sanitary condition of the premises is to form the basis of the decision then practically a very large number of Natives could be allowed to reside in Cape Town.'[30]

Gregory's opinions were taken seriously and many of his proposals were agreed to. But W.G. Cumming, Secretary for Native Affairs, challenged his call for district-wide enforcement by asserting that urban Africans could be forced into locations merely by prohibiting urban employment to anyone without a pass. In this respect, the government had its eye cocked towards a major source of opposition to the new Bill: farmers. Farm labour must be exempted from a location pass law. Thus Cumming evaded Gregory's real point, which was the necessity to apply the law to all Africans over extensive areas. Here, the Prime Minister, Sir Gordon Sprigg, also temporized, not wishing to add wider pass and police powers. 'Leave it to Regulations', he said.[31]

Sprigg as leader of the Progressive Party, the inheritors of Rhodes's imperial mantle, knew he faced vigorous opposition in parliament from such liberal anti-Progressives as J.W. Sauer and John X. Merriman backed by H.T. Tamplin and J.T. Molteno, all from the eastern Cape where a large African as well as rural vote existed. In presenting the Bill for debate, Sprigg appealed for wide support on the basis of segregation, saying that with the plague now receding there was no longer 'any [lawful] reason for refusing to allow the natives to associate with the white population'.[32] Under the proposed law, the natives would emerge from barbarism 'so that they might no longer be a source of danger'. At Uitvlugt, for example, things were not so bad as alleged. There was a free hospital, churches were allowed, some 'better class' huts were being put up and liquor was to be forbidden as in the Transkei.

But Sauer struck at ultimate implications, professing to be aghast at the Bill's 'extreme and oppressive' powers to invade 'the rights and freedoms of individuals – whether white or black'. He argued for a non-racial test on civilized standards: 'There were many natives who were fitted by education, by their habits and mode of life, to live where other civilized people lived'. Edgar

Harris Walton of Port Elizabeth tried to counter Sauer's point by noting that registered voters were to be exempt, but Sauer replied that many of the Africans they actually would put into locations could qualify for the franchise, and there were many unqualified to vote, perhaps without education, who were otherwise respectable citizens. To Sauer and other critics, 'the real crux of the bill was the powers which it gave the Government'. They were too great, notwithstanding Dr Gregory's views, for they implied the establishment of labour locations anywhere in the country, threatening Africans and the white employers of farm labour far beyond the municipalities, and allowing expropriation of white and black alike.[33]

Both Sauer and Merriman represented rural interests against the big towns, and Merriman launched his attack on economic as well as humanitarian grounds. Who should pay? It was a 'monstrous doctrine' to tax the colony generally to supply labour at sweated wages to urban employers. Let the municipalities pay. It was a question of responsibility. 'These men in Cape Town who had made big piles should be made to pay. They dragged these people from the farms and then left them to go body and soul to ruin in Cape Town. ... A man could have a horde of barbarians sent down from the Transkei and ... [then] send them down to the dog kennels at [Uitvlugt]'.[34]

These critics, however, were not opposed to separating the mass of Africans, the 'raw natives' or 'barbarians', from the corruptions of the town. The conflict was really over how to segregate, under what conditions and at what cost. For example, Walton, though he strongly favoured locations and supported the Bill, sided with Sauer in opposing criminal sanctions against rent defaulters and pass violators (already a major headache of location administration). In this regard he believed the Bill would fail. It would simply create a class of convicts. Others, however, hailed the prospect of jail for defaulters, since, in their view, the Africans were paid too much and simply squandered their money. Some wanted the towns to control locations for reasons exactly opposed to Merriman's: not because towns ought to pay for what advantaged them, but because locations could be a source of municipal income. Still others, on the other hand, joined Walton and Sprigg in calling for the government to avert such exploitation. In the end, though divided on details, parliament nevertheless agreed (Sauer least willingly) on the main issue: urban segregation had become necessary to save both Africans and the cities from each other. It was 'absolutely impossible for the sanitation of the town to be attended to under present conditions'.[35] The Attorney-General, Graham, reminded his colleagues vividly of why they had acted already to establish Uitvlugt in the plague emergency:

> The condition of affairs which then prevailed in Cape Town was a disgrace to any country in the civilized world. Whole streets were inhabited by natives, and in some houses close to the leading thoroughfares the cellars were occupied by large numbers of men – Europeans, Malays, and raw Kafirs – all sandwiched together, living in a state of the utmost neglect, disease, and vice ... and it was essential that the natives should be removed from the city. ... The Premier and himself came to the conclusion that it was absolutely necessary to bring in a measure dealing with the natives in large centres. ... The idea was to benefit the natives, and to keep them away from the contaminating influences of the town, and also indirectly to assist the labour market.[36]

In sum, the sanitation syndrome was everyone's point of reconciliation. Beyond this point Sauer and Merriman prevailed over Dr Gregory, for the Bill was watered down, and its original powers of compulsory location were drastically limited to areas *within* municipal boundaries and the locations themselves.[37] The Native Reserve Locations Act (No. 40 of 1902) therefore left Africans free of control right up to the borders of the towns, as the municipality of Port Elizabeth discovered to its dismay.

IV

Traditionally 'Cape Liberalism' is thought to have drawn a line among Africans between the barbarous and the civilized, yet Cape urban policy well before 1910 sought to link them together. Officials like Stanford and Scully were interested in African 'improvement' as well as amelioration but they were fundamentally paternalist and segregationist. They wished to protect the 'barbarians' while they evolved, and the European towns at least until they evolved, but there would be no end to the process and, in common with parallel developments elsewhere in South Africa, these initiatives became the seed bed of urban segregation.

In conclusion, Cape Town's and Port Elizabeth's experience with bubonic plague transcended its purely epidemiological dimensions. The plague had been identified with their black populations and they with it. Steps taken to stop the plague persisted after the emergency. Sanitation and public health provided the legal means to effect quick removals of African populations; they then sustained the rationale for permanent urban segregation.

The locations themselves, at first perceived as the means to remove a medical menace from white towns, came to be viewed as an equal danger. Alarm mounted at obvious degeneration in the mushrooming urban locations and slums after 1912, and most dramatically in the frightful influenza epidemic of 1918 when over 130,000 Africans died. In 1914 the Union government's Tuberculosis Commission condemned locations and slums together as 'a menace to the health of their inhabitants and indirectly to the health of those in the town', and identified white slumlords as a major problem whose property interests prevented action by local authorities. African property rights were equally condemned. In general, private property of either description was seen as a stumbling block to improvement and protection of urban Africans. Officials wished to break this economic nexus of African 'squalor'. They prescribed government control or laws enjoining municipalities to enforce sanitation and eschew profit motives in location management.[38] The 1918 Influenza Commission did recommend 'security of tenure' for householders to encourage better housing, but the 1923 Natives (Urban Areas) Act abandoned this possibility in favour of allowing municipal funding of improvements through the revenues of the native beer monopoly system.[39] In promoting legislation the Union Native Affairs Department noted that 'The Influenza Epidemic [had been] ... a startling revelation [of African conditions] and to what extent these conditions were a standing menace to the health of our whole population.'[40]

The essential point was not that locations were wrong, but that uncontrolled and insanitary locations were wrong, and that municipalities and private interests were responsible. The constant aim of official policy remained to reinforce segregation by seeking to make locations more viable in serving their isolating function along the lines of the medico-social analogy already so familiar. The unresolved issues of 1902–5 would come to a head

in future times of critical growth, ever larger in scope and more
daunting in their implications.

NOTES

1 The research for this article was made possible by grants from Yale
   University, The American Philosophical Society and Miami
   University of Ohio.
2 M.W. Swanson, 'Urban Origins of Separate Development', *Race*, X
   (1968), 31–40, esp. 37; 'Reflections on the Urban History of
   South Africa', in H.L. Watts (ed.), *Focus on Cities* (Durban, 1970),
   142–9, esp. 147; '"The Durban System": Roots of Urban Apartheid
   in Colonial Natal', *African Studies*, XXXV, 3 and 4 (Dec. 1976),
   159–76.
3 K. David Patterson, 'Disease and Medicine in African History',
   History in Africa, I (1974), 142.
4 William L. Langer, 'History's Next Assignment', *American Historical
   Review*, LXIII, 2 (Dec. 1957), 283–304.
5 Gareth Stedman Jones, *Outcast London: A Study of the Relationship
   Between Classes in Victorian Society* (Oxford, 1971), 13–16, 167, 188–93,
   256ff., 289–98, 306–12, 330–2.
6 *Natal Mercury*, 24 March, 13 December 1870; Durban *Mayor's
   Minutes*, 1891, 1870–93 *passim*.
7 Robert H. Huttenback, *Gandhi in South Africa* (Ithaca, NY, 1971), 53ff.
   and 77ff.; P.S. Joshi, *The Tyranny of Colour* (Durban, 1942), 57.
8 Huttenback, *Gandhi*, 107ff. and 128; Joshi, *Tyranny*, 50ff.
9 *Natal Mercury*, 2 and 3 December 1886.
10 William Jameson (Durban Borough Councillor) to Theophilus
   Shepstone, and Shepstone to Jameson, 3 and 5 August 1881, Natal
   Archives, Shepstone Collection, Box 17. Cf Freda Wolfson, 'Some
   Aspects of Native Administration under Theophilus Shepstone
   1857–1865', unpubl. MA thesis (Witwatersrand, 1946), 67–8.
11 For the process by which urban apartheid was precipitated in Natal
   at this time see M.W. Swanson, '"The Durban System": Roots of
   Urban Apartheid in Colonial Natal'.
12 R. Pollitzer, *Plague*, The World Health Organization (Geneva, 1954),
   ch. 1
13 Cape Town *Mayor's Minutes* (*MM*), 1900–1, 169–70 and
   CXXXIX–CXLI, Report of the Medical Officer of Health (MOH).
14 A term used by the Police Superintendent of Durban, describing
   conditions in that city to the *South African Native Affairs Commission,
   1903–5* (*SANAC*), *Evidence*, III, 640–58.
15 *SANAC*, 205; *MM*, 1904–5, Appendix 10 (Census of 1904).
16 *MM*, 1900–1, CXL, 172–3.
17 *MM*, 1899–1900, 53; *MM*, 1900–1, 179–80. See J.W. MacQuarrie (ed.),
   The Reminiscences of Sir Walter Stanford, vol. II (Cape Town, 1962), 213.
   Stanford gives the impression that the Uitvlugt location was established before the plague, but the commission's recommendation

did not appear until after the city council had appealed to the government on 14 February 1901.

18 Public Health Act (No. 4 of 1883) as amended by Act No. 23 of 1897. Section 15: 'In cases of urgent necessity arising from the prevalence or threatened outbreak in any district of infectious disease . . . it shall be lawful for the Minister to make and proclaim such regulations to be in force within such districts as may be required to prevent the outbreak, or check the progress of, or eradicate such disease'. Cape of Good Hope, *Acts of Parliament* 3741–70. Cf Stanford's *Reminiscences*, II, 214, n. 3.

19 *MM*, 1900–1, 180. Cape of Good Hope, *Native Affairs Blue Book (NABB)* 1901 [G25–1902], 81–9, 'Report on Uitvlugt Location'. NA598/1525, 'Papers Relating to Natives Living Outside Locations in Urban Areas, 1901–6', Govt Notices 237, 12 March 1901, and 577, 24 June 1901. (All archival citations are from Cape Archives.)

20 *MM*, 1900–1, 169–79.

	Cases	Deaths
Whites	204	69
Coloureds	431	244
Africans	172	76
	807	389

21 Cases in point were the Indwe Company's coal mines near Molteno in the eastern Cape and the DeBeers dynamite factory at Somerset West near Cape Town. NA625/1988, 'Matters in Connection with Native Location Acts, 1893–1906', Minute Paper No. 304, W.E. Stanford (Supt of Native Affairs) to Prime Minister, 6 June 1899.

22 *Cape Times*, 27 July 1899, 'Second Reading Debate, Native Labour Locations Bill', NA625/1988.

23 Ibid.

24 Note 18 above.

25 NA598/1525, W.G. Cumming (SNA) to Prime Minister (PM), 6 December 1901; Municipal Clerk, Sea Point, to Cumming, 21 March 1902; file of petitions, certificates and memoranda *in re* exemptions.

26 *NABB* 1902 [G29–1903], 94–6, 'Reports on Ndabeni Location'. *NABB* 1903 [G12–1904], 94, 'Report on Condition of Ndabeni'. NA533/617, 'Papers Relating to Native Reserves Location Bill, 1902', memoranda of Acting Assistant Resident Magistrate, Uitvlugt, 27 May 1902; W.G. Cumming to PM, 28 July 1902; Dr A. John Gregory (Colonial MOH), 2 August 1902. See also Alfred G. Seller to editor, *Cape Times*, 23 July 1902.

27 NA598/1525, esp. memos by W.G. Cumming to PM, 6 December 1901, and Noel Janisch (Under Col. Sec.) to Town Clerk, Sea Point, 27 March 1902. NA 533/617, W.G.C. to PM, 28 July 1902.

28 As note 27.

29 As note 27, Gregory to Colonial Sec., 2 August 1902. Stanford, *Reminiscences*, 214–15, says Uitvlugt was renamed Ndabeni, using the name Africans had given to himself, at the request of black

leaders, though Sprigg thought it was to celebrate his own role in the settlement.

30 NA598/1525, Gregory to Cumming, 8 October 1902.
31 NA533/617, Gregory to Col. Sec., 2 August 1902, Memorandum by W.G.C., 11 August 1902.
32 Cape House of Assembly (H of A), *Debates*, 144–7, 8 September 1902.
33 H of A, *Debates*, 145, and 326–7, 29 September 1902.
34 H of A, *Debates*, 146.
35 H of A, *Debates*, 145.
36 H of A, *Debates*, 329.
37 H of A, *Debates*, 654. Act 40 of 1902 was promulgated 18 November 1902. Cape Government *Gazette*, Supplement, 21 November 1902, 88–91.
38 *Report of the Tuberculosis Commission, 1914* (UG 34–'14), 125, 129, 13–39, 323. [UG denotes Union of South Africa, Parliamentary Papers Series. It is followed by the number and the year – Eds.]
39 For an early review of the growth of urban policy see J.S. Allison, 'Urban Native Administration', *Race Relations*, VII, 4 (1940), 54–62. For the 1923 Urban Areas Act and 'liberal' proposals for freehold and amelioration, cf T.R.H. Davenport, 'African Townsmen? South African Natives (Urban Areas) Legislation Through the Years', *African Affairs*, vol. 68, issue 271 (April 1969), 98–100, and Peter Kallaway, 'F.S. Malan, the Cape Liberal Tradition, and South African Politics 1903–1924', *J. Afr. Hist.* XV, I (1974), 113–29, esp. 123–8. For the beer monopoly, see note 2 above.
40 *Report of the Native Affairs Department 1919–21* [UG 34–'22], 13.

2

BRITISH HEGEMONY AND THE ORIGINS OF SEGREGATION IN SOUTH AFRICA, 1901–14*

Martin Legassick

This paper by Martin Legassick is one of three that the scholar and political activist presented to the Southern African Seminar at the Institute of Commonwealth Studies, London University, in 1972–3. Though widely influential and often cited in academic works, none has been published before and all are 'unfinished'. The historiographical importance of this paper lies in its location of the origins of segregation in terms of British imperial policy in the decade after the South African War of 1899–1902. Legassick shows how the British conquest of South Africa created unprecedented opportunities for the rational administrative and political 'reconstruction' of the former British colonies and Afrikaner republics. Central to the vision of the new South Africa was a concerted attempt to define 'native policy'. The South African Native Affairs Commission of 1903–5, headed by Sir Godfrey Lagden, represented a key document in this regard. It served to articulate some of the main premises of what later emerged as 'segregation': territorial separation between whites and blacks; a controlled flow of cheap African labour to the white cities and mines; and a political system that excluded Africans from direct representation in government. Legassick locates core elements of segregationist theory within wider imperial debates. And he indicates that these ideas retained influence in the interwar period when segregation was fully realized and implemented by an Afrikaner-led government.

* * *

The fact is we have all been moving steadily from the Cape idea of mixing up white, brown and black and developing the different grades of colour strictly along the lines of

43

European civilization, to the very opposite conception of encouraging as far as possible the black man to separate from the white and to develop a civilization, as he is beginning to do in Basutoland, on his own lines. For that reason we have been apt to attach great importance to maintaining the sanctity of the native reserves and not breaking them up as Botha wishes to do. We want to see them kept as places to which in the future the black man can retreat if as we believe the tendency will be for the white man to push him out.

Lionel Curtis to Patrick Duncan, 26 November 1907

I

The policy of racial segregation in South Africa, more recently known by the terms apartheid, separate development and multinational development, has had at different times and for different groups a multiplicity of meanings and functions. Segregation operates at the levels of ideology, of social control, of reproduction of labour and so on. Yet if there is a common thread which unites these meanings it is at the level of the imperative for separate territorial/residential poles as the focus of black and white activities in South Africa, coupled with the idea that black and white have different wants and requirements in the fields of social, cultural and political policy. Some of those who have examined segregation have found its roots at the commencement of white settlement, with van Riebeeck's attempt to build a hedge to separate white and Khoisan. Others see it, or, more strictly, apartheid, as the product of Afrikaner nationalist thought, specifically since the 1930s. I would argue that the crucial formative period for the policy of segregation was between the South African War of 1899–1902 and the First World War.

It is true that aspects of the totality which is 'segregation' can be discovered in earlier periods. Dr John Philip was termed by W.M. Macmillan the first and greatest segregationist. He was concerned chiefly with the Khoisan, but (as Francis Wilson has noted) the same policy applied to Africans in the Cape may be found in parliamentary reports from the 1870s. David Welsh and Maynard Swanson, among others, have seen the roots of segregation in nineteenth-century Natal, Shepstonian and post-Shepstonian. Yet in neither case was there quite the same totality created of ideological rationalization, economic functions and legislative-administrative policy. Symptomatically, segregation only acquired its name, by diffusion (it would seem) from the American South, after the turn of the century. My chronology, though not developed fully in my argument, is similar to that of Van den Berghe, Roskam or the Simons's.[1] But Van den Berghe regards segregation as a competitive industrial (rather than patriarchal pre-industrial) form of racism created by a white urban working class; while the Simons's view the policy almost entirely at the level of social control, as a response to the changing focus of African protest and resistance from 'tribal society' to the framework of colonial society. These I would see only as aspects of a wider policy, its ideological, political and economic levels the specific product of the birth of capitalist social relations in a colonial society.

II

The conquest of the Transvaal and the Orange Free State in 1900 inaugurated six years of British supremacy in South Africa before Campbell-Bannerman's so-called magnanimous gesture set things moving towards political independence for the Union in 1910. But in those six years Milner[a] and his administrative appointees had, as they consciously understood, the opportunity to 'reconstruct' the institutions of South Africa with a power greater than that wielded before or since by Britain. Of course this reconstruction had its limits – and many aspects of Milner's failure to match ideal to action have been dealt with recently by Denoon.[2] Administrators are always constrained by the institutions and structures which they inherit. They usually find a whole range of processes at work which are totally outside their control. The changes they make are often trivial or superficial, or are blocked or modified, or unanticipated in their effects at different levels of the system. Yet – and in this period of reconstruction many polemicists were to insist on this point – if there was an overall vision, appropriate action could initiate *trends* in one direction or another. And where so-called natural or inevitable processes were at work, they could sometimes be guided and directed towards ends beneficial or harmful to 'the society'. Thus, within the sphere of legislation or administration, certain things could be achieved or not achieved. But more

45

important perhaps was the elaboration of the vision as the pre-
liminary to achievement. Those in power in this period knew
their time was limited. The best they could hope for was to create
an intellectual climate and the formal and informal institutions to
support that climate, which would encourage legislation and
administration to proceed along desirable lines in the future.

The key aspects of that vision were enunciated by Milner in a
famous letter to that archetypal articulator of the political interests of deep-level gold mining, Percy Fitzpatrick: 'The ultimate
end is a self-governing white community supported by well-
treated and justly governed black labour from Cape Town to the
Zambezi.' And, as Blainey, Denoon and others have convincingly
argued (and whatever the nuances of the relationship between
the British imperial regime at this point and mining capital), the
immediate beneficiary of these ends assigned to government was
the gold-mining industry.[3] British power, in short, was called in
to destroy a state based on feudal relations of production in the
Transvaal, and to create throughout South Africa the conditions
for securing a sufficiency of black labour at a suitably low price.
The state was to *stimulate* or *initiate* certain kinds of processes.
Equally, it was to *guide* or even *inhibit* others. For directly and
indirectly the mining industry had already qualitatively
increased the numbers of those dependent on wages for their
subsistence (and it had already drawn a dividing line between
the unskilled who were black almost exclusively, and the skilled
who were almost entirely white). Other forms of capitalist
economic activity were burgeoning: railway construction, commerce, secondary industry in some degree, capitalist agriculture.

Among the central aspects of the creation of this vision for
the new kind of society in South Africa was the area of 'native
policy': that is, of policies of social welfare and social control for
those socially defined as 'native'. The Selborne Memorandum is
only the most familiar of the documents to insist that a unified
South African state must be created so that a common 'native
policy' could be implemented. At the Intercolonial Conference
of 1903, the first such gathering since the war, summoned to
consider a common customs policy, Milner himself introduced
'the Native Question' and 'Alien Immigration' to the agenda. He
was partly paving the way for the introduction of Chinese labour
(by emphasizing the labour shortage) and he was partly (argues
Denoon) concerned that the customs discussions would break

down. But he also hoped, if not for the immediate drafting of a 'common Native code', at least

> an agreement on certain general principles which, being adopted by a body like this, would undoubtedly possess very high moral authority and could not fail to exercise a good influence on the future legislation of the several States and on their administrative action in matters affecting the Native races.

Such general principles as were agreed were chiefly on the question of labour supply. But it was also decided to establish a Commission with two representatives from each colony, and one each from Rhodesia and Basutoland, which would 'gather accurate information on affairs relating to the Natives and native administration, and ... offer recommendations to the several Governments concerned with the object of arriving at a common understanding on questions of native policy'. (It may be noted that the Anthropological Institute in Britain had recommended a similar inquiry to the Colonial Secretary three years earlier, on the grounds – a refrain much heard in South Africa – that contact with 'civilization', in particular the mines, was dissolving 'tribal restraints' without imposing new ones, thus rendering them 'difficult to manage' unless governments framed regulations 'in accordance with the customs and institutions' of those concerned.)

This Commission, the South African Native Affairs Commission (SANAC), reported in February 1905 and was widely acclaimed (except, perhaps, by diehard nineteenth-century liberals in the Cape). Thus two of the leading 'friends of the natives' in the American Board of Foreign Missions regarded it as 'very liberal and broad-minded', 'admitted on all sides to be sane and statesmanlike', 'without local prejudice or ulterior motive'. 'You can hardly realize what pleasant reading it is after the rabid stuff we are constantly reading about ourselves and our people in the newspapers. ... It appears that the Commission stands strongly for nearly every principle of treatment that missionaries stand for.' And SANAC enunciated numerous aspects of what was to emerge as the policy of segregation. It advocated racially exclusive occupation of separate land areas, and the political representation of blacks and whites by separate means. Yet it was no protagonist of *total* separation. If there was emphasis on the preservation and development of an agriculturally based African society, SANAC was equally clear that black labour was needed by the South African mining and urban economy. Its chairman was Sir Godfrey Lagden, an upwardly mobile and reactionary High Tory, who had served as Resident Commissioner in Basutoland before his appointment by Milner to run Native Affairs in the Transvaal (where his chief task was to secure labour for the mines). In an article contemporary with SANAC's report, Lagden emphasized that it could not be 'deemed of advantage for an inferior race, struggling upwards, to be brought up in the notion that its only means of subsistence must be the land: it narrows the vision of hopeful evolution . . . success in the struggle for existence lies in learning handicrafts and pursuing callings which offer a ready and comfortable return for industry'.

SANAC believed that the supply of black labour could be increased locally: it rejected direct compulsion but maintained also that

> Any recommendation as to higher wages is quite out of place. In the first place, any departure from the principle that the rate of wages must be a free contract . . . is unsound.
>
> Further, it has been stated, and the Commission feels that there is a measure of truth in the suggestion, that while increased wages might have the effect of tempting a larger number of labourers in to the market, on the other hand, such increased gains would enable them to remain for a longer period at their homes.

The task, in fact, and it is made fairly explicit at the 1903 Intercolonial Conference and other commentary of that time, was 'to compel indirectly', to *create* a *voluntary* supply, to proletarianize. Over the long run, as Lagden wrote, 'as population increases and the thirst for land to cultivate is no longer so keenly felt, they may be expected to become continuously industrious workmen looking on their land as mere gardens to supplement the comforts of living'. Socially and culturally SANAC's general feeling was that 'advance cannot be stayed, but must be conducted under civilized guidance'. It was 'assisted evolution' and

> evolution, to be sound and healthy, must, following the dictates of Nature, be of slow growth. Unnatural development of the human species creates the same sort of impression as is formed in the mind of the cultivator at the sight of a

spurious and weedy plant – the genus does not commend itself for propagation.

In the initial stages, at least, it seemed, 'the rational policy . . . is to facilitate the development of aboriginals on lines which do not merge too closely into European life, lest it lead to *enmity* and stem the tide of healthy progress'. In the sphere of education this meant that 'the character and extent of aboriginal teaching should be such as to afford opportunities for the natives to acquire that amount of elementary knowledge for which in their present state they are fitted'.

III

SANAC issued its report in a period of transition. Milner left South Africa some two months later, to be replaced by Selborne. Lagden went on six months' leave and returned shortly before the Liberal government came to power in Britain over the Chinese labour question. By the end of that year, 1906, the Transvaal had a new self-governing constitution on the basis of the recommendations of the Ridgeway Committee; and by the end of that year the Kindergarten, spearheaded by Lionel Curtis, had launched its campaign for Closer Union.

SANAC is clearly an important landmark in the evolution of the 'native policy' of the South African state, though it could be argued that it represented the sum of local and not metropolitan wisdom. SANAC was prepared as a guidebook for future reference in the best imperial tradition through a synthesis of imperial guidelines with local expertise. The measure of the influence of the period of British hegemony is the extent to which its recommendations were disseminated, adopted and implemented; and the extent and manner in which this was done by Imperial representatives.

A large step to this end was taken by Lionel Curtis in a paper written in 1906–7 (at the same time as the draft Selborne Memorandum) to be presented to the Fortnightly Club, the same forum at which Feetham launched the Closer Union campaign. The Club was apparently established by the Kindergarten, and limited to forty members. Curtis's paper was titled 'The Place of Subject Peoples in the Empire' but its purpose was clearly South African. It contains the first use of the word 'segregation' that I have yet traced in the South African context, and it sets the policy within a more coherent ideological framework than did SANAC.

The core of Curtis's argument was the distinction between 'Indian' and 'Australian' models of colonial government, and the identification of the South African situation as an amalgam of the two. The origins of this argument need further research. Elements of it can be found in writings of the 1880s and 1890s in South Africa, and it was given a wider authority, or perhaps its first coherent presentation, in James Bryce's *Impressions of South Africa* (1897):[4] South Africa was a society

> in which the native race is, on the one hand, numerous and strong enough to maintain itself in the face of Europeans, while, on the other hand, there is plenty of room left for a considerable European population to press in, climatic conditions not forbidding it to spread and multiply.

It was this juxtaposition which constituted the specificity, even the existence, of a 'native problem' or 'native question' in South Africa. As the Intercolonial Conference of 1903 resolved, 'the Native Question embraces the present and future status of all aboriginal natives of South Africa, and the relation in which they stand towards the European population'. Or, as Lagden put it:

> What is understood as the native problem existing today may be divided under a few heads – those which affect aboriginal contact with whites in a country which, formerly inhabited only by aboriginal races, has now been reclaimed by Europeans of higher intellect, with the fixed and determined purpose of permanent occupation and development.

Indeed the very construction of this model requires probing at a level more systematic than I intend here. The model grew out of and reacted back on a social system, emphasizing certain features and ignoring others, shaped by the system and reshaping it. There was, to begin with, the deliberate and conscious conflation of racial and cultural distinctions. 'Turn it over as you will', wrote Lagden in private, 'there is and must be a dividing line between semi-barbarism and civilization. You needn't say it is between black and white, but for the time being it means the same thing.' The viewpoint was a common one: the capacity of individual 'natives' was irrelevant to the treatment of the native problem as a whole. The dynamics of the situation were created by such factors as comparative rates of racial population increase, the degree and character of miscegenation and the extent and character of the workrole distribution in industry (by skills and race). The contradictions which created these dynamics permitted South Africa to be seen as an Indian–Australian amalgam, and in turn the model ('white man's country', 'black man's country') reacted back to be utilized by actors in the struggle.

Yet here I am concerned with the effects, and not the origins, of this model. Bryce drew the significant conclusion that:

> the general difficulty of adjusting the relations of a higher and a lower race, serious under every kind of government, here presents itself in the special form of the construction of a political system which, while democratic as regards one of the races, cannot safely be made democratic as regards the other. . . .

For classic nineteenth-century liberalism, from which milieu Bryce sprang, these ideas were, or should have been, difficult to swallow. Yet (as Curtis pointed out) they were also argued by J.S. Mill:

> If the smaller nationality supposed to be the more advanced in improvement, is able to overcome the greater . . . there is often a gain to civilization; but the conquerors and the conquered cannot in this case live together under the same free institutions. The absorption of the conquerors in the less advanced people would be an evil; these must be governed as subjects, and the state of things is either a benefit or a misfortune according as the subjugated people have or have not reached the state in which it is an injury not to be under a free government, and according as the conquerors do or do not use their superiority in a manner calculated to fit in the conquered for a higher state of improvement.

Bryce was slightly more defensive; he situated himself between the old faith in equality and democracy and the imperatives of the new imperial era. The so-called disaster of Southern Reconstruction was on his mind (and on those of white South Africans from at least the 1890s), and he was conditioned by the viewpoints of South African 'progressives' – the Lovedale missionaries, Johannesburg mine-owners and those who were turning away from Cape ideals. 'It is easy for people in England',

51

he wrote, 'who have no experience of the presence among them of a semi-civilized race, destitute of the ideas and habits which lie at the basis of free government, to condemn the action of these Colonies in seeking to preserve a decisive electoral majority for the white.' Yes, it was wrong to exclude voters merely on the score of their race, and the 'coloured' should have *some* representation (though he did not explicitly mention identical qualifications to white); 'but to toss the gift of political power into the lap of a multitude of persons who are not only ignorant, but in mind children rather than men, is not to confer a boon, but to inflict an injury'.

Curtis's argument was more coherent and less defensive. Sometimes, he conceded, the Imperial government had 'yielded to the temptation to justify itself to the subject peoples' on the basis of the 'will o' the wisp of equality' – but only because of pressure from self-governing Englishmen, few of whom came in contact with subject races. But were such a principle to be effected 'the British Empire would tumble down like a pack of cards'; the conflict between myth and reality meant that 'Colonial history is strewn with broken pledges and contemptible compromises'. Realistically, the mission of the Empire was 'the forceful maintenance of the best system of government in each community compatible with its local conditions' or at least 'better government than it could otherwise have enjoyed'. The white community must become self-governing; the black population must be ruled autocratically. The next problem was who should rule the blacks? Specifically, could the self-governing white community be entrusted with this task?

In the nineteenth century this issue had been a matter of conflict not only between the Imperial power and the local community, but between interest groups in that community. There had been, and remained, a powerful strain of local thought which wanted to preserve and even reseparate black areas under Imperial rule. Two kinds of arguments could be used to justify the transfer (or maintenance) of government in local hands: moral arguments, and arguments of power balance. It may have been the Ridgeway Committee which was the first body to articulate a theme which was voiced increasingly as Union approached: that local settler control was justified. They had been assured by Lagden, they said, that 'during the past few years there has been a wholesome change in public opinion on Native questions'. It was 'moving in the right direction and is tolerant in character.' Curtis used the argument of greater local realism, and implicitly a recognition, at the time of the Bambatha rebellion, of black leverage. Unlike the Indian commercial community, South Africans could not 'abandon the country in a few weeks' and would not because they regarded it as home. They would therefore seek a workable local solution to 'the native problem'.

Yet there was a second argument, on which the Ridgeway Committee and Curtis reached apparently contradictory conclusions. The fact that the 'native was indispensable in the social as well as the industrial economy of the two Colonies', insisted Ridgeway, ensured white self-interest would lead to his fair and benevolent treatment. 'If he were ill-treated he might leave the Colony, and certainly he would not migrate into it.' But for Curtis it was the fact that white and black interests were 'entangled . . . at a hundred different points' which placed difficulties in the way of just treatment. He compared the situation in 'the best of the reserves' like Basutoland (Lagden's stamping ground, on which Lagden would publish a book, in fact, in 1909) with areas where 'black and white are indiscriminately mixed together' like the Natal of Bambatha. The Basuto 'are showing unmistakable signs of progress but their advancement though influenced by white civilization is less on European lines than in a direction of their own', while in Natal

> the native is increasing in numbers but not in advancement. As the area of white cultivation increases there is a tendency to crowd the native off the land which takes the form of raising the rent he pays for squatting. Unhappily sexual intercourse is tending to degrade both races. Moreover the natives are encumbered with debts to the white and Indian populations.

The solution, for Curtis, was segregation. Given a single authority in South Africa, controlling all black-occupied as well as white-occupied areas, given the deliberate adoption of 'the ideal . . . of allowing the white and black races each to develop on their own natural lines, the policy pursued should aim steadily at the separation of the two races into different areas . . . by a well-conceived set of laws'. Curtis suggested, for example, that it should be a principle that fixed property be held only by whites in white areas, etc. 'When a white owner of a property in a black reserve or the black owner of a property in a white reserve, died, the property might be made to revert to the Government who would hand the money value to the heirs.' On the franchise, he suggested that each race have the vote in its own areas to elect to the central parliament, but with black representation fixed in number (and not on the basis of population) as recommended by SANAC.

IV

Give or take some of the details, this is an extraordinarily precise foreshadowing of the situation which a 'well-conceived set of laws' began to establish in South Africa. It is interesting to note Curtis's remarks that 'Personally I was at issue with Mr Pim when he suggested this policy (separation) because I could not apprehend the practical steps by which it could be carried out but they have since been suggested to me by a leading authority on native affairs.' If the identity of this leading authority (Lagden?) is uncertain, that of the later 'liberal' Howard Pim is not, and it is tantalizing to find his name associated with the origins of segregation. Here, in concluding, there are two matters with which to deal briefly: (a) given that Curtis had in fact resigned from the Transvaal administration in October 1906 to launch the Closer Union campaign, how far do his views represent, and how far did they come to represent, British policy in South Africa? (b) what were the means by which 'segregationism' was diffused through white South African opinion so that it became the official policy of the Labour Party, the Nationalist Party and the South African Party by at the latest 1913, and was even debated by the Unionists? Both are large questions, but some brief remarks are in order.

(a) The implicit evidence for the adoption of a segregationist perspective by British policy-makers, or the British authorities, in South Africa is contained in the writings of R. Hyam.[5] If he does not draw these conclusions, it is because of a tendency characteristic of imperial historians to limit his perspective to Public Record Office sources, i.e. to correspondence which would often omit shared assumptions or uncontroversial matters, etc. As Hyam argues, Britain gradually placed less emphasis on the insertion of a non-racial franchise in the Act of Union, in favour of encouraging black representation through Glen Grey-like 'native councils' (and a national council of this kind was first

54

suggested, so far as I am aware, by F.E. Garrett to the Ridgeway Committee), and of securing viable conditions for the transfer of the Protectorates. In other words there was a recognition that the securing of separate territorial/residential areas for Africans (the Basutoland/Transkei model) was more important than political power at the centre (the 'Cape model').

Already in his letter to Duncan of November 1907 Curtis was recommending that Swaziland *not* be transferred immediately to the Transvaal:

> It is a cardinal point in our idea that when South Africa has united, that the South African Government shall take the place of Downing Street so far as Native Protectorates are concerned and we are in hopes that some responsible English Statesman will soon see his way to enunciating this policy openly. If however more Zululands are to be handed over to more Natals to make a mess of this policy it becomes increasingly difficult. From conversations I have had with General Botha I think that he lays more store on getting hold of Swaziland than on Union or anything else and if Swaziland is incorporated with the Transvaal I think that you will feed the undoubted ambition of the average Het Volker of making the Transvaal independent of the rest of South Africa.

And if the Protectorates were *not* transferred immediately, the reason was indeed partly to retain (as Hyam has argued) a bargaining power over South African policy. In part this was power over 'native policy': the desire being, indeed, that segregationism (the securing of land guarantees to Africans of a limited kind not inhibiting migration) be more fully implemented against the class interests of landless whites. Hence Athlone and Harcourt welcomed the Natives Land Act of 1913. And representation was to be through Councils. Thus Buxton welcomed, and perhaps even encouraged, the Native Affairs Act of 1920. When Hertzog came to power in 1924 it was his secessionism[b] and not his 'native policy' which was of most concern to Britain, and one suspects (though this must be examined more closely) that the critique of Hertzog's 'native policy' was always more vociferous among the new South African 'liberals' than in British policy-making circles, at least after the Imperial Conference of 1926. Finally, Britain welcomed the moves towards coalition and fusion by Hertzog and Smuts in the 1930s; one of the premises of their agreement was the passage of the 1936 segregationist legislation.[c]

(b) From about May 1907 Curtis began to press the idea of a newspaper to propagandize for closer union, and specifically to advance the position of the 'British' party, demoralized by the 'Boer' electoral victories. If the principles were contained in the Selborne Memorandum (and would be represented in *The Government of South Africa*, published by Curtis in 1908) 'the facts and the details constantly change and require to be explained' (as Kerr put it). The paper was to be a part only of the Closer Union movement but Curtis hoped it would get sufficient financial backing to enable it to take 'such measures as will make that weekly article circulate not only among the Schreiners, Macintoshes, Maydon's and Pim's but will carry it into the slums of Durban and the uttermost parts of Prieska'. It was to fill what was the 'greatest need', for 'some consistent thinking and preaching outside party politics'.

In the event the paper was not launched until January 1909, when the National Convention was still functioning, so that two issues, but two issues alone appeared before the Convention's report. It was monthly rather than weekly, and though Curtis had spent a part of 1908 seeking financial support for it in Britain, and obtained some, it was largely guaranteed by Abe Bailey.[d] The editor was Philip Kerr who had spent much of 1908 writing the report of the Transvaal Indigency Commission, returned home, been advised by Milner and Lyttelton to be in South Africa for the drafting of the constitution, been unable to participate in the Convention, and thus resigned from government service. The 'non-party-political' nature of the journal was supposedly guaranteed by Howard Pim, who was to refuse to sign financial requisitions if party-political nuances were to rear their heads. F.S. Malan and Mr Crawford were a 'court of appeal'.

So far as 'native policy' was concerned, *The State* in some respects took its heritage from Curtis and the Fortnightly Club, but it also entered a debate already in progress, partly a narrow one on the franchise issue, but also over the whole broad field. Besides writing in newspapers and pamphlets, two central institutions for this debate were the Native Affairs Reform Societies established in Johannesburg and Durban, nearly simultaneously, in January 1908. In Natal the initiative came from the American Board of Foreign Missions, the Congregationist Union and some of those involved in SANAC and the post-Bambatha Natal Native Affairs Commission. Natal may have influenced Johannesburg, but the first Committee in the latter place included, from the Fortnightly Club, Pim, Quinn, Perry, Napier, Furse. Moreover in 1908 two crucial Transvaal Commissions reported: one (on which Philip Kerr was largely instrumental) concerned with the 'poor whites'; and the other concerned with racial allocation of work in the gold-mining industry in the aftermath of the 1907 strike, and which essentially advocated a 'white labour policy'. Indeed it was the period in which the organized sections of the white working class (and elements of the petty bourgeoisie) began moves towards the formation of a Labour Party.

The consequence was that *The State*'s attempt to 'weigh' the issues as between segregation and assimilation, and to push a policy derived from the SANAC–Curtis–Lagden ideas, was outflanked by *total* segregationists, on the one hand, and by a temporary reassertion of Cape liberalism, on the other. And *total* segregation, unlike the policy of Curtis, usually involved a critique of the forced labour practices of the mining industry. The total segregationists were those like Wybergh (writing in *The State*) or F.W. Bell, who captured control of the Transvaal Native Affairs Society. Meanwhile *The State*, with the departure for Britain (and a tour of America with special reference to the South) of Philip Kerr, became more openly partisan under the editorial hand of B.K. Long. And with Curtis and Kerr gone to launch the *Round Table*, the advocacy of Kindergarten positions in South Africa fell on men like Duncan. In 1911–12 Hertzog, perhaps independently, perhaps through people like Bell, perhaps through *The State*, began to advocate segregation – though more on the Curtis model than that of Bell. Deliberately or not, the Unionists[e] chose to label Hertzog a total segregationist, and in 1912 Duncan wrote a pamphlet titled *Suggestions for a Native Policy* which he tried to have accepted as official by the Unionist Party Congress that year. It stressed the imperative of economic 'integration' between white capital and black labour, wanted white workers to achieve their superiority by greater efficiency rather than legislation on 'job colour bars', remarked that the process of 'civilizing' the 'native' to European ways could be guided but not stopped, and pressed for white immigration. (Indeed Duncan, along with the Communist-to-be

Sidney Bunting, had been committee members of a White
Expansion Society founded in 1909.) It was in this context that
Botha began to speak of segregation, and the South African Party
brought to parliament the Natives Land Bill in 1913.

Duncan, as well as others whose South African connections
began with the Milner administration, played an important role
in South Africa throughout the interwar period. Tying his for-
tunes to those of Smuts from 1920, he became a cabinet minister
and eventually Governor-General. In 1927 he republished his
Suggestions for a Native Policy. I have found it remarkable how
through the continuation of his connections with Britain and the
establishment of connections with the United States (he became
with C.T. Loram the South African representative of the Carnegie
Foundation, for example), he crosses the path of almost every
significant commentator on 'native affairs' in the period. To what
extent his emphasis on 'civilization' conflicted with the principles
of segregation, or whether it was not simply a dialectical complement to the dangers of interpreting segregation too 'totally',
must be left for examination on another occasion. Meanwhile the
last word may go to Philip Kerr who, as Secretary of the Rhodes
Trust, visited South Africa (with Lionel Curtis) for the first time
since 1909 in 1926. He expressed his views in two articles in *The
Observer*, the second one on the 'native question', in which
Hertzog's proposed legislation gave evidence 'that the South
African people are beginning to consider the real fundamentals
of the white and black problem which confronts them'.

> Complete segregation of the two races ... is manifestly
> impossible, for geography and economics forbids it. But
> some degree of segregation is desirable, especially in the
> tenure of land, for the gulf between the outlook and civiliza-
> tion of the two colours is so wide that too intimate an associ-
> ation is bad for both. For many years to come the two races
> must develop to a large extent on the lines of their own.

This he did not find inconsistent with maintaining that 'in the
long run ... the Bantu is for good and all the fellow-citizen of
the white South African, and that South Africa itself can only rise
if all its human inhabitants rise together'. What the white man
has to remember is the truth long indicated by experience that
'the civilized Community on contact with a barbarian either
raises it to its own level or sinks'.

EDITORS' NOTES

a Sir Alfred Milner was High Commissioner of South Africa at the time of the South African War of 1899–1902. An uncompromising British imperialist, he was one of the chief instigators of the war against the Boer republics and the leading exponent of 'Anglicization' policies in the postwar period.

b J.B.M. Hertzog was leader of the National Party. He became Prime Minister in 1924 in coalition with the Labour Party. Secessionism refers to anti-imperial Afrikaner sentiment which sought to reform or break links with Britain.

c In 1934, J.B.M. Hertzog's ruling National Party and Jan Smuts's opposition South African Party 'fused' to become the United Party. The United Party, with Hertzog as Prime Minster and Smuts as Deputy Prime Minister, held power until the outbreak of world war in 1939. Several writers consider that the act of 'fusion' helped to precipitate parliamentary acceptance of the key 1936 segregationist acts.

d Sir Abe Bailey was a leading mining magnate.

e The Unionist Party was the official opposition party after the first South African elections in 1910. It was in favour of the imperial connection and was sympathetic to mining and commercial interests.

NOTES

* This seminar paper was originally presented without references. The editors have added some endnotes for the benefit of readers, but it has not been possible to track down references to primary material – Eds.

1 P.L. Van den Berghe, *South Africa: A Study in Conflict* (Berkeley, CA, 1970); K.L. Roskam, *Apartheid and Discrimination* (Leiden, 1960); H.J and R.E. Simons, *Class and Colour in South Africa, 1850–1950* (Harmondsworth, 1969).

2 D. Denoon, *A Grand Illusion: The Failure of Imperial Policy in the Transvaal Colony during the Age of Reconstruction, 1900–1905* (London, 1973).

3 D. Denoon, 'The Transvaal Labour Crisis, 1901–6', *Journal of African History*, 8 (1967), 481–94; D. Denoon, '"Capitalist Influence" and the Transvaal Government during the Crown Colony Period, 1900–06', *Historical Journal*, 11 (1968), 301–31; G.A. Blainey, 'Lost Causes of the Jameson Raid', *Economic History Review*, 18 (1965), 350–66.

4 J. Bryce, *Impressions of South Africa* (London, 1897).

5 R. Hyam, *Elgin and Churchill at the Colonial Office, 1905–08* (London, 1968).

3

CAPITALISM AND CHEAP LABOUR POWER IN SOUTH AFRICA:

From segregation to apartheid[1]*

Harold Wolpe

More than any other single work, Harold Wolpe's discussion of the cheap labour and reserve-subsidy thesis became central to the radical analysis of segregation. Wolpe had been an opposition activist in South Africa at the time of the political upheavals before and after Sharpeville (1960). He escaped imprisonment to establish himself as a politically committed academic in Britain. Wolpe argued that cheap labour in the South African context was best procured through the system of migrant labour and that key elements of segregation policy reinforced this arrangement. The migrant labour system ensured that the mines pre-dominantly used the labour of adult males whose families remained in rural areas. Capitalists were able to pay African workers meagre 'bachelor' wages because the costs of both the physical and social repro-duction of the labour force were borne by their families who remained primarily responsible for maintaining subsistence agriculture in the reserves. Wolpe's analysis was innovative in that it recognized the in-adequacy of a simple class analysis of South African society and attempted to theorize the relationship between segregation, the labour market and reserves. If this system was to survive, reserves for African people had to be entrenched (as envisaged in the 1913 Land Act); mass urbanization, he implied, would undermine the cheap labour supply. Wolpe's article continues to examine how the reserves strategy was pur-sued in the middle years of the century when the capacity of these areas to provide subsistence for their inhabitants was undermined. He sug-gests that the more directive and coercive homeland policy post-1948, by which the state intended to exclude Africans through tighter control of population movements rather than development of the reserves, resulted from the collapse of subsistence production in these areas.

INTRODUCTION

There is undoubtedly a high degree of continuity in the racist ideological foundations of apartheid[2] and of the policy of segregation which prevailed in the Union of South Africa prior to the election of the Nationalist Party to power in 1948. It is, perhaps, this continuity which accounts for the widely held view that fundamentally apartheid is little more than segregation under a new name. As Legassick expresses it: 'after the Second World War segregation was continued, its premises unchanged, as *apartheid* or "separate development"'.[3] According to this view, such differences as emerged between segregation and apartheid are largely differences of degree relating to their common concerns – political domination, the African reserves and African migrant labour. More particularly, the argument continues, in the political sphere, apartheid entails a considerable increase in White domination through the extension of the repressive powers of the state; the Bantustan[a] policy involves the development of limited local government which, while falling far short of political independence and *leaving unchanged the economic and political functions* of the reserves, nevertheless, in some ways, goes beyond the previous system in practice as well as in theory; and, in the economic sphere apartheid 'modernizes' the system of cheap *migrant* labour and perfects the instruments of labour coercion:

> *Apartheid*, or separate development, has meant merely tightening the loopholes, ironing out the informalities, eliminating the evasions, modernizing and rationalizing the inter-war structures of 'segregationist' labour control.[4]

While it will be necessary, at a later stage, to question this characterization of the differences between segregation and apartheid, it is relevant to consider at this point how the variance between the two 'systems' summarized above has been explained.

Generally, the explanations advanced account for the increased racial oppression manifested by apartheid on the basis of the contention that the governing Nationalist Party's ideology is more racist than that of its predecessors, and for the intensified political repression by reference to the Party's totalitarian ideology. According to this view, the government, in pursuance of its racist ideology, and even at the cost of economic rationality, introduced a series of measures which extended racial discrimination to its limits. The effect of this was to produce widespread opposition which the government met, acting in pursuance of its totalitarian ideology, by a drastic curtailment of political rights and an elaborate system of state security. This set in train a vicious cycle of resistance and repression which led, in due course, also to international condemnation of, and pressure on, South Africa. The Bantustan policy of separate development was the response to these combined internal and external political pressures and was designed both to divert opposition and to transfer conflict out of the 'white' urban areas to the African rural 'homelands'.[5]

Legassick, however, has proposed a far more complex account of apartheid, at least in so far as the control of the labour force is said to be the main area of change, but ultimately his explanation is also unsatisfactory. He argues that the main components of the policy of segregation are:

> restrictions on permanent urbanization, territorial separation of land ownership, and the use of traditional institutions as providers of 'social services' and means of social control ... [and] Along with other mechanisms of labour coercion ... the system of migrant labour which characterized South Africa's road to industrialization.[6]

This system, which emerged in a period in which 'gold' and 'maize' were the dominant productive sectors of the economy, undergoes rationalization and 'modernization' in the context of an economy in which massive 'secondary industrialization' is occurring. Apartheid is the attempt of the capitalist class to meet the expanding demand for cheap African labour in the era of industrial manufacturing capital; at the same time it is the realization of the demand of White workers for protection against the resulting increased competition from Black workers. The outcome of the 'modernization' of segregation in the African rural areas (the Bantustans) is to leave the 'economic and political functions (of the reserves) ... unchanged' and thus to preserve the economic and social foundations of the system of cheap migrant labour. This is complemented in the urban industrial areas by the refinement of the mechanisms of labour coercion which guarantees the cheapness of African labour. Legassick describes the situation in graphic terms:

apartheid has meant an extension to the manufacturing economy of the structure of the gold-mining industry. In the towns, all remnants of African land and property ownership have been removed, and a massive building programme of so-called 'locations' or 'townships' means that the African work force is housed in carefully segregated and police controlled areas that resemble mining compounds on a large scale. All the terms on which Africans could have the right to reside permanently in the towns have been whittled away so that today no African . . . has a right to permanent residence except in the 'reserves'.

The attempt to relate alterations in policy to changes in social conditions – primarily the development of a class of manufacturing industrialists – unquestionably represents an advance over the simplistic view that apartheid is the result of ideology. Intense secondary industrialization *does* have a bearing on the development of apartheid but the mere fact that it occurs does not explain why it should lead to the attempt to extend the 'structures of gold-mining' to the economy as a whole. Legassick is clearly correct in arguing that secondary industrialization intensifies the demand for a *cheap* African labour force at various levels of skill and that this is accompanied by new problems of control for the capitalist state. The problems of control (including the control of wage levels) are *not*, however, simply or primarily a function of the *demand* for labour power which is cheap, but crucially a function of the conditions of the production and reproduction of that labour power. It is in this respect that the crucial gap in Legassick's analysis appears, for by focusing largely on the development of secondary industrialization and by assuming that the economic and political functions of the reserves continue unchanged and, therefore, that the migrant labour system remains what it has always been, he fails to grasp the essential nature of the changes which have occurred in South Africa. The analysis of these essential changes – the virtual destruction of the pre-capitalist mode of production of the African communities in the reserves and, therefore, of the economic basis of cheap *migrant* labour power and the consequent changes in and functions of 'tribal' political institutions – will constitute the subject matter of the third and subsequent sections of the paper.

IDEOLOGY, POLICY AND CAPITALISM IN SOUTH AFRICA

A few exceptions apart,[7] the literature – radical, liberal and racist alike – analyses and describes the society in terms of racial concepts.[8] Even where the relationship between classes is incorporated into the discussion, race is nevertheless treated as the dominant and dynamic force.[9] 'Racial segregation', 'separate development', 'racial discrimination', 'racial groups' (African, White, coloured and Asiatic), 'colour bar', 'White ruling class', 'race relations', etc., etc. – these are the concepts of the analysis of South Africa. The predominance of these concepts can, no doubt, be attributed to the opaqueness of racial ideology, which is reflected, *inter alia*, in the formulation of laws in racial terms, in the content of the mass media, in the policies and ideological statements of all the political parties and organizations (both Black, White and also mixed) and in almost the entire intellectual product of the society.

The overwhelming importance accorded to race in these approaches is apparent, above all, in their treatment of the relationship between racially oriented action and 'the economy'. Thus, on the one hand, the content of 'Native' or 'Bantu' policy (to use the official terms) which can be found in the legislative programmes, government policies and commission reports both before and after 1948, is analysed in its own terms and treated as being concerned solely with the regulation of 'race relations'. On the other hand, whether the economy is conceived of in terms of liberal economics,[10] or in Marxist terms as a capitalist mode of production,[11] racial beliefs are treated as a force external to, but productive of, distortions in the otherwise rational economic system. In its most advanced form this leads to the 'theory' of the plural society which both reflects the dominant ideology and provides an apparently scientific corroboration of it.[12] This approach accepts, precisely by reference to the racial or ethnic content of the laws, policies and ideologies current in the society, the critical salience of race to the exclusion of the mode of production. The basic structure of the society is seen, in this and the other analyses referred to, in the relationship between a dominant White group and a dominated Black group.

It is of fundamental importance to stress that in this perspective the state in South Africa comes to be treated as the instrument of oppression of Whites over Blacks but (precisely because class relationships are not normally included in the analysis) as neutral in the relationship between classes. It in no way detracts from the conception of the state as an instrument of White domination, however, to insist that the South African state is also an instrument of class rule in a specific form of capitalist society. Indeed, while there have been, of course, variations in emphasis and detailed policy (variations which stem, in part, from the specific class composition of and alliances in the parties which have ruled from time to time), nevertheless, since the establishment of the Union of South Africa in 1910 (to go back no further), the state has been utilized at all times to secure and develop the capitalist mode of production.[13]

It is not possible in this paper to discuss in detail the historical evidence which demonstrates this. First, the state has acted directly through the law (e.g. Land Bank Act which provides for subsidies and grants to White farmers), through special agencies (for example, the Industrial Development Corporation which has been important in the growth of, *inter alia*, the textile industry), through the development of state enterprises and in other ways to foster capitalist development.[14]

Second, the repressive apparatus of the state (police, army, prisons, courts, etc.) has been used broadly in two ways. First, as the occasion arose, to coerce workers, whether Black or White, on behalf of or in support of employers. A small selection of the more dramatic examples of this would include the 1914 White mineworkers' strike, the 1922 general strike (Rand Revolt) of White workers, the 1946 African mineworkers' strike and the 1972 Ovambo workers' strike. Second, to enforce the laws which either overtly guarantee the perpetuation of capitalism – laws such as the Industrial Conciliation Act 1924, the Masters and Servants Act, the Native Labour (Settlement of Disputes) Act 1953, the Native Labour Regulation Act 1911, and so on, or (as in the case of most laws affecting Africans) which covertly perform the same functions – for example, the Natives Land Act 1913, and the Native (Abolition of Passes and Co-ordination of Documents) Act 1952.

It is precisely from the racial terms that are employed in these laws that their ideological function can be determined. The enactment of laws, the express purpose of which is the regulation of relationships between racial groups and the ordering of the conduct of the members of legally defined racial categories, is both an expression of racist ideology and a means of reinforcing that ideology. This is so because not only do racial laws, in common with other laws, appear as neutral to the capitalist structure of the society by taking that structure as given, but more importantly, like other laws but in a different way, they actively operate to mask both the capitalist nature of the society altogether and the consequences of their provisions for the functioning of that system.

The history of South Africa shows the emerging *dominance*, first through British imperialism, and then also through internal capitalist development, of the capitalist mode of production. The development of this dominant mode of production has been inextricably linked with two other modes of production – the African redistributive economies and the system of labour-tenancy and crop-sharing on White farms. The most important relationship is between capitalism and the African economies and although it is not entirely satisfactory to do so, for reasons of space the discussion which follows is restricted to this relationship. These two modes of production may be briefly characterized as follows.

(a) First, the capitalist mode of production in which (i) the direct labourers, who do not own the means of capitalist production, sell their labour power to the owners of the means of production who are non-labourers, and (ii) the wages the labourer receives for the sale of his labour power are met by only a portion of the value of the product he actually produces, the balance being appropriated as unpaid labour (surplus value) by the owners of the productive means.

(b) Second, the mode of production in the areas of African concentration (particularly, but not exclusively, the reserves) in which (i) land is held communally by the community and worked by social units based on kinship (the enlarged or extended family), and (ii) the product of labour is distributed, not by exchange, but directly by means of allocation through the kinship units in accordance with certain rules of distribution.

This is *not* to argue either that other forms of production were not developing in the interstices of the African societies or that they were not continuously undergoing profound changes.[15] On the contrary, as will be elaborated later, the central argument of the present paper is based on the occurrence of such transformations. What must be stressed, however, is that in the period of capitalist development (from, say, 1870) African redistributive economies constituted the predominant mode of rural existence for a substantial (for much of the period, a majority), but continuously decreasing number of people.

The simultaneous existence of two modes of production within the boundaries of a single state has given rise to the notion of the 'dual economy'.[16] As Frank and others have shown for Latin America, however, the assumption that different modes of production can be treated as independent of one another is untenable.[17]

In South Africa, the development of capitalism has been bound up with, first, the deterioration of the productive capacity and then, with increasing rapidity, the destruction of the pre-capitalist societies. In the earlier period of capitalism (approximately 1870 to the 1930s), the rate of surplus value and hence the rate of capital accumulation depended above all upon the maintenance of the pre-capitalist relations of production in the reserve economy which provided a portion of the means of reproduction of the migrant labour force. This relationship between the two modes of production, however, is contradictory and increasingly produces the conditions which make impossible the continuation of the pre-capitalist relations of production in the reserves. The conse-, quence of this is the accelerating dissolution of these relations and the development, within South Africa, towards a single, capitalist, mode of production in which more and more of the African wage-labour force (but never the whole of it) is 'freed' from productive resources in the reserves. This results in important changes in the nature of exploitation and transfers the major contradiction from the relationship *between* different modes of production to the relations of production *within* capitalism.

Here we arrive at the critical point of articulation between ideology, racial political practice and the economic system. Whereas segregation provided the political structure appropriate to the earlier period, apartheid represents the attempt to maintain the rate of surplus value and accumulation in the face of the disintegration of the pre-capitalist economy. Or, to put it in another way, apartheid, including separate development, can best be understood as the *mechanism specific to South Africa* in the period of secondary industrialization, of maintaining a high rate of capitalist exploitation through a system which guarantees a cheap and controlled labour force, under circumstances in which the conditions of reproduction (the redistributive African economy in the reserves) of that labour force are rapidly disintegrating.

THE AFRICAN RESERVES – THE SOCIAL AND ECONOMIC BASIS OF CHEAP MIGRANT LABOUR POWER

In commenting on the conceptions of the 'subsistence' economy in the dual economy thesis, Laclau stressed that:

> The latter (i.e. the 'subsistence' economy) was presented as completely stagnant and inferior to the former in capital, income and rate of growth. All relations between the two were reduced to the provision by the backward sector of an unlimited supply of labour to the advanced sector. It has now been repeatedly shown that this model underestimates the degree of commercialization which is possible in rural areas, as well as the degree of accumulation in peasant enterprises.[18]

Arrighi, Bundy and others have shown that the processes of commercialization and accumulation were, no less than in Latin American societies, occurring in African rural economies in Rhodesia and South Africa.[19] It is none the less true that by not later than 1920 the overwhelming economic and political power of the capitalist sector had succeeded, whether through unequal terms of trade or otherwise, in underdeveloping the African economy so that it no longer presented any significant competitive threat to White farmers. Production, in the African reserves, of a marketable surplus became increasingly rare, finally disappearing altogether. Unlike some other situations elsewhere, therefore, the capitalist sector was unable to extract the (non-existent) surplus product *directly* from the African pre-capitalist sector. The relations between the two sectors were, indeed, '... *reduced* to the provision by the backward sector' of a supply of labour power to the capitalist sector. The peculiar feature of this labour force is that it is migrant and temporary, returning to the reserves in between periods of work, and retains means of production in the African economy or has a claim on such means. The exploitation of migrant labour power of this kind enables the capitalist sector to secure an increased rate of surplus value. How is this effected?

A number of attempts have been made to explain why it is that Africans who are in possession of agricultural means of production in the reserves nevertheless enter wage employment in the capitalist sector. It is unnecessary for present purposes to consider these explanations which, in any event, are generally inadequate. What *is* relevant is the conventional conceptualization of wage labour as the means of supplementing deficiencies in the income derived from production in the reserves. In this view the need to supplement income arises from inefficient farming methods, inappropriate values, an outmoded social system and so on which lead to underproduction – the only relationships between the capitalist sector and the traditional economy are territorial and through the market for western consumer goods which capitalism introduces into the latter economy. Underlying this conception is, thus, the dual economy thesis in which there is no place for an analysis of the way in which capitalism enters into, lives off and transforms the rural African economy.

If, however, the African economy and society is treated as standing in an ancillary relationship to the capitalist sector, then a different analysis follows. When the migrant labourer has access to means of subsistence, outside the capitalist sector, as he does in South Africa, then the relationship between wages and the cost of the production and reproduction of labour power is changed. That is to say, capital is able to pay the worker *below* the cost of his reproduction. In the first place, since in determining the level of wages necessary for the subsistence of the migrant worker and his family, account is taken of the fact that the family is supported, to some extent, from the product of agricultural production in the reserves, it becomes possible to fix wages at the level of subsistence of the individual worker. Arrighi has shown this to be the basis of cheap labour in Rhodesia, and Schapera has argued this for South Africa on the basis of the following quotation from the Chamber of Mines' (the largest employer of migrant labour) evidence to the Witwatersrand Native Mine Wage Commission (21/1944):

It is clearly to the advantage of the mines that native labourers should be encouraged to return to their homes after the completion of the ordinary period of service. The

HAROLD WOLPE

maintenance of the system under which the mines are able
to obtain unskilled labour at a rate less than ordinarily paid
in industry depends upon this, for otherwise the subsidiary
means of subsistence would disappear and the labourer
would tend to become a permanent resident upon the
Witwatersrand, with increased requirements.[20]

In the second place, as Meillassoux has pointed out:

The agricultural self-sustaining communities, because of
their comprehensiveness and their *raison d'être* are able to
fulfil the functions that capitalism prefers not to assume . . .
the functions of social security.[21]

The extended family in the reserves is able to, and does, fulfil
'social security' functions necessary for the reproduction of the
migrant workforce. By caring for the very young and very old,
the sick, the migrant labourer in periods of 'rest', by educating
the young, etc., the reserve families relieve the capitalist sector
and its state from the need to expend resources on these necessary functions.

The accessibility to the migrant worker of the product (and of
the 'social services') of the reserves depends upon the *conserva-
tion*, albeit in a restructured form, of the reciprocal obligations of
the family. The interest of the capitalist sector in preserving
the relations of the African familial communities is clear – if the
network of reciprocal obligations between migrant and family
were broken neither the agricultural product nor the 'social
services' of the African society would be available to the worker.
It is no accident that the South African state has consistently
taken measures, including the recognition of much of African law
and custom, the recognition of and grant of powers to chiefs, the
reservation of areas of land, etc., aimed at preserving the 'tribal'
communities.

In passing it may be noted that the pressures towards retain-
ing the family communities in a restructured form came also
from the migrant labour force. As Meillassoux puts it:

the capitalist system does not provide adequately for old-
age pensions, sick leave and unemployment compensations,
they have to rely on another comprehensive socio-economic
organization to fulfil these vital needs. . . . It follows that
the . . . preservation of the relations with the village and the

70

familial community is an absolute requirement for wage-earners, and so is the maintenance of the traditional mode of production as the only one capable of ensuring survival.

However, the preservation of the social relations of the familial community is, quite obviously, only one aspect of the migrant cheap labour system. The social obligation to provide subsistence and security is only of relevance to both migrant and employer if that obligation can actually be met from the agricultural product. But this requires both the retention of the pre-capitalist mode of production, at least in so far as this guarantees the allocation of productive land to all members of the community, and the maintenance of certain levels of production. Both of these raise strategic problems for the capitalist sector.

The first problem relates to the tendency in capitalist development for ownership of land to become concentrated and the consequent development of a landless class 'free' of means of production. The importance of this stems from the obvious fact that landless families would be unable to supplement the migrant's wages.

The drive towards land acquisition came from sections of both the African and White groups and the threat that this might lead to a landless class of Africans was met by two different sets of measures.

The Natives Land Act 27/1913 defined (or scheduled) certain areas as African reserves and laid down that no African could henceforth purchase or occupy land outside the reserves. Simultaneously the Act prohibited Whites from acquiring, or occupying, land in the reserves. It was stated in parliament, at the time, that the purpose of the Act was to ensure the territorial segregation of the races. This stated purpose has generally been accepted, by politicians as well as social scientists, as a sufficient explanation for the Act which has come to be regarded as the cornerstone of territorial segregation. Recently, however, some writers have argued that the Act can be interpreted as an attempt to remedy the shortage of African labour on White farms, and to prevent Africans utilizing communal or private capital from repurchasing European owned land which had been acquired by conquest.[22]

Be that as it may, the consequences (possibly unintended) of the section of the Act which prohibits the purchase and occupation by

71

Whites of land in the reserves have been consistently ignored or misconstrued. The effect of this provision was very far-reaching – it halted the process, whether through the market or otherwise, by which more and more land was wrested from or made unavailable to Africans. Since the reserves (particularly with the additions made in terms of the Native Trust and Land Act 1936) roughly coincided with the rural areas into which Africans had already been concentrated, the Act had the effect of stabilizing the existing distribution of land. Liberal historians have stressed the 'protection' this provided against a further diminution of the land held by Africans, but the importance of this 'protection' in preventing the economic basis of migrant labour power from being undermined through landlessness has been almost completely overlooked.

The removal of reserve land from a market open to White capital did not eliminate the possibility of land becoming concentrated in the hands of a relatively small class of *African* landowners. Indeed, the fact, already mentioned, that Africans were beginning to repurchase land outside of the then *de facto* 'reserves', is proof that some Africans had the necessary resources for land purchase. No doubt, an immediate effect of the Natives Land Act would have been to lead these potential purchasers to search for suitable land in the reserves, but here there were other obstacles in their way. The Glen Grey Act of 1894 and various other proclamations and enactments (which were to be extended and elaborated from time to time until the 1930s) laid down the rule of one-man-one-plot in the reserves. This rule impeded the concentration of land.

The second strategic problem arises from the necessity to maintain production in the reserves at a level which, while not too low to contribute to the reproduction of migrant workers as a class, is yet not high enough to remove the economic imperatives of migration. While, as Arrighi has shown, there is no simple relationship between production levels in the rural economy and the *rate* of migration – social, political and other economic conditions may affect this – none the less low levels of agricultural and craft production constitute a necessary condition of labour migration. This is so because both the demands of and the economic returns from high output farming would tend to render the population immobile. At the same time, if output is allowed to drop too low then the reserve product becomes relatively a less important

72

element in subsistence and, unless wages are increased, threatens the reproduction of migrant workers.

In the earlier period (roughly prior to 1930) the state in fact did extremely little to develop or assist agriculture in the reserves. Statistics of food and other agricultural production are extremely sparse. Clearly, by the mid-1920s surpluses were either extremely small or non-existent and continued to decline. Thus the Director of Native Agriculture estimated that the income from the sale of produce (after consumption needs had been met), for a family unit of five in the Transkei, to be £4 per annum in the period before 1929. In the Northern Transvaal, Van der Horst points out:

> The extent to which grain was purchased to supplement domestic production resulted in there being practically no income from the sale of farm produce for the purchase of other food, and clothes, or for the payment of taxes and school fees.[23]

Nevertheless, the evidence as a whole shows that the drop in the level of production to this point did not yet threaten the migrant system.

The level of production is not, however, the only point. What is equally important is the extent to which productive activities and, therefore, means of subsistence are distributed among all the families in the reserves and, in particular, among the families with which migrant wage workers are connected. This is so since the product of the reserve economy will only be available to contribute to the reproduction of the migrant labour force if the migrant's family (given that he remains in a relationship of reciprocal obligation with them) is in fact producing means of subsistence in the reserves. There is virtually no data specifically on this point but it nevertheless is possible to infer from the situation as a whole that few wage workers, up to say 1920 or so, did not have a supplementary source of subsistence for themselves and their families in the reserves.

Table 3.1 shows the clear predominance of Africans in the mining industry as compared to other major sectors of the economy in the period 1910–40. Practically all African mineworkers were (and are) recruited through the Chamber of Mines recruiting organizations from the reserves (and also from territories outside South Africa – up to 50 per cent in the years covered by Table 3.1), and returned to their homes on completion of a term of service

Table 3.1 African employment in mining, private industry and the
South African Railways and Harbours

Year	Mining	Private industry	South African Railways and Harbours
1910	255,594	?	24,631*
1915	240,397	35,065	29,130*
1918	255,897	51,870	37,218*
1919	250,953	?	29,286
1920	265,540	?	32,104
1925	266,912	71,858	34,620
1930	312,123	69,895	25,415
1935	355,563	89,613	16,497
1940	444,242	130,597	45,413

* These figures include coloured and Asiatic workers as well, numbering
probably about 6,000 in each year shown.

of a year or so. From this, and from our knowledge of the
general economic situation of the areas from which mineworkers
were recruited, it can be inferred that they retained economic
links with their kin in the reserves.

The conclusion can thus be drawn that in the early period of
industrialization in South Africa (the period of gold mining) the
reserve economy provided the major portion of Africans
employed in capitalist production, at any given moment, with
supplementary subsistence and was thus a crucial condition of
the reproduction of the migrant working class. The crucial function thus performed by the policy of segregation was to maintain
the productive capacity of the pre-capitalist economies and the
social system of the African societies in order to ensure that these
societies provided a portion of the means of reproduction of the
migrant working class.

THE CORROSION OF THE SOCIAL AND
ECONOMIC BASIS OF CHEAP MIGRANT
LABOUR POWER

The production and reproduction of the migrant labour force thus
depended upon the existence of a rough equilibrium between
production, distribution and social obligation in the reserves – the
level of production in the reserves together with wages being *more
or less* sufficient to meet the (historically determined) subsistence

requirements of migrants and their families, while land tenure and familial community relationships ensured the appropriate distribution of the reserve product. This equilibrium was, however, inherently fragile and subject to irresistible pressures.

Given the developed incapacity of the reserves to generate a surplus product, the limited area of land available (fixed by the Natives Land Act), the increasing pressure of population and, therefore, congestion on the land, the loss, at any given time, of a large proportion of the economically active adults to temporary employment in the capitalist sector, the relatively backward and inefficient farming methods, the only possibility of ensuring appropriate levels of agricultural production is through investment by the capitalist sector. In fact, as was pointed out earlier, the state's expenditure on agricultural development in the reserves has always been extremely low, increasing only marginally as conditions of production worsened. The immediate consequence of all this was a rapid decline in the agricultural product in the reserves.

By the 1920s attention was already being drawn to the deterioration of the situation in the African areas and in 1932 the Native Economic Commission Report (1930–2) commented at length on the extremely low productivity of farming in the reserves, on the increasing malnutrition and on the real danger of the irreversible destruction of the land through soil erosion. Every subsequent government commission dealing with the reserves reiterated these points and drew attention to the decline in output.[24] By 1970, Gervasi summed up the situation:

There is good evidence that the standard of living of Africans in the Reserves has actually fallen over the last two decades. The condition of the Reserves can only be described as one of abject poverty. There is a mass of other evidence corroborating the income statistics. According to a survey conducted in 1966, almost half the children born in most Reserves were dying before the age of five. In fact mortality of this kind is unknown in any other industrial country. It can only mean that the vast mass of the population in the typical Reserve is living well below the level of subsistence most of the time.[25]

The conclusion which emerges is that, overall, production in the reserves provides a declining fraction of the total subsistence of migrant labourers.

75

The level of production, however, is not the only relevant aspect; the way in which the product is distributed must also be considered. Capitalist development produced further changes which had the effect of altering the pattern of distribution so that the diminishing agricultural product became more and more unequally distributed and less and less available to wage labourers. The development of classes in the reserves (or, perhaps, strata within classes), which had already begun in the nineteenth century, was intensified and broadened. There can be little doubt that the processes leading to the concentration of land-holding in the hands of a relatively restricted class have been continuous and that, correlatively, the class of landless rural dwellers is substantial and growing. The Native Laws Commission (1948), among other studies already referred to, has provided some data concerning these developments. The Commission reported, for example, on the Ciskei:

> What goes on in the Reserves? Nearly ⅓ of all families have no arable land. The average land-holder works, what is, under the climatic conditions obtaining in the Ciskei, a sub-economic unit of land. He owns what is, because of its poor quality, sub-economic numbers of stock. Above him is a relatively small favoured class of bigger owners. It is known that there are individuals who own 100 head of cattle and as many as a thousand sheep. Below him are thousands who own nothing. In Keiskama Hoek, before the drought, 29% of all married men owned no cattle, another 33% from one to five head.

The Tomlinson Commission (1956) [see n. 24 – Eds], also reported finding substantial numbers of landless inhabitants of reserves. In addition the Commission provided evidence of striking inequalities (12.7 per cent of the families earn 46.3 per cent of the total income accrued inside the reserves) thus adding to the picture of income-less or very low income groups. It follows from this that a proportion of the families living in the reserves produce either very little or, in the case of the landless and cattleless, no means of subsistence.

Thus far I have discussed the economic changes in the reserves which undermined, to a significant degree, the economic basis of the migrant labour system and, by the same token a substantial economic prop of cheap labour power. The essence of the argument has been that the amount of subsistence available to the migrant labour force and their families in the reserves has either diminished because the overall decline in production has resulted in a decrease in the product *per capita* or has virtually disappeared because of the partial or total loss, in the case of some families, of means of production.

This, however, is only one aspect of the process, for, in the second place, the product of the reserves may no longer be available to the migrant as a means of subsistence for himself and his family in the reserves by reason of the termination of the reciprocal social obligations of support between the migrant and his kin in the reserve, even where the latter continues to produce subsistence. An important condition for this change is the permanent urbanization of a substantial number of workers. The process of secondary industrialization and the development of the tertiary sector of the economy provided the opportunity for the development of, and was accompanied by, an ever-increasing, permanently urbanized, industrial proletariat.

The first point to note is that the percentage of the African population in the urban areas increased from 12.6 per cent in 1911 to 23.7 per cent in 1946 and by 1971 was approximately 38 per cent.

It is unnecessary to detail the growth of manufacturing – it contributes today more than gold mining and agriculture combined to the national product. What is more pertinent is the data showing the changes in African urbanization and employment in manufacturing.

In Table 3.1 figures of African employment in private industry were set out for some years in the period 1910–40. The changes between 1940 and 1970 are shown in Table 3.2 following:

Table 3.2 African employment in private industry

Year	Number
1945	207,797
1950	307,671
1955	433,056
1970	864,300

The significance of these figures derives from the fact that, in contrast to Africans employed in mining, those employed in secondary industry are not brought into employment (or returned to the reserves) through recruiting organizations. They are, of course, subject to the pass laws and other legal provisions restricting their right of residence in urban areas, laws which have become increasingly rigorous over time. Nevertheless, employment in manufacturing coupled with residence in 'locations' and townships undoubtedly enabled large numbers of African workers to settle permanently in the urban areas and in due course to raise families there.

It is, once again, extremely difficult to calculate with any accuracy what proportion of urban industrial workers have become fully dependent upon wages for subsistence, that is to say, how many are fully proletarianized.[26] Not only are the statistics incomplete and unsatisfactory but in addition very little analysis has been made of the relationship between permanently urbanized workers and the African societies in the reserves.[27] Despite this, however, there can be no doubt that during the period 1910–70 (and particularly in the period during and since the Second World War) the number of Africans in the urban areas having no relevant links with the reserves has grown steadily and rapidly and that they today constitute a significant, if not major, proportion of African industrial workers.

APARTHEID: THE NEW BASIS OF CHEAP LABOUR

The focus in the two previous sections has been largely on the economic foundation of cheap migrant labour power in the reserve economy and on the processes which have continuously and to an ever-increasing degree undermined this foundation. The immediate result of the decline in the productive capacity of the pre-capitalist economies was a decrease in the agricultural product of the reserves resulting, therefore, in a decrease of the contribution of the reserves towards the subsistence necessary for the reproduction of the labour force. This threatened to reduce the rate of surplus value through pressure on wages and posed, for capital, the problem of preventing a fall in the level of profit.

The solution, for capital, to this problem must take account of the complementary effect of the erosion of the economic foundations of cheap migrant labour power upon both the African rural societies and the urbanized industrial proletariat. I have already shown that the system of producing a cheap migrant labour force generated rural impoverishment, while at the same time it enabled extremely low wages to be paid to Africans in the capitalist sector. But increasing rural impoverishment, since it removes that portion of the industrial workers' subsistence which is produced and consumed in the reserves, also intensifies urban poverty. This twofold effect of capitalist development tends to generate conflict, not only about wages, but about all aspects of urban and rural life and to bring into question the structure of the whole society. This broadening and intensification of conflict is met by political measures which in turn lead to an increasingly political reaction.

This struggle began long before 1948 when the conditions discussed above began to emerge (and control measures to be taken), but the particularly rapid urbanization and industrialization fostered by the Second World War sharpened and intensified the trends we have been discussing and the resultant conflicts. The 1940s were characterized by the variety and extent of the industrial and political conflicts especially in the urban, but also in the rural areas. In the period 1940–9 1,684,915 (including the massive strike of African mineworkers in 1946) African man-hours were lost as compared with 171,088 in the period 1930–9. Thousands of African workers participated in squatters' movements and bus boycotts. In 1946 the first steps were taken towards an alliance of African, coloured and Indian political movements and this was followed by mass political demonstrations. Towards the end of the 1940s a new force – militant African intellectuals – appeared on the scene. There were militant rural struggles at Witzieshoek and in the Transkei. These were some of the signs of the growing assault on the whole society (and the structure of cheap labour power which underpinned it) which confronted the capitalist state in 1948.

For English-dominated large-scale capital (particularly mining but also sections of secondary industry), the solution both to the problem of the level of profit and to the threat to their political control implicit in growing African militancy was to somewhat alter the structure of segregation in favour of Africans. Indeed, the 1948 recommendations of the Native Law Commission (appointed in 1946 by the United Party government precisely in response to the changing nature of African political struggle) for an alternative mode of control of African labour which included certain restricted reforms and modifications of the racial

79

political-economic structure, were accepted by the United Party as its policy in the 1948 election in which it was defeated by the Nationalist Party. The implementation, had it occurred, of that policy might possibly have had consequences for both the Afrikaner petit bourgeoisie and, also, the White workers which would have led them into a collision with the state. The point is that reforms which would have resulted in higher real wages and improved economic conditions for Africans could only be introduced without a corresponding fall in the rate of profit provided they were bought at the cost of the White working class – that is to say, either through a drop in the wages of White workers or the employment of Africans, at lower rates of pay, in occupations monopolized, until then, by White workers. Historically the latter aspect has been at the centre of the conflicts and tension between the White working class and large-scale capital – conflicts which also reached their peak in terms of strikes in the 1940s.

The alternative for the Afrikaner working class, resisting competition from African workers, for the growing Afrikaner industrial and financial capitalist class, struggling against the dominance of English monopoly capital, and, perhaps, for a petit bourgeoisie threatened with proletarianization by the advance of African workers (and the Indian petit bourgeoisie), was to assert control over the African and other non-White people by whatever means were necessary. For the Afrikaner capitalist class, African labour power could be maintained as cheap labour power by repression; for the White worker, this also guaranteed their own position as a 'labour aristocracy'. Thus the policy of apartheid developed as a response to this urban and rural challenge to the system which emerged inexorably from the changed basis of cheap labour power. What was at stake was nothing less than the reproduction of the labour force, not in general, but in a specific form, in the form of cheap labour power.

At the most general level, that of control of the African political challenge, apartheid entails the removal of the limited rights which Africans and coloureds had in the parliamentary institutions of the White state; the revision of old and the introduction of a whole complex of new repressive laws which make illegal militant organized opposition (e.g. Suppression of Communism, Unlawful Organizations and Sabotage Acts, etc.), and the building of all-powerful agencies of control – security police, Bureau of State Security, the army, and police and army civilian reserves, etc.

In the economic sphere measures have been introduced to prevent or contain the accumulation of pressure on the level of wages. Most obvious in this regard is the Natives (Settlement of Disputes) Act which makes it illegal for Africans to strike for higher wages or improved working conditions. This, coupled both with the fact that African trade unions are not legally recognized and that their organization is impeded also by other measures, has effectively prevented the emergence of an African trade union movement capable of having any significant effect on wages. The decline in industrial strikes since 1948 and the tendency of real wages for Africans to fall indicates the success of government policy.

Less obvious, but having the same purpose of controlling the development of strong African pressure for higher wages, are the important measures introduced by the Nationalist government relating to African job and geographical mobility. The nature and meaning of these measures has been obscured by the terms of the relevant laws and the government's policy statements to the effect that Africans were to be regarded only as temporary migrants in the urban areas, there only as long as they ministered to White needs.

The pass laws and the Native Urban Areas Act 1923 which regulated the right of residence in urban areas, were, of course, available in 1948. The 'modernization' of the pass laws under the Native (Abolition of Passes and Coordination of Documents) Acts and the establishment of labour bureaux which serve to direct African workers to where White employers require them has been effected through a battery of amendments to old laws and the introduction of new laws which give the state exceptionally wide powers to order Africans out of one area and into another. There are practically no legal limitations on these powers which can be used to remove 'excess' Africans from areas where their labour is not required or 'troublesome' Africans to outlying, isolated areas where they will be politically harmless. All Africans are, legally, only temporary residents in the urban areas.

In its application to the urban areas, apartheid appears predominantly and with ever-increasing thoroughness in its coercive form. In its application to the reserves it has undergone a number of changes in content – culminating in the programme of self-development – in which the attempt both to establish forms of control which Africans would regard as legitimate and to institutionalize conflict has been an increasingly important ingredient although coercion is never absent. This policy towards the reserves has been, whatever other purpose it may have had in addition, centrally concerned, as in the past, with the control and supply of a cheap labour force, *but in a new form.*

The idea of the total separation of the races, although an integral element of the Nationalist Party's programme, was not regarded as an attainable objective by the government. The impossibility of achieving total separation was underlined by the Tomlinson Commission which estimated (or rather, as we now know, grossly overestimated) that by the turn of the century, if all its recommendations for the reconstruction of the reserves were implemented, there would be *parity* of Whites and Africans in the 'White' areas.

Nor, in the early years of its regime, did the government accept the possibility of the reserves becoming *self-governing and autonomous* areas. In 1951 Verwoerd (then Minister of Native Affairs) told the Upper House of Parliament that the Opposition had tried to create the impression that:

> I had announced the forming of an independent Native State . . . a sort of Bantustan with its own leader . . . that is not the policy of the Party. It has never been that, and no leader has ever said it, and most certainly I have not. The Senator wants to know whether the series of self-governing areas will be sovereign. The answer is obvious. How could small scattered states arise? We cannot mean that we intend by that to cut large slices out of South Africa and turn them into independent states.

There is, in fact, little to suggest that, in the first few years of rule, the Nationalist Party had a fully worked-out policy in relation to the reserves or one which differed significantly from that of earlier governments. There are, however, two important points to be noted.

First, the government already had clearly in mind the establishment of an apparatus of control which would be cheap to run and acceptable to the African people. The 1951 Bantu Authorities Act which strengthened the political authority of the (compliant) chiefs, subject to the control of the state – indirect rule – was the first (and, at the outset, very conflictual) step in that direction. Second, political control in the reserves was obviously recognized to be no solution to the problem of the never-ending enlargement of a working class totally removed from the reserves.

The rather modest proposals of the Tomlinson Commission to spend £104 million over ten years for the reconstruction of the reserves, to end one-man-one-plot in order to create a stable class of farmers and a landless class of workers, and to develop the reserves economically through White capital investment on the borders and in the reserves themselves, were not accepted by the government. There are probably two reasons for this rejection. First, facts brought to light by the Commission showed that to implement the Commission's recommendations relating to agricultural development would have served simply to hasten the ongoing processes which were obviously resulting in the formation of a class of landless rural dwellers and to intensify the migration of workers to the urban centres resulting in a class of workers unable to draw on the reserves for additional subsistence. Consequently, expenditure on agricultural improvement may have seemed pointless and even dangerous since it would exacerbate the pressures and conflicts in the towns. Second, the abolition of restrictions on land-holding and the assisted development of a class of 'kulaks', as recommended by the Commission, also carried with it certain possible dangers. On the one hand, this could lead to a resurgence of African competition to White farmers which it had been one of the purposes of the Natives Land Act of 1913 to destroy. On the other hand, the emergence of an economically strong class of large peasants presented a potential political threat to White domination.

Whatever the reasons, by 1959 the government's policy began to change in significant respects. Without attempting to set out a chronological record, I want to analyse the emergence after 1959 of separate development as the mode of maintaining cheap labour in the reserves (complementing that in the urban areas) which takes as given the changes in the African 'tribal' economies and erects, under the overarching power of the capitalist state, an institutionalized system of partial political control by Africans. That is to say, the practice and policy of separate development must be seen as the attempt to retain, in a modified form, the

HAROLD WOLPE

structure of the 'traditional' societies, not, as in the past, for the purposes of ensuring an economic supplement to the wages of the migrant labour force, but for the purposes of reproducing and exercising control over a cheap African industrial labour force in or near the 'homelands', not by means of preserving the pre-capitalist mode of production but by the political, social, economic and ideological enforcement of low levels of subsistence.

In 1959, in the parliamentary debate on the Promotion of Bantu Self-Government Act, the Prime Minister Dr Verwoerd stated:

> if it is within the capacity of the Bantu, and if those areas which are allocated to him for his emancipation, or rather, which are already his own, can develop *into full independence*, then it will develop in this way.
>
> (Hansard, 1959, col. 6520)

This was echoed by Vorster in 1968 (Hansard, 1968, col. 3947):

> We have stated very clearly that we shall lead them to independence.

Significantly, the ideological shift from White supremacy to self-determination and independence was accompanied by a parallel alteration in the ideology of race. Thus, whereas in all its essentials Nationalist Party ideology had previously insisted upon the biological inferiority of Africans as the justification for its racialist policies, as the government was impelled towards the Bantustan policy so it began to abandon certain of its previous ideological positions. Now the stress fell upon ethnic *differences* and the central notion became 'different but equal'. In 1959 the Minister of Bantu Affairs an Development, De Wet Wel, stated:

> There is something ... which binds people and that is their spiritual treasures, the cultural treasure of a people. It is those things which have united other nations in the world. That is why we say that the basis of our approach is that the Bantu, too, will be linked together by traditional and emotional bonds, by their own language, their own culture, their national possessions. ...
>
> (Hansard, 1959, col. 6018)

More and more the term 'race' gives way to 'nation', 'ethnic group', *'volk'*.

There is an obvious necessity for this ideological change since

84

a policy of ethnic political independence (for each of the eight ethnic groups identified) was incompatible with an ideology of racial inferiority. Nor would the latter have facilitated the attempt to set up the complex machinery of government and administration intended, in fact, to institutionalize relations between the state and the reserves *and* to carry out certain administrative functions necessary for economic development in the reserves. What all this amounts to, as one writer has expressed it, is 'racialism without racism'.

The Transkei Constitution Act was passed in 1963 and provided for a legislative assembly to exercise control over finance, justice, interior, education, agriculture and forestry, and roads and works. The Republican government retains control, *inter alia*, over defence, external affairs, internal security, postal and related services, railways, immigration, currency, banking and customs. It need hardly be stressed that this arrangement in no way approaches political independence. At the same time it must not be overlooked that within limits, set both by the Constitution and the available resources, the Transkeian government exercises real administrative power. By this means the South African state is able to secure the execution of certain essential social control and administrative functions at low cost particularly as a considerable portion of government expenditure can be obtained through increased general taxes. Thus in 1971 the Transkeian government's budget was £18 million of which £3½ million was obtained through taxation of Transkeian citizens.

It is, however, in the sphere of economic development that the emerging role of the reserves can be seen most clearly. I am not here referring to the rather minor role of the various development corporations (Bantu Development Corporation, Xhosa Development Corporation and so on) in fostering economic development in the reserves. In fact, up to the present they have largely served to assist small traders and commercial interests by means of loans – that is, they appear to be instruments for the nurturing of a petit bourgeoisie and have little to do with economic growth in the reserves. Far more important is the state's policy of industrial decentralization.

This policy which has been the subject of government commissions and legislation is also the concern of a Permanent Committee for the Location of Industry. At all times the policy of decentralization has been tied to the Bantustan policy and this meant, at first, the establishment of 'White' industries on the borders of the Black 'homelands'. Between 1960 and 1968 some £160 million was invested in industrial plant in the border areas and approximately 100,000 Africans were employed in these industries which were absorbing 30 per cent of Africans entering jobs each year by 1969. By 1971 there were plans for a rapid expansion (including car factories and chemical plants) of industrial development in the border regions. I would suggest that the policy of border industrial development can only be understood if it is seen as an alternative to migration as a mechanism for producing cheap labour power. There are three aspects of the situation which need to be stressed.

First, neither the provisions of the Industrial Conciliation Act nor Wages Act determinations made for other regions apply to the border industries. This is extremely important in two respects. Since the Industrial Conciliation Act is inapplicable, Section 77 which empowers the minister of labour to reserve certain jobs for particular racial groups also does not apply and neither do the provisions of industrial agreements which reserve the higher-paid skilled jobs for White workers. This being so it becomes possible to employ Africans in jobs which, in the 'White' areas, are the exclusive preserve of White workers. The effect of this, in conjunction with the inapplicability of wage determinations for other areas, is that a totally different and much lower wage structure becomes possible and has arisen.

Second, as elsewhere, African trade unions are not recognized and the provisions of the Natives (Settlement of Disputes) Act apply.

The third, and in some ways perhaps the most important aspect, relates to the conditions of life of the African workers in the border industries. Not only, as has already been indicated, is the level of subsistence extremely low in the 'homelands' but in addition there are virtually no urban areas which might tend to increase this level. The assessment by the state, employers' organizations and so on, of African subsistence requirements in the reserves is much lower than in the main industrial centres. This fact is not altered (or, at least will not be altered for a considerable period) by the necessity of establishing townships of some kind for the housing of workers employed in industry. It is an interesting index of the state's policy that a major item of expenditure for the so-called development of the reserves has been for town planning. A United Nations Report (No. 26, 1970, p. 15) stated:

> Town planning has throughout been a major portion of expenditure. Thus in 1961 a five-year development plan for the reserves was inaugurated which projected an expenditure of £57 million, but *two-thirds* of this amount was allocated for town planning, while the next largest item – £7.3 million – was for soil conservation.

The towns planned will be, no doubt, simple in the extreme, supplying little in the way of the complex services and infrastructure of the 'White' urban areas. Despite the state's expenditure all the indications are that what will be established will be rural village slums.[28]

Recently, the government reversed its previous rejection of the Tomlinson Commission's recommendation that Whites be allowed, under certain conditions, to invest capital in the reserves. As in the case of the border industries various incentives are held out to induce investment. These include 'tax holidays', tariff reductions, development loans and so on. All the considerations discussed above in relation to the border industries apply with equal force to industrial development within the reserves. It is still too soon to say anything about the likely level of investment inside the reserves although some investment has already occurred. Nevertheless, the change in policy must be seen as a further significant step towards the establishment of an extensive structure of cheap labour power in the reserves.

CONCLUSION

The argument in this paper shows that apartheid cannot be seen merely as a reflection of racial ideologies and nor can it be reduced to a simple extension of segregation.

Racial ideology in South Africa must be seen as an ideology which sustains and reproduces capitalist relations of production. This ideology and the political practice in which it is reflected is in a complex, reciprocal (although asymmetrical) relationship with changing social and economic conditions. The response of the dominant classes to the changing conditions, mediated by these ideologies, produces the two faces of domination – segregation and apartheid.

HAROLD WOLPE

The major contradiction of South African society between the capitalist mode of production and African pre-capitalist economies is giving way to a dominant contradiction *within* the capitalist economy. The consequence of this is to integrate race relations with capitalist relations of production to such a degree that the challenge to the one becomes of necessity a challenge to the other. Whether capitalism still has space (or time) for reform in South Africa is an issue which must be left to another occasion.

EDITORS' NOTE

a Bantustan: the term applied in the 1950s to areas reserved for African occupation. Many of these had existed since the nineteenth century and, although a small proportion of the total area of the country, they included the heartlands of some old African chiefdoms. The Nationalist government intended to extend and consolidate them into ten units, pushing the total area to over 13 per cent of the land surface. They were given a form of self-rule which was later intended to become political independence. Bantustan, initially used by H.F. Verwoerd, was taken up by the opposition critical of the balkanization of the country, as a disparaging term for these mini- and micro-states.

NOTES

* [The footnotes for this article have been altered from the original Harvard system to endnotes for consistency. Both notes and text have been shortened – Eds.]
1 In revising an earlier draft of this paper I have benefited from criticisms and comments made by a number of people. I am particularly grateful to S. Feuchtwang, R. Hallam, C. Meillassoux and M. Legassick.
2 Although the term 'apartheid' has more or less given way to 'self-development' in the language of the Nationalist Party, it remains the term mostly widely used to characterize the present system in South Africa.
3 M. Legassick, 'South Africa: Forced Labour, Industrialization, and Racial Differentiation', later published in R. Harris (ed.), *The Political Economy of Africa* (Boston, 1975). See also A.P. Walshe, 'The Changing Content of Apartheid', *Review of Politics*, XXV (1963), 360; B. Bunting, *The Rise of the South African Reich* (London, 1964), 305.
4 Legassick, 'Forced Labour'.
5 M. Szeftel, 'The Transkei: Conflict Externalization and Black Exclusivism', *Collected Seminar Papers on the Societies of Southern Africa in the 19th and 20th Centuries*, vol. 3, Institute of Commonwealth Studies, University of London (1972).

6 Legassick, 'Forced Labour'.
7 M. Legassick, 'Development and Underdevelopment in South Africa', unpublished paper, Royal Institute of International Affairs (1971) and 'Forced Labour'; H. Wolpe, 'Industrialization and Race in South Africa', in S. Zubaida (ed.), *Race and Racialism* (London, 1970); S. Trapido, 'South Africa in a Comparative Study of Industrialization', *Journal of Development Studies*, 7, 3 (1971); F. Johnstone, 'White Prosperity and White Supremacy in South Africa Today', *African Affairs*, vol. 69, issue 275 (1970), 124–40.
8 H.J. and R.E. Simons, *Class and Colour in South Africa 1850–1950* (London, 1969); S. van der Horst, 'The Effects of Industrialization on Race Relations in South Africa', in G. Hunter (ed.), *Industrialization and Race Relations* (London, 1965); P. Van den Berghe, *South Africa: A Study in Conflict* (Berkeley, CA, 1967); N.J. Rhoodie, *Apartheid and Racial Partnership in South Africa* (Pretoria, 1969).
9 Simons and Simons, *Class and Colour*, 614–15.
10 Van der Horst, 'The Effects'; Van den Berghe, *South Africa*; R. Horwitz, *The Political Economy of South Africa* (London, 1967).
11 Simons and Simons, *Class and Colour*; A. Asherson, 'South Africa: Race and Politics', *New Left Review*, 53 (1969), 55–67. For a critique, see Wolpe, 'Industrialization and Race'.
12 Van den Berghe, *South Africa*; L. Kuper and M.G. Smith, *Pluralism in Africa* (Berkeley, CA, 1969).
13 See L. Althusser, 'Ideology and Ideological State Apparatuses', in his *Lenin and Philosophy* (London, 1971); N. Poulantzas, 'The Problem of the Capitalist State', *New Left Review*, 58 (1969), 67–78.
14 See Horwitz, *Political Economy*, 355.
15 There is a serious lack of adequate material on, or analysis of African societies. It is clear that no adequate account of the dynamics of South African society can be arrived at without a proper history of these societies.
16 D. Hobart Houghton, *The South African Economy* (London, 1964).
17 G.A. Frank, *Capitalism and Underdevelopment in Latin America* (London, 1967).
18 E. Laclau, 'Feudalism and Capitalism in Latin America', *New Left Review*, 67 (1971), 19–46.
19 G. Arrighi, 'Labour Supplies in Historical Perspective: A Study of the Proletarianization of the African Peasantry in Rhodesia', *Journal of Development Studies*, 6 (1970), 197–234; C. Bundy, 'The Emergence and Decline of a South African Peasantry', *African Affairs*, vol. 71, issue 285 (1972), 369–88.
20 Arrighi, 'Labour Supplies'; I. Schapera, *Migrant Labour and Tribal Life* (London, 1947).
21 C. Meillassoux, 'From Reproduction to Production', *Economy and Society*, 1, 1 (1972), 102.
22 F. Wilson, 'Farming', in M. Wilson and L. Thompson (eds), *Oxford History of South Africa*, vol. 2 (Oxford, 1971); Legassick, 'Forced Labour'.
23 S. van der Horst, *Native Labour in South Africa* (London, 1971).

24 Union of South Africa, Report No. 9 of the Social and Economic Planning Council, *The Native Reserves and their Place in the Economy of the Union of South Africa* (U.G. [Union Government Parliamentary Papers] 32/1946); *Report of the Native Laws Commission* (U.G. 28/1948); Union of South Africa, *Summary Report of the Commission for the Socio-Economic Development of the Bantu Areas within the Union of South Africa* (U.G. 61/1955) – the Tomlinson Commission. [The Report appears to have been published in 1955, but the document and attached White Paper appear to have been released in 1956 – Eds.]

25 S. Gervasi, *Industrialization, Foreign Capital and Forced Labour in South Africa* (United Nations ST/PSCA/Set A./10, 1970).

26 Hobart Houghton, *South African Economy*, 86–7.

27 But see P. Mayer, *Townsmen or Tribesmen* (London, 1962).

28 The appendix to Mayer, *Townsmen*, 2nd edn (1971) provides an account of a 'dormitory' town.

4

NATAL, THE ZULU ROYAL FAMILY AND THE IDEOLOGY OF SEGREGATION

Shula Marks

Shula Marks initially trained as a historian in South Africa but emigrated to Britain and established a thriving centre of southern African studies at the University of London in the 1970s and 1980s. Working in the context of the rapidly developing subdiscipline of African History, for which the School of Oriental and African Studies was an important centre, she and her students emphasized African initiatives in the making of South African society to a greater degree than the neo-Marxist analysts of capital and the state. She notes that the establishment of African reserves and the survival of African chieftaincy as central elements of segregation originated not in the Boer republics, but in Natal, the most British of colonies. The Natal or Shepstonian system devolved substantial local control to African chiefs who were seen as the best guarantors of a stable social order, a forerunner of the practice of indirect rule developed elsewhere in colonial Africa. Although the Zulu kings were initially exiled and lesser chiefs appointed to control the area, Marks argues that the colonial authorities became increasingly concerned about 'detribalization' in Natal and Zululand. By the 1920s, the king – whose supporters were ambitious for him – came to be viewed by segregationists not as a threat, but as a possible bulwark of communalism in the face of growing popular protest in town and countryside. The Zulu-speaking Christian élite, formerly hostile to the royal family, now began to give the monarchy political support. This reflected the fact that their attempts to gain equal rights within a common society were being thwarted by the rise of segregationist sentiment among whites and they sought instead to secure political influence by working through the chieftaincy. Marks therefore suggests that the Zulu monarchy was revived largely because the segregationist state afforded it the political space to do so. But she recognizes the capacity of the king to win broader Zulu national support as well.

* * *

On 18 October 1913 Dinuzulu ka Cetshwayo, son of the last Zulu king, died in exile on a farm in the Middelburg district of the Transvaal. In response to the condolences of the government conveyed by the local magistrate, Mankulumana, his aged adviser, who had shared Dinuzulu's trials and had voluntarily shared his exile, remarked with some justification:

> It is you [meaning the government] who killed the one we have now buried, you killed his father, and killed him. We did not invade your country, but you invaded ours. I fought for the dead man's father, we were beaten, you took our King away, but the Queen sent him back to us, and we were happy. The one whom we now mourn did no wrong. There is no bone which will not decay. What we now ask is, as you have killed the father, to take care of the children.[1]

For the next twenty years Dinuzulu's son and heir, Solomon, engaged in a prolonged struggle, first to be recognized as chief of the Usuthu, as his father's most immediate followers were known, and then to be recognized as the Zulu paramount, by the Natal authorities and the Union government. Despite the fact that he gained considerable support both at the level of central government and from a coalition of interests in Zululand itself, the strong opposition of the Natal administration prevented the realization of his demands; after his death and during the minority of his potential heirs, his brother Mshiyeni, who had worked for some time in Natal, and who was believed to be 'most anxious to obtain the good opinion of the government and most amenable to the control of the Native Commissioner',[2] was accorded some wider recognition as Social Head of the Zulu Nation and Regent. After a prolonged succession dispute between Solomon's heirs in the 1940s Cyprian was recognized as chief of the Zulu section in 1948;[3] a couple of years later the Nationalist government installed him 'with great acclamation' as paramount, in response to their new imperatives.[4]

Given the importance of members of the Zulu royal family in the contemporary politics of the Republic, and of the role of chiefs in general in the various forms of control in twentieth-century southern Africa, the earlier years of this struggle for recognition and the political alliances it generated are not without interest. Not only does the story contribute to recent discussion on the origins and dynamic of segregationism in South Africa, and perhaps illuminate through its narrow focus some relatively neglected aspects of this debate; at a wider level it would also appear to provide support for Poulantzas's view that 'dominant ideology does not simply reflect the conditions of the existence of the dominant class ... but rather the concrete relations between the dominant and the dominated classes in a social formation'.[5]

In a series of important articles, Martin Legassick first set out the proposition that segregation was a set of policies specifically designed to cope with the strains of a society in the throes of industrialization, an ideology most clearly formulated initially during the reconstruction period in South Africa and devised to resolve the problems aroused in the context of the mining industry by the increased proletarianization of the African workforce.[6] More recently he has shown the role of key thinkers like Howard Pim, C.T. Loram and R.F. Hoernlé in refining this ideology in the interwar years.[7] Paul Rich has pointed to yet another strand in segregation policies in this century; in an unpublished seminar paper he has related this to what he terms 'the agrarian counter-revolution in the Transvaal, as an intrinsic part of a political response by the white polity in the Transvaal to the challenges from non-whites in the agrarian sector', in the years before the 1913 Land Act.[8]

Certainly by the end of the First World War, segregation in some form or other had become the accepted convention within which solutions or resolutions of class conflict in South Africa were sought. Valuable as these formulations have been, they do open up certain further questions: questions, as Legassick has pointed out, about the relative autonomy of the political and ideological levels,[9] and related to that, why it was that the particular ideological form of segregation was seen as the most suitable for an industrializing South Africa. Moreover, by focusing on the period after the South African War, as the time when these policies were formulated for a wider South Africa, the earlier origins of the ideology of segregation have to some extent been lost sight of.

It has frequently been remarked that of all the colonies of South Africa, Natal's policies in the nineteenth century were closest to twentieth-century notions of segregation. Not only were many of the key ideologues of segregation in this period Natal men – M.S. Evans, C.T. Loram, E.H. Brookes in his earlier phase, and G. Heaton Nicholls – most of them also explicitly looked back to Sir Theophilus Shepstone, Diplomatic Agent to the Native Tribes and Secretary for Native Affairs in Natal between 1845 and 1875, and the policies he devised:[10] the allocation of reserved lands for African tribal occupation; the recognition of customary law; administration through acceptable traditional authorities; the exemption of Christian Africans from customary law; and the attempt to prevent permanent African urbanization through the institution of a *togt* labour system.[11] It is these features of Natal's nineteenth-century policies which led David Welsh to entitle his book on the Shepstone era in Natal *The Roots of Segregation*.[12]

At first sight the coincidence of form is puzzling. At a deeper level, however, it is perhaps not so strange. It can after all be argued that it was in Natal more than in any other of the territories of South Africa that in the nineteenth century colonists were forced in the first instance to come to terms with the strength of the pre-capitalist mode of production and utilize it for their own purposes of surplus extraction and control. Of course one must be careful in this kind of analysis to note that though the forms remain the same, the features of Natal policy in the nineteenth century are used in the twentieth for very different purposes, and that whereas in the mid-nineteenth century surplus was being extracted from the pre-capitalist mode of production in the form of rent, tribute or tax, now the same ideology is being used to legitimate the extraction of surplus directly in the form of labour power.[13]

In Natal the forces of colonization were weak and had to come to terms with existing structures. The destruction wrought by the *Mfecane* [see Glossary – Eds] and the very fact that Africans were already producing tribute for a Zulu state meant that in some respects whites were able to utilize the pre-colonial structures for their own ends. Moreover, the very fact that in Natal, as Henry Slater has shown so well, it was the absentee landowners who were the dominant white class, meant that surplus value was extracted through rent, which could be produced without a major restructuring of African society.[14] The resilience of African society and the weakness of settler forces together with the unwillingness of the British government to pay the cost of totally changing African society meant that even the sugar planters had to rely for labour on indentured Indians. This again reinforced the tendency towards conserving African society, while at the same time providing certain other kinds of models for labour control which were to be utilized in the context of the late nineteenth–early twentieth-century mining industry.

In the trekker republics of the north, Boer supremacy was based on the outright expropriation of Africans: where this was not possible because Boer 'eyes were big but their teeth were poor' there was uneasy co-existence of separate social formations within a single geographical arena.[15] Boer ideology was undoubtedly based on notions of racial superiority – but not on principles of segregation. This can be seen as late as 1903 in General Botha's evidence (among others) to the Transvaal Labour Commission, when he suggests that the solution to the labour shortage in the Transvaal would be to 'break up the locations' of Basutoland, Swaziland and Zululand in order to *directly* release their land and labour for the white man – a solution which was unacceptable to the Milner administration, which feared the expense and possible disruption involved.[16] In the Cape, too, where the forces of colonialism were far stronger and the disintegration of pre-colonial structures more thoroughgoing, at least within the colonial 'frontiers', there was little material base for an ideology of segregation. There, as Stanley Trapido had pointed out, a liberal, assimilationist ideology emerged out of the dominance of the mercantile class, interested in fostering a stable and prosperous African peasantry: a peasantry which could only be 'produced' by a partial restructuring of pre-colonial society, though the *Mfecane*, the flight into the Cape of the Mfengu[a] and later the 1856 cattle-killing[b] undoubtedly facilitated the process.[17]

None of these, then, could provide ideologies which 'could serve to rationalize or reproduce bourgeois social relations' in the new industrializing context of early twentieth-century South Africa with its massive black proletariat.[18] That Natal could provide the model was, however, quickly realized by Sir Alfred Milner, High Commissioner and Governor of the Cape Colony; as early as November 1897, in a letter to Asquith – at that time front-bench member of the Liberal Party – he categorized the various colonies and territories of southern Africa in relation to their treatment of the black man:

The best is Natal, for here the black population is so enormous, compared with the white, that though they are kept in subjection, prudence, apart from all other considerations, would necessitate their not being treated too harshly. Besides, the white men are mainly of British race.[19]

Despite the racial interpretation (i.e. the implication that 'British is best') and Milner's emphasis on 'treatment', it would appear that the High Commissioner was quick to realize the utility of Natal forms for his own 'modernizing' policies: the constraints on using force to expropriate Africans in order to provide the necessary labour supply for gold mines or the land for white farmers were to be features of his reconstruction administration in common with the early days in Natal, and, given the earlier expedients, it was clearly simpler to adapt these than to start from scratch.

I am not, of course, suggesting that segregation can in any way solely be seen as a result of Natal's prior experience: this would be absurd reductionism. Apart from all else, the ideology came to be more and more clearly formulated in the newly industrializing context of South Africa. Moreover, it was a many-faceted policy made up of varying components which could be and were subtly shifted in response to circumstance and to the needs of different interests of the dominant white group in South Africa. Indeed its great strength as an ideology was its very elasticity, its ability to serve the needs of very many different interests and to absorb 'elements stemming from the way of life of classes and fractions other than the dominant class or fraction'.[20]

It is indeed to these latter aspects that I now wish to turn through a closer examination of the relationship of the Natal government to the Zulu royal family. In Natal, as we have seen, the control of the African population had been premised since the mid-nineteenth century on the rule of chiefs. The conquest of Zululand in 1879, its annexation by Britain in 1887 and its final takeover by Natal in 1897 posed problems, however, in the control of the African population. The war of 1879 was undertaken in the first instance largely to destroy the power of the Zulu king and thus release the resources and manpower of the tributary state for white exploitation. It was, however, far more difficult to fill the power vacuum left by the removal of the king in Zululand than it had been in Natal earlier in the century. Despite the British victory at Ulundi, in fact the imperial army never totally destroyed the Zulu kingdom,[21] nor were the imperial authorities willing to take on the costs of direct administration of the territory. The Zulu king posed far too great a threat to be recognized as a ruler, and the settlement after the war therefore meant finding the most compliant alternatives. Only the broad details of this need be rehearsed here: the 'Kilkenny cats' settlement after the Zulu War; the return of the king as simply one of the many chiefs of Zululand in 1883 in an attempt to end the civil war which had erupted in his absence; the trial of Dinuzulu, his son and heir, for rebellion in 1887, and his exile to St Helena; the non-recognition of Dinuzulu's position as Zulu king on his return from exile and the perennial fears which his presence aroused among white officials in Natal and Zululand until his second trial and exile in 1908 for alleged complicity in the Bambatha rebellion.[22]

Thereafter, for the next six years of his life, Dinuzulu remained in exile. The Natal government continued its paranoia about the influence of the Zulu kings and strenuously opposed any suggestion that he be allowed to return to Zululand; they looked with suspicion on the activities of messengers to and fro from his family, and it was only the more relaxed attitude of the Union government which left him to live out his last days on a farm in the Middelburg district of the Transvaal.[23] After his death a decision had to be taken about the position of his son and heir, Solomon. Again the attitude of the Natal government was passionately against any form of recognition of the special position of the Zulu kings. Indeed, it was only in 1917 that Solomon was recognized as chief of the Usuthu section of the Zulu, but again any further hopes he might have had of wider recognition of paramountcy were sternly frowned upon by the Natal administration.[24]

In 1916 there was one of those flurries of hysteria to which Natal was prone when the support which the Zulu kings enjoyed became manifest. As a result of a misunderstanding, Solomon had called a ritual hunt to 'cleanse the nation' after the period of mourning for Dinuzulu had ended. The Chief Native Commissioner in Zululand was convinced that this was yet another ploy by the Zulu kings to gain recognition from their people.[25] It was only the intervention of the central government which prevented the removal of Solomon from Zululand and a heavy fine in cattle being imposed.[26] As late as 1920 the Chief Native Commissioner in Zululand was very concerned by the visit of Solomon's brother David to Cetshwayo's grave – news of which 'thundered through the country'.[27] The Commissioner warned the keepers of the grave against the consequences of 'continuing to be a hindrance to the Government and getting mixed up in political matters. They had had a lesson during the rebellion and now they were deliberately courting trouble again by becoming mixed up with royal youngsters'.[28]

Nevertheless, by the mid-1920s there was clearly a perceptible change in attitude. Although this was not to be given full administrative expression until later, it is none the less of considerable significance, particularly as it was associated with a class alliance between the Zulu royal family, the Natal African petty bourgeoisie and the Zululand planters.

On the white side, the key figure was George Heaton Nicholls, at that time Member of Parliament for Zululand and President of the South African Planters' Union and its affiliate, the Zululand Planters' Union.[29] By far one of the most articulate proponents of segregation, and at this time one of the most influential in terms of the political power he achieved, George Heaton Nicholls's role in the formulation of the policies of segregation has been curiously underestimated, notwithstanding – or perhaps because of – the significance he himself attached to it.[30] An important member of the Joint Select Committee appointed to take evidence and formulate revised policy on Hertzog's 1926 native legislation, Heaton Nicholls as a member of the Native Affairs Commission was also responsible in 1937 for publishing as an appendix to the Native Affairs Commission Official Report a major interpretation of segregationist principles.[31]

In the late 1920s and early 1930s he set out his ideas in a series of revealing private letters and memoranda. He had little doubt what the alternatives to segregation would be. As he wrote to J.H. van Zutphen in May 1929, just as tension was mounting in Durban over an African beerhall boycott, which was to lead in the following month to the deaths of six Africans and two whites and the injury of another 108 Africans:

> We must come back to the real essence of native life – communalism – a very different thing to communism. If we do not get back to communalism, we will certainly arrive very soon at communism. . . . We cannot long continue as a white aristocracy or black proletariat. . . . We end ultimately I think in the not too distant future in the class war.[32]

He elaborated this further in an undated fragment probably written about 1931:

> An adaptionist policy demands as its primary concept the maintenance of chieftaindom, without which the tribal society cannot exist. The institution is the necessary pivot around which all tribal evolution must take place. . . . The adaptionist policy assumes a difference between the Abantu and the Europeans. It assumes some measure of territorial segregation. It assumes what is in effect the growth of a national consciousness amongst the Abantu themselves. . . . The opposite policy of assimilation substitutes class for race, and if continued on its present basis must lead to the evolution of a native proletariat, inspired by the usual antagonisms of class war. The process of assimilation has already gone very far and unless some effort is made to stem the tide of tribal disintegration, it will soon be too late.[33]

He was very concerned with what he saw as the discrepancy between the treatment the government handed out to the Industrial and Commercial Workers Union (ICU) organizers, at that time active in Natal, and the lack of respect accorded to traditional authority: in the same fragment he continued, 'the Governor-General on a visit to Durban a few years ago shook hands with Champion[d] in the sight of thousands of Zulus assembled ... by the municipal authorities, while Solomon ka Dinuzulu was a few days later talked down to and reprimanded before his people in Zululand by the Governor-General, and his Chief's stipend stopped for a year because of some assumed disrespect'.[34] In yet another letter at around the same time he set out his views if anything even more explicitly:

> The policy of a Bantu nation, as distinct from that of a black proletariat – and that stripped of all verbiage, that is the real issue in Africa – obviously brings in its train a pride of race. The most race-proud man I know is Solomon. He glories in his race and its past prowess; and there is no native in the Union who is so earnestly desirous of maintaining a Bantu race purity.[35]

Heaton Nicholls as an outsider was well aware of the possibilities which were being shut down by the government's refusal to acknowledge the position of Solomon: he had in his Northern

Rhodesian days had the task of training the Barotseland Native Constabulary and was doubtless aware of the role as paramount played there for the British South Africa Company by Lewanika, king of the Lozi.[36] According to Nicholls, in Zululand

> many of the magistrates had the Zulu war plus the Bambatha rebellion mentality and resented the influence of Solomon, the Zulu king in their district, although they all knew that he was the undoubted paramount chief of the Zulus. The Government made no use of Solomon on some idea as out of date as an assagai that it was dangerous to create officially a paramount chief. Solomon himself was disgruntled. He asked merely to be used. When deadlock was reached between the Administration and the natives at Mtunzini in connection with their cattle, the Administration called Solomon in to help them. 'Is that all', said Solomon. . . . He went himself and settled the dispute in five minutes which had been going on for over a year.[37]

If one prong of Heaton Nicholls's policy was to restore 'Bantu-race pride' and make use of the unemployed talents of the Zulu royal family, the other was the co-option of the Natal African petty bourgeoisie, under the leadership of John Dube. This was very clear both in the schemes he laid before the Joint Select Committee, and in his correspondence with Dube on the Hertzog legislation. Again, unlike his predecessors earlier in the century, who saw John Dube as a 'pronounced Ethiopian' who ought to be watched,[38] an attitude which persisted until well after the First World War when the Durban municipal authorities were convinced that Dube was behind the unrest among workers in that city in 1918–19, and should be reprimanded,[39] Heaton Nicholls perceived the conciliatory and conservative role which Dube could play. In this, indeed, he may have been preceded by the Chief Native Commissioner for Natal and Zululand, C.A. Wheelwright, who was described in 1923 as Dube's 'strongest supporter'.[40] Again, too, the perceptible shift in attitude comes in the early twenties as new and more dangerous class forces begin to emerge.

What Heaton Nicholls recognized was the need to co-opt the Natal *kholwa* (African Christians) if his schemes for the Hertzog legislation were to have any chance of success. His connection with John Dube may well have come through their common con-

tact with the Zulu king and their common antagonism to the ICU
– though I have no direct evidence of this as yet. In 1931 through
John Dube he sought and obtained the agreement of a number of
prominent African leaders to a scheme entitled 'The Land
Settlement' which set out 'the principle of creating reserves in
which Natives will be "enabled to attain a high standard of economic production under a system of local self-government"'. The
reserves were to be compact and large enough for Africans 'to
develop a real national life . . . a becoming race-consciousness'.
Each reserve was to have, in addition, a local council with powers
greater than those of the Transkeian Bhunga, the civil service
was to be open to 'competent natives' and the 'fullest facilities for
trading by Natives in the reserves should be allowed'. There
was to be a Union Native Council elected from members of the
provincial councils to 'deal with all matters affecting the native
people as a whole'. In return for the disappearance of the Cape
franchise with the present voters, there were to be eight Africans
elected on equal terms with the Europeans to the Senate.[41]

In his autobiography, Nicholls was thus able to assert with some
confidence that Natal's effort to find a solution to Hertzog's legislation 'met with the full approval of a number of the leading
natives'.[42] It was indeed the success of Nicholls's manoeuvres
which led to Albert Luthuli's first lesson in politics, which he
entered when invited to attend a Conference of chiefs and leaders
to discuss the Hertzog Bills in 1935. The Regent was the Chairman,
with Dube acting for him. According to Luthuli, the Revd
Mtimkulu, one of the 'old guard', was appointed to head a
committee to report on the findings of the conference, but Luthuli
acted in his place. When it came to report, however, Mtimkulu
rejected the committee's findings and presented instead a statement which Luthuli describes as 'inspired unofficially by a clerk
in the NAD' – it was more than likely that it was inspired by
Heaton Nicholls.

> The upshot was that Natal Africans appeared completely
> indifferent to the fate of their disenfranchised brothers in
> the Cape and the conference appeared to accept without
> criticism the proposals relating to land. . . . We younger
> men were shocked and taken aback, but we did not see how
> to make an issue of it with a politically entrenched older
> man.[43]

I do not wish here to dwell on this rather later aspect of the story. I have set out elements of this in my article, 'The Ambiguities of Dependence: John L. Dube of Natal'.[44] Here what is important to show are the interconnections both at the level of Heaton Nicholls's policy formulations and in terms of the alliance between the Natal petty bourgeoisie and the Zulu royal family.

In the late 1920s Heaton Nicholls began to elaborate his ideas on segregation. This was not simply the accidental result of his becoming the Natal representative on the Select Committee, nor because he later became a member of the Native Affairs Commission. In the 1920s there were more fundamental reasons why the representative of farming interests in Zululand should take such a particular interest in schemes for bolstering the powers of chiefs and resuscitating the reserves. For it is clear that it was at this point that Zululand began to show really major strains as a result of the expansion of white capitalist farming, class formation within the African population, and overstocking and overgrazing – the latter ecological concomitants of the first two factors taken together with the consequences of the eradication of East Coast Fever by about 1920.

Although as Jeff Guy has pointed out, proletarianization in Zululand probably began with the destruction of the Zulu kingdom in the 1880s,[45] this was still a very uneven and jagged process. Some of the southern districts were feeling stress at the beginning of the century; yet as late as 1925 magistrates in Zululand could comment on the good year Africans had had, and the abundance of cattle and grain after the rains. In some areas to the north, indeed, settlers and magistrates maintained that the Africans had never been more prosperous.[46] One must be wary of taking these reports at their face value. Though there clearly were individuals with herds of two to four hundred in Zululand at this time, they were undoubtedly the privileged few.[47] For the majority, the effects of poverty were only too evident.

Above all, these were the years in which white farming activities expanded rapidly in response to world demand for tropical commodities: cotton and sugar expanded along the coast, wattle and sheep in the thornveld of the Zululand interior and the northern districts of Natal. And both forms of expansion had major repercussions for the African peasant. In the old Republican districts of Vryheid, Utrecht and Paulpietersberg –

annexed to Natal after the South African War with their relations of production (if such they can be termed) virtually intact – rural relationships were now radically restructured for the first time.[48] The result was massive evictions:[49] Chief Mgizo, grandson of the Zulu king Mpande, put it vividly when he talked of 'the yawning crack which empties forth human beings'.[50] Many of these 'homeless wanderers'[51] found their way to Zululand where chiefs tried to squeeze them on to already overcrowded lands – lands which had seen a steady influx of Africans from Natal not only since the passage of the 1913 Land Act, but even since the 1880s as a result of the British 'settlement' of southern Zululand.

The effects in the coastal areas were different but no less traumatic. These areas had always been thinly populated – with good reason. As the cotton and sugar plantations extended, and the railway was built to service them, a malaria epidemic of major proportions raged.[52] It was not to be brought under control until the 1930s. No wonder, then, that in the 1930s Max Gluckman found that the whites 'were accused of having introduced malaria into a Zulu arcady':[53] according to the Medical Officer of Health in Natal, who was greatly concerned by the casual attitude of the Department of Railways to the loss of life in building the new line, and the spread of the disease into Natal and even the eastern Cape by non-immune labour, 'there is no other part of the Union with such a large labour force engaged in the conduct of extensive agricultural operations in such an unhealthy area'.[54]

It is against this background that the response of the Zulu to the spread of the ICU in rural areas has to be understood. As Peter Wickins has shown, the move of ICU headquarters to Johannesburg and Durban in 1926 led to 'a proliferation of branches in the countryside'. Kadalie was able to rely very heavily on Durban financially and this became the bastion of the ICU in 1926.[55] Wickins attempts to explain this by saying that it was through the 'efforts of A.W.G. Champion, who had a genius for making himself unpleasant to those in authority and for fastening upon and exploiting grievances'.[56] While the role of Champion was undoubtedly important, particularly in Durban itself, far more significant was what was happening in the countryside. As *The Times* noted in October 1927, 'thousands of Zulu are joining up. The red ticket of promise is everywhere'.[57] And it was among wage labourers and labour-tenants that ICU propaganda gained most response. The reaction of Natal farmers was immediate. At a special Congress in 1927 policy was discussed of evicting ICU members from the farms, and it seems as though many farmers were doing precisely this. In August, it was resolved to take special measures, if possible in the form of a Farmers' Vigilance Association, for the protection of farmers 'against unreasonable actions of trade union organizations and communistic bodies'. White resentment erupted in violence in Bergville, Greytown, Weenen, Kranskop and Pietermaritzburg itself.[58] In 1929 and 1930 the rural unrest found its counterpart in urban disturbances in Durban. Again it is no coincidence that the Communist Party's anti-pass demonstration gained its greatest support in Durban itself that year.[59] The urban and rural disturbances were reflections of a single reality: the increasing impoverishment of the African population in the rural areas and their proletarianization.

If, however, one of the responses of the African population was to join the ICU in an attempt to find a solution of their problems in these years, it would seem equally clear that for many Africans the Zulu king constituted an alternative answer. After all, in the Zulu state the king had represented the unity of the community, its father and redistributor. He personified the community and had the role of 'representing and defining the common interests of all members of the community'.[60] At the ideological level he and his ancestors had ensured the integrity and well-being of the people on both their natural and supernatural plane.[61] Therefore in a situation of crisis it was perhaps natural, especially at a time when the majority of Africans had not accepted the new ideology of the whites and certainly did not see the white state as in any way representing their interests, that they should turn again to the Zulu royal family.[62]

It is always difficult to explore mass consciousness, and the perceptions held by the masses of the people of the Zulu royal family are far from clear, particularly as these perceptions are reported and refracted through hostile colonial officials on the one hand and through the literate African élite and the far from disinterested royal family itself on the other. Moreover, it can be argued that the very processes which the administration used to manipulate the subordinate chiefs in Natal to undermine the Zulu royal family, in fact strengthened the latter's position. Whereas the subordinate chiefs came to be seen as 'the government's "boys"', the royal family could in some sense be seen, like the people, to be the victims of the colonial administration.[63] The cleavages, which Shepstone had picked up in the nineteenth century in Zululand,[64] were in the process of being papered over by the Natal government's very obduracy in regard to the royal family. At a time when the subordinate chiefs were becoming increasingly unpopular and their power crumbling as a result of the abuse of power, the Zulu royal family, as Max Gluckman has remarked, 'had no power to abuse'.[65] And while this probably overstates the case – for power was not simply to be measured in the authority granted by the colonial government – ironically the very attempt to strip the royal family of its 'pretensions' increased its popularity. In the 1920s, when so many of the lesser chiefs were becoming impoverished and losing their land base through evictions – from which chiefs on private lands were no more immune than their followers – the appeal of 'the good old days' when the Zulu kings had an abundance of land and cattle with which to reward their followers must have been considerable.

Nor were Solomon and his advisers unaware of the importance of sustaining through positive action their popular appeal, though it is almost impossible to distinguish cause and effect through the inadequacy of the sources. Thus, soon after his return to Zululand, at the time of the notorious 'hunt'[66] Solomon was called up before the Chief Native Commissioner in Zululand who told him 'to leave the Zulu alone' until the government had decided how to define his status:

His replies were most characteristic, and his demeanour ... although ... extremely courteous left not the slightest doubt in my mind that his aspirations are to become head of the Zulus. He kept repeating 'I do not ask these people to follow me and show me any sort of respect; wherever I go, they recognize me as the representative of the Zulu House and accord me the respect due thereto [Solomon then asked for the restoration of his ancestral lands]. ... I told him to disabuse his mind of any hopes of the resurrection of the situation which formerly existed. .... At present, Solomon is attempting to build up his status as a leader of the Zulu people with the connivance of Mnyaiza [his cousin, and chief adviser].[67]

In the 1920s, as we shall see, the evidence that the royal family were manipulating traditional forms and popular feeling to secure recognition of the 'paramount' position of Solomon is clearer; there is nevertheless also considerable evidence of the hold the monarchy had in popular consciousness. To some extent this can be gauged through the recurrent rumours long after his death that Dinuzulu was still alive and about to bring a fresh army into Zululand, or that he was – very threateningly for the Natal administration – in alliance with the Germans during the First World War.[68] The rumours continued until at least 1920.[69] In 1923 the missionary Oscroft remarked, after observing a meeting of the newly formed Zulu National Council, Inkatha,[70] that

> the real object is to unite all black races ... they consider that the native is victimized in many ways and receives unfair and unjust treatment from the white man; that this will continue as long as the natives are divided; that the native peoples will never be strong until there is unity among them. They are casting around for a rallying point – a central figure – and that figure would seem to be Solomon.[71]

In the 1920s at a meeting of magistrates, all admitted that the power of Solomon in their district was 'extraordinary, and that no chief could act contrary to his wishes'.[72] Most strikingly, in 1930 before the Native Economic Commission Archdeacon Lee of Vryheid maintained:

> I may say that the present very serious political condition of Zululand – one which cannot be exaggerated – I do not want to be alarmist – may lead to trouble before many years are over. The political conditions are due to one thing ... and it is ... that while Solomon is recognized by the people as their King, he is not recognized by the State. He has all the responsibilities of kingship and none of the authority. There is no political question which is ever debated amongst the Zulu people which is not brought to Solomon, and he has instituted ... more with the connivance of the Government than its recognition a large committee of Zulu people which he calls Inkata ka Zulu.[73]

The origins and development of Inkatha owed as much to the deliberate resuscitation by the Zulu royal family of traditional forms as to any spontaneous reaction of the Zulu people. Founded in 1922–3, by a group of Solomon's advisers including the redoubtable Mankulumana and Mnyaiza, but also a group of *kholwa* including John Dube of Natal,[74] Inkatha ya ka Zulu was a deliberate attempt to make use of traditional forms in the establishment of a council of chiefs and 'important men' in Zululand. It was closely associated with the raising of a Zulu National Fund – alleged to have £3,000 banked at Vryheid in 1923, and used to pay off the debts of the Zulu royal family (which were considerable, and which led to much snide magisterial comment) as well as 'to be used for the benefit of the Zulu nation from time to time'.[75] At a five hundred-strong meeting of Inkatha in 1924 the matters discussed included the building of a national church to be called the 'Chaka Zulu's Church', 'to commemorate Chaka, who is looked upon as the founder of the Zulu nation and power'; the Zulu National Fund; the division between the Mandhlakazi and Usuthu sections of the royal family – a division which went back to Cetshwayo's day; and, most significantly, opposition to the introduction of the council system on the Transkei model into Zululand – the meeting maintained that 'the present means of government through Solomon and the chiefs should not be interfered with'.[76] Not surprisingly, Heaton Nicholls was an enthusiastic supporter of Inkatha in the late 1920s, urging that

> The Inkata is their very own. All the Natives belong to it. ... It is based upon the old Zulul. [*sic*] national system which existed under their old kings and I think it would go far to win the confidence of the Zulu if the government would adopt the Inkata instead of creating the stereotyped council of the Cape. . . .[77]

As the missionary L.E. Oscroft appreciated, the role of 'educated natives from outside' in the creation of Inkatha was considerable.[78] In some respects, indeed, Inkatha can be seen – as can this alliance between the Zulu royal family and the Natal *kholwa* involved in its inception – as a deliberate attempt to reduce the tensions which had arisen within Zulu society as a result of the growth of internal social stratification.

For if the general picture in these years is one of impoverishment, as I have already suggested,[79] it is also evident that the same processes had brought into being a class of prosperous black farmers employing outside labour, a process which had begun in Natal in the mid-nineteenth century but which found its parallel in Zululand to an increasing degree in the 1920s. Thus at a time when there is increasing evidence that in certain areas of Zululand, congestion, overstocking and erosion, with the consequent impoverishment of the people was the norm, there is also evidence of a stratum of increasingly wealthy farmers. The process even in Zululand had its roots in the late nineteenth century, but the spread and scale of the problem appear new. According to Archdeacon Lee before the 1930–2 Native Economic Commission, 'there are people now in Zululand who have herds of three hundred and four hundred'.[80] More revealingly, he added, 'One of the obstacles in the way of the more economic use of land is through the land-grabbing by men of importance in the community.'[81] Many of these were dependent on the use of outside labour, and offered the same terms as white farmers.[82] By the second half of the 1920s, they were also threatened, as the white farmers were, by the rise of the ICU. This indeed was recognized by Solomon in a bitter attack on the union in August 1927. Reported in *Ilanga lase Natal* in Zulu, the editor (Dube) took the opportunity of the English translation to make the message even more explicit:

the organization would be a good thing in industrial centres if the ideal aimed at was the amelioration of conditions under which the natives labour, and to secure those means by cooperation of both Natives and Europeans. But he [Solomon] regards the activities of the leaders ... as very dangerous. ... The I.C.U. are exploiting poor Native workers. ... The leaders are irresponsible they do not understand the relations of capital to labour, the need for investment, ... what workers are they looking for in the native areas and reserves? Are any of their leaders engaged in business employing a number of people for farming and paying 8 shillings a day to their workers? How about that for the men of Groutville, Amanzimtoti and Ifafa! Are they prepared to pay their employees that wage? How long can they raise cane at a profit if they pay such wages?[83]

It is indeed to this alliance between the Zulu royal family and the Natal petty bourgeoisie that we must now turn. At first sight it would indeed appear to need some explanation. After all, in the nineteenth century it was the Natal *kholwa* who were recruited to fight against the Zulu during the 1879 war. During the Bambatha rebellion, the *kholwa* were regarded as *amambuka* – traitors to the white man.[84] It was frequently held that they had a very different set of values, and were antagonistic to traditional authorities. In some cases, in the nineteenth century they deliberately cut themselves off from their fellow Africans in their adoption of a new ideology and a new way of life – and indeed the whole policy of mission reserves in Natal was designed to do precisely this.[85] Nevertheless, nothing is more incorrect than to imagine that there was an inevitable and invariable rift between the new élite of teachers, preachers, clerks, lawyers and prosperous farmers and the old élite of chiefs: as has now frequently been pointed out, on many occasions the new élite were indeed the old in new guise, the sons of chiefs and the aristocracy having had preferential access to the resources necessary for the acquisition of education and modern skills. John Dube was the descendant of a chiefly family, as was the equally distinguished S.M. Molema; Pixley ka Isaka Seme was married to the daughter of Dinuzulu and both Stephen Mini and Martin Luthuli, leaders of the Natal Congress at the beginning of the twentieth century, were Christian chiefs. Both, too, had served as clerks and interpreters to the royal families of South Africa: Mini to the Swazi royal family, Luthuli to Dinuzulu both in the 1880s and during his exile on St Helena.[86]

The royal families, moreover, also offered not only opportunities of employment but also financial resources to the new petty bourgeoisie. The South African Native National Congress was heavily dependent on financial support from the major royal families – the Swazi royal family funded its newspaper *Abantu-Batho*, for example,[87] while S.T. Plaatje hoped that his book *Native Life in South Africa* would be financed by a grant from the Rolong chief, Lekoko.[88] With the foundation of the South African Native National Congress the alliance took on an even more concrete form: the special role of chiefs was recognized in the creation of a separate upper house, while many of the royals were recognized as honorary vice-presidents. Dinuzulu himself was clearly in close touch with the founders of the SANNC.[89]

It was indeed during Dinuzulu's second trial that the support of the *kholwa* community, expressed through its most outstanding member in Natal at that time, John Dube, became most explicit, and it is in their connection during the trial that the origins of the later alliance between Dube and the Zulu royal family must

probably be sought. Both Dube and Seme were heavily involved
in the affairs of the Zulu royals in Middelburg in the Transvaal,
and after Dinuzulu's death Dube continued as adviser to the
young princes and especially to Solomon, his heir – a fact which
caused some alarm to the Chief Native Commissioner in Natal,
who remarked on Solomon's accession 'that he was one who may
confidently be expected to lead a quiet life unless led away by the
headmen and agitators such as John Dube, Seme and others'.[90]

To some extent the royal family could play a function for the
new petty bourgeoisie which the subordinate chiefs could not:
a nationalist role – in the sense of a pan-Zulu nationalism; a
modernizing role – the position could be, and was, conceived
of, as similar in some way to that of the British constitutional
monarchs; while their central position as the 'pivot of Zulu
cultural life'[91] could tie in very fruitfully later on with a revival
of Zulu national consciousness. This was most explicit in the
foundation in the 1930s of the Zulu society, ostensibly a cultural
union for the promotion of Zulu cultural identity.[92] It is no coincidence that John Dube was its founder and first president, and
Mshiyeni its honorary patron.

Above all, it can be argued that with the sharpening of class
conflict in Natal and Zululand in the 1920s, the Zulu royal family
and the traditionalism it represented constituted a bulwark
against radical change: a bulwark for the African petty bourgeoisie as for the ideologues of segregation. There are several
ironies in the situation. Whereas in the 1880s it can be argued that
it was the 'new men', 'entrepreneurs' like Sibhebhu of the
Mandhlakazi or the king's cousin, Uhamu, or the intrusive Hlubi
in Nqutu district, who were at the same time most closely
involved in the colonial economy and the king's bitterest enemies,
by the 1920s and 1930s, the unrecognized king was coming to act
as their spokesman. Even the deep-seated rivalry with the
Mandhlakazi was resolved with Mankulumana's death when
the Zulu royal family petitioned the government for Bhokwe, the
son of Sibhebhu, to join Matole Buthelezi, son of Tshanibezwe,
son of Mnyamana, Cetshwayo's last hereditary prime minister, as
joint adviser to Solomon.[93]

The Natal *kholwa* attitude, too, had undergone equally pro-
found changes: as late as 1912, John Dube could write in his
'Address to the Chiefs and Gentlemen of the South African
Native National Congress':

Upward! into the higher places of civilization and Christianity – not backward into the slump of darkness, nor downward into the abyss of antiquated tribal systems.[94]

This was a far cry indeed from the views of the *kholwa* who gave evidence to the 1930–2 Native Economic Commission on behalf of the chiefs and headmen in the northern districts of Natal that 'everything in tribal custom was good, except the practice of witchcraft',[95] and the appeals in 1938 of Charles Mpanza, secretary of the Zulu Society (a decidedly *kholwa*-dominated organization) that the paramountcy of the Zulu chief be recognized:

> It was unanimously felt at that meeting [of the Zulu Society in Durban] that according to the customs and traditions, the preservation of our wholesome Traditions and Customs and Rule of Etiquette . . . should centre around and receive the support of the Head of the Principal family of the Zulu whose status today was that of an ordinary chief officially.[96]

From the white point of view, the turnabout was even more complete. Whereas in the 1870s and 1880s, the Zulu royal family had to be destroyed if Zululand was to be 'opened up' for white exploitation, now that the real powers of the Zulu kings had been removed, their regiments dismantled and their economic position undermined, the residual hold they had at an ideological level was to be used to make Zululand safe for the sugar planters! To quote Heaton Nicholls once more in his advocacy of the recognition of Solomon as paramount:

> The recreation and the maintenance of the old native aristocracy is essential to the growth of the adaptionist ideal . . . if native policy could be directed to capturing the latent loyalties of the Zulu race by recognizing the Royal House as paramount, it would go far to satisfy native opinion and to reorient that opinion in the direction of building up a native society in the reserves. . . . [97]

EDITORS' NOTES

a Mfengu: term applied to African communities, originally from a number of different chiefdoms in Natal and Zululand, who migrated or fled to the eastern Cape in the 1820s and 1830s to escape the consequences of Zulu power and more generalized conflict. Some became 'colonial Africans' adopting Christianity and mission education, fighting alongside colonial militia and working as peasants or labourers in the colonial economy. The term was thus sometimes used to indicate African people who were more assimilated into colonial society.

b The cattle-killing of 1856–7 is South Africa's best-known and most tragic millennial episode. Some Xhosa and neighbouring chiefdoms, who bore the brunt of colonial encroachments on the eastern frontier, responded to the vision of a young woman, as interpreted by her uncle and the political authorities, by slaughtering their own cattle and destroying grain stores in anticipation of a new and less troubled society. As a result, over 30,000 died and many more sought work in the Cape Colony.

c Cetshwayo: the Zulu king or paramount chief who ruled from 1872 to 1884 during the last phase of Zulu independence.

d A.W.G. Champion: an educated African political leader of Zulu origin who became head of the Industrial and Commercial Workers' Union in Natal during the late 1920s.

NOTES

1 Pretoria Archives, Native Affairs Department (henceforth NA) 290 2151/F727. Report G.W. Kinsman, Assistant Magistrate, Babanango, to Chief Native Commissioner (CNC), 28 October 1913. There was some debate over the 'inflammatory nature' of this speech, and in particular over the somewhat obscure phrase 'There is no bone which will not decay'. It was accepted in the end that the term 'kill' had a more general sense of 'ruin' and the phrase meant 'Let revenge cease'. For Natal's antagonism to the Zulu royal family see my *Reluctant Rebellion* (Oxford, 1970), parts II and IV. The attempts to destroy the royal family after the Bambatha rebellion are described on pp. 353ff.

2 Heaton Nicholls Papers, Killie Campbell Library, Durban (henceforth Ms. Nic. 2.08.1) KCM 3303 d, Carbon fragment, Folder 2, nd.

3 Native Affairs Department, *Annual Report*, 1948–9, 36.

4 NAD, 1951–2 (Pretoria, 1955), 13.

5 N. Poulantzas, *Political Power and Social Classes* (London, 1973), 203.

6 These were first presented as three papers under the general title 'Ideology and Social Structure in 20th Century South Africa' to a postgraduate seminar at the Institute of Commonwealth Studies, London, in 1973. The final paper was published in revised form in the *Journal of Southern African Studies*, 1, 1 (1974), 5–35 under the title 'Legislation, Ideology and Economy in Post-1948 South Africa'. [See Legassick's contribution in this volume – Eds.]

7 The papers on Pim and Loram are as yet unpublished; that on Hoernlé 'Race, Industrialization and Social Change; The Case of R.F. Hoernlé' was published in *African Affairs*, vol. 75, issue 299 (1976), 224–39. The quotation comes from the latter article, p. 229.

8 'The Agrarian Counter-Revolution in the Transvaal and the Origins of Segregation: 1902–1913', University of Witwatersrand, 1976.
9 'Race, Industrialization and Social Change', 229.
10 Cf M.S. Evans, *Black and White in South East Africa*, 2nd edn (London, 1916), 242; E.H. Brookes, *The History of Native Policy in South Africa until 1924* (Pretoria, 1927), 10, 26–31,41–74; G. Heaton Nicholls, *South Africa in My Time* (London, 1961), 278, 282.
11 Legassick, 'South Africa: Forced Labour, Industrialization, and Racial Differentiation', in R. Harris (ed.), *The Political Economy of Africa* (New York, 1975), 250 defines segregation as 'restrictions on permanent urbanization, territorial separation of land ownership, the use of traditional institutions as providers of "social services" and means of social control'.
12 This is subtitled *Native Policy in Natal (1845–1910)* (Cape Town, 1971). Cf p. 322: 'It is a myth that apartheid is the exclusive product of Afrikaner nationalism: its antecedents are to be found in Natal rather than in any of the other provinces. A long line of segregationist writers and politicians from Natal did much to create the climate of opinion in which segregation became acceptable to white electorates . . .'. Welsh does not, however, try to explain why this should have been so.
13 See Maurice Godelier, 'The Non-Correspondence between Form and Content in Social Relations: New Thoughts about the Incas' in his recently translated *Perspectives in Marxist Anthropology* (Cambridge, 1977), 186–96.
14 H. Slater, 'Land, Labour and Capital in Natal: The Natal and Colonisation Company, 1860–1948', *Journal of African History*, XVI, 2 (1975), 257–83, esp. 263–5.
15 For attempts to characterize the Boer mode of production, see S. Trapido, 'The South African Republic: Class Formation and the State, 1850–1900', *Collected Seminar Papers on the Societies of Southern Africa in the 19th and 20th Centuries*, vol. 3, Institute of Commonwealth Studies, London (1973) (henceforth, *CSP*) and his 'Aspects in the Transition from Slavery to Serfdom' in *CSP*, vol. 6 (1976). For the 'uneasy coexistence', I have drawn on my reading of Philip Bonner's PhD thesis, 'The Rise, Consolidation and Disintegration of Dlamini Power in Swaziland between 1820 and 1889: A Study in the Relationship of Foreign Affairs to Internal Political Development' (London, 1976) [published as *Kings, Commoners and Concessionaires* (Johannesburg, 1983)].
16 *Transvaal Labour Commission*, Evidence (Pretoria, 1903), 505.
17 S. Trapido, 'Liberalism in the Cape in the 19th and 20th Centuries', *CSP*, vol. 4 (1974); for the emergence of the Cape peasantry, see C. Bundy, 'African Peasants and Economic Change in South Africa 1870–1913, with Particular Reference to the Cape', DPhil (Oxford, 1976).
18 Legassick, 'Race, Industrialization and Social Change', 228.
19 For a full transcription of this document and a commentary upon it see J. Butler, 'Sir Alfred Milner on British Policy in South Africa in

1897', in J. Butler (ed.), *Boston University Papers in African History*, 1 (Boston, MA, 1964), 245–70. The quotation is on p. 248.

20 Poulantzas, *Political Power and Social Classes*, 203.

21 For a full account of the Zulu War and its aftermath, the civil wars in Zululand, see J.J. Guy, 'The Destruction of the Zulu Kingdom: The Civil Wars in Zululand, 1879–1884', PhD (London, 1975), published Johannesburg, 1979. Guy shows convincingly that the British victory at Ulundi was illusory – it was more of a tactical withdrawal by the Zulu – and that the real destruction came five years later at the second battle of Ulundi between the Usuthu supporters of Cetshwayo and the Mandhlakazi supporters of Zibhebhu. As we shall see this breach was only partially healed in the late 1920s.

22 See *Reluctant Rebellion*, sections II and IV for these events.

23 *Reluctant Rebellion*, 303.

24 See below.

25 NA 289 2151/F727 esp. Secretary to Native Affairs to Minister of Native Affairs 24.2.16 and CNC, R.H. Addison Natal to W. Dower Pretoria, 27 January 1916. See also Notes of a Meeting at Magistrate's Office Nongoma, 28 February 1916 in connection with the attempt by Solomon to hold an unauthorized hunt.

26 As note 25, CNC to SNA 27 January 1916; E. Barrett to SNA, Cape Town, 15 February 1916.

27 Pietermaritzburg Archives, Secretary for Native Affairs (henceforth SNA) 1.9.5. Notes of an Enquiry by the CNC, Natal, regarding the visit of David to Cetshwayo's grave, Nkandhla, 24 May 1920.

28 As note 27.

29 See his autobiography, *South Africa in My Time, passim*.

30 See the somewhat snide way in which Alan Paton refers to Heaton Nicholls in his biography of *Hofmeyr* (Oxford , 1964), 230.

31 *Report of the Native Affairs Commission, 1936* (UG 48, 1937). Legassick, 'Hoernlé', 236 cites this to show the continuity with Hoernlé's thought in 1909. As the next quotation but one reveals, it is extremely close to Heaton Nicholls's writings in 1929–31 – which is not surprising as Nicholls probably composed the *Report*.

32 Ms. Nic. 2.08.1 KCM 3348, 28 May 1929.

33 Ms. Nic. 2.08.1/Folder 3, Pencil draft, nd/KCM 3323.

34 As note 33. See also Ms. Nic. 2.08.1 KCM 3330d. Carbon fragment, p. 10. A.W.G. Champion was the leader of the ICU in Natal.

35 Ms. Nic. 2.08.1 KCM 3362d. Carbon copy of a letter, nd, no addressee.

36 Heaton Nicholls, *South Africa in My Time*, 43–6, 56–61.

37 Nicholls, 155.

38 CO 179/235/22645, Gov. to Sec. St. 30.5.06. For Dube's earlier career, and the Natal government's attitude towards him see *Reluctant Rebellion*, 72–6; for this period, my 'The Ambiguities of Dependence; John L. Dube of Natal'; in *Journal of South African Studies*, 1, 2 (1975), 162–80. As will be apparent, my current interpretation is, however, rather different.

39 See especially NA 214 723/18/F473, J.H. Nicholson, Mayor of

Durban to PM and MNA, General Botha, 9 August 1918 and enclosures; *Natal Mercury*, 12 August 1918.

40 See Pim Papers, C.A. Wheelwright to Howard Pim, 14 December 1923 (University of Witwatersrand Library).

41 Ms. Nic. 2.08.1 KCM 3350. Document entitled 'The Native Land Settlement' (Copy, with signatures in Dube's hand).

42 *South Africa in My Time*, 290.

43 A. Luthuli, *Let My People Go* (London, 1962), 95–6.

44 Marks, 'The Ambiguities of Dependence', 176–9.

45 'The Destruction of the Zulu Kingdom'.

46 See e.g. evidence C.A. Wheelwright before the 1930–2 *Native Economic Commission*. Wheelwright had just retired as CNC, having served in Natal–Zululand since the 1890s.

47 [See p. 108 – Eds.]

48 See for example the evidence before the 1930–2 *Native Economic Commission* of the Kambule Farmers' Association, 1632.

49 Report of SC 19–'27 (1928) Evid. C.A. Wheelwright, 210; Evidence *Native Economic Commission*, e.g. 1612, 1664ff; See also Champion Papers (University of Cape Town) BC 581/B3.76: A.W.G. Champion to Hertzog, 24 September 1927.

50 *Native Economic Commission*, 1778.

51 Champion Papers: A.B. Ngcobo, Eshowe, to Champion, Durban, 30 August 1927.

52 House of Assembly, Ann. 452–'26 (unpublished paper laid on the table of the House), Memo on Plantation labour in Natal, G.A. Park Ross to C.A. Wheelwright, 15 October 1925.

53 *Analysis of a Social Situation in Modern Zululand* (The Rhodes Livingstone Papers, No. 28, reprinted by Manchester University Press, 1968; first published 1940–2), 50.

54 Ann. 452–'26.

55 P.L. Wickins, 'The Industrial and Commercial Workers Union of Africa', unpubl. PhD (University of Cape Town, 1973), 343–4; C. Kadalie, *My Life and the ICU: The Autobiography of a Black Trade Unionist in South Africa* (edited, with an introduction by S. Trapido, London, 1970), 159.

56 Wickins, 'Industrial and Commercial Workers Union'.

57 10 October 1927. Cited in Wickins, 270.

58 Kadalie, *My Life*, 159; Wickins, 379–82; *Ilanga lase Natal*, 24 June 1927.

59 See E. Roux, *Time Longer than Rope* (Wisconsin, 1964), 248; J. Simons and R. Alexander, *Colour and Class in South Africa* (Harmondsworth, 1969).

60 Godelier, 'The Non-Correspondence between Form and Content in Social Relations', 189, talking of chiefs among the Andean peoples.

61 Gluckman, *Analysis of a Social Situation*, 34.

62 Gluckman, 43–4.

63 Harriette Colenso noted this in a letter to a Mr Pollock, Colenso Correspondence Collection (Natal Archives) 140, Vol. III, 27 August 1908.

64 See *Reluctant Rebellion*, 96–8, which also sets out the royal family view as argued by the Colensos – perhaps too uncritically.

SHULA MARKS

65 *Analysis of a Social Situation*, 44.
66 See p. 97.
67 NA 289 2151/F727 CNC to Dower, 4 May 1916.
68 Pretoria Archives, Department of Justice (henceforth DJ) 221 4/65/15 P. Binns, Chief Magistrate, Durban to J. de V. Roos, Secretary of Justice, 11 February 1915.
69 Pietermaritzburg Archives, SNA 1/9/5, Carbon copy CNC 2261/920, Interview with Manzolwandhle ka Cetshwayo (Dinuzulu's half-brother), 24 June 1920.
70 This should, of course, not be confused with the National Cultural Liberation Movement founded recently by Chief Gatsha Buthelezi also called *Inkatha yakwa Zulu*, or simply *Inkatha*. A connection between the two organizations is, however, alluded to in the Constitution of the new movement which has, at the head of its constitution, 'Founded in 1928 – by: King Solomon ka Dinuzulu'. The decision to use the same name is surely not accidental, and in both cases the deliberate manipulation of tradition is manifest. An *inkata* or *inkatha* is literally 'a grass coil placed on the head for carrying a load'. The *inkatha yezwe*, or 'grass coil of the nation', according to James Stuart's informant, Baleni ka Silwana, in 1914, was an actual ritual object, 15 or 18 inches in diameter which was inherited by Shaka's successors, and kept at the royal headquarters. According to Baleni, 'The *inkata*'s purpose is to *keep our nation standing firm*. The binding round and round symbolizes the binding together of the people so *that they should not be scattered.*' C. de B. Webb and John Wright, *The James Stuart Archive* (Natal, 1976), I, 40–1. The italicized phrases have been translated by the editors from Stuart's original Zulu; the definition of *inkatha* I owe to the editors' footnote 49, p. 51.
71 DJ 3/953/23/1. Report of a meeting of Inkatha, 8 October 1924 by Revd L.E. Oscroft.
72 Ms. Nic. 2.08.1 KCM 3323: Fragment; Draft memorandum, mainly in pencil, nd, Folder 3.
73 *Native Economic Commission*, Evidence, 1473.
74 See DJ 6/953/23/1 Report.
75 As note 74. See also Deputy Commissioner, Natal Police to Deputy Commissioner, CID, Pretoria, 25 November 1924.
76 DJ 6/953/23/1 Report.
77 Ms. Nic. 2.08.1 KCM 3362 d fragment, nd, no addressee, carbon. Also sim. KCM 3362.
78 DJ 6/953/21/1 Report.
79 See note 78.
80 *Native Economic Commission*, evidence 1486.
81 See note 80. See also the evidence of the Kambule Farmers' Association (Vryheid) 1642 and of Mkwintje and Kumalo, themselves 'progressive' farmers and traders, Nongoma, 1807.
82 See e.g. evidence of Mkwintye, Nongoma, *Native Economic Commission*, 1821, who sometimes had forty to sixty 'assistants' working for him on a seasonal basis, and whom he paid one shilling a day.

83 *Ilanga lase Natal*, 12 August 1927.

84 *Reluctant Rebellion*, 326–7 for the very divided response of the *kholwa* to the 'rebellion'. Cf also Welsh, *Roots of Segregation*, 282–4 for the cleavage between the chiefs and the *kholwa*.

85 For the origins and repercussions of the policy of creating mission reserves, see N.A. Etherington, 'The Rise of the Kholwa in South East Africa: African Christian Communities in Natal, Pondoland and Zululand, 1835–80', PhD thesis (Yale University, 1971), published as *Preachers, Peasants and Politics in Southeast Africa* (London, 1978); see also Welsh, 45–50. Welsh emphasizes the cleavage in the nineteenth century, which reinforces one's impression of change in the period under discussion.

86 For Dube, Mini and Martin Luthuli, see *Reluctant Rebellion*; for Molema and Seme, see T. Karis and G. Gerhart, *From Protest to Challenge*, vol. 4, *Profiles of African Politics in South Africa, 1882–1964* (Stanford, CA, 1977).

87 E. Roux, *Time Longer than Rope*, 111.

88 B. Willan, Introduction to a new edition of *Native Life* published in Johannesburg, 1982.

89 Not only was he made an Honorary Vice-President of Congress; at the first meetings of the SANNC called in Zululand and addressed by leaders like Dube and Saul Msane, 'Natives well-known supporters of the Usutu who are not in the habit of attending at the promulgation of Government laws or notices or at the visit of any Ministers or high officials were noticed amongst the assembled', NA 268/3098/12/7639. CNC Zululand to CNC, Natal, 10 December 1912.

90 CNC, Natal (R.H. Addison for a short period) to SNA, Pretoria, 13 November 1913.

91 The phrase occurs in a letter from Charles Mpanza, Secretary of the Zulu Society (ZS Papers) to its President, A.W. Dhlamini, as the conservative answer to the changes resulting from urbanization and proletarianization. See next note.

92 See the Charter of the Zulu Society, issued by the Zulu Society, Natal, 1st edn, 1937; 2nd edn, 1939. The papers of the Zulu Society are in the Natal Archives, Pietermaritzburg.

93 Ms. Nic. 2.08.1 KCM 3305, Carbon, nd. Address to the Rt Hon General Hertzog, PM and SNA. Signed 'By authority of the Nation, Mnyaiza ka Ndabuko and Franz Zulu'. (The bulk of the document is an appeal for the recognition of the paramountcy.)

94 Papers of the Aborigines Protection Society, Rhodes House, Oxford: Mss. Brit. Emp. S 19/D2/3 Written from Ohlange for the opening meeting of the SANNC, 2 February 1912.

95 See evidence, M.L.O. Maling *et al.*, *Native Economic Commission*, 1655.

96 ZS III/1/2 Charles Mpanza to E.H. Braatvedt, Magistrate, Nongoma, 22 August 1938.

97 Ms. Nic. 2.08.1 KCM 3323, Draft, fragment, nd.

5

MARXISM, FEMINISM AND SOUTH AFRICAN STUDIES*

Belinda Bozzoli

Belinda Bozzoli's article represents one of the first attempts to insert a systematic feminist perspective into South African historiography. Based in the sociology department at the University of the Witwatersrand in Johannesburg, she has been a major contributor to the History Workshop movement in South Africa – a group which has greatly extended the scope of popular history, labour history and African history. Her article does not merely argue that historians should write about women, but that patriarchy and gender roles have had a far-reaching impact on the structure of South African society. Patriarchy was not a single power relationship but a 'patchwork quilt' reflecting the diverse societies that made up South Africa. In respect of African societies, pre-colonial controls over women and the division of labour by gender were carried over into the twentieth century. While African men migrated to work they were able to keep African women at home in the countryside. Here they continued to work the fields, thereby underpinning the survival of African rural society. The development of labour migrancy on a large scale, as well as segregation more generally, can therefore be seen as in part the (unintended) result of gender divisions within African society.

* * *

INTRODUCTION

Our understanding of South African society has been radically revised and deepened over the past decade – but the recent radical revision of South African history, sociology and politics has not, by and large, been interwoven with feminist reinterpretations of conventional wisdoms.

118

There has, of course, recently been a growth of interest in the study of women in South Africa. But this field has remained largely segregated, with all its attendant risks of ghettoization. Thus with a few outstanding exceptions, there is a lack of awareness on the part of many radical South African scholars not concerned centrally with issues of gender, of the major issues which feminists have raised about social explanation. And, concomitantly, writers concerned centrally with the analysis of gender have not often extended their findings into wider fields of social analysis.

The resulting loss to both Marxism and feminism may in part be attributed to the absence of a significant South African feminist movement. Just as the 'prior insights' of bourgeois political economy provided Marx with the basis for many of his own discoveries, so the thrusting and revolutionary insights of radical feminists in western Europe and the United States have provoked a spate of original and creative thought. On the basis of their uncompromising insistence on the need to conceptualize gender relations, socialist and Marxist feminists have revised and deepened our understanding of the wider relations between gender, class and capitalism – and have been led to challenge some of Marxism's own unquestioned tenets. Had radical feminists of the stature of Firestone[1] or Millett[2] been confronted with the South African reality, their first aim would have been to establish the 'patriarchal' (to use their term) character of this society. This is not difficult to do. On the cultural level the *Sunday Times*, self-appointed arbiter and defender of male domination against the (usually mythical) attacks on it by lunatic libbers, provides an excellent starting point for the analysis of female oppression of the English-speaking variety; while the proclamations of Afrikaner nationalist spokesmen about *volk, vaderland en vroumens* would surely reveal that Afrikaner patriarchy has a (hitherto unexplored) character of its own. Black culture too provides easy evidence of sexist assumptions and ideologies, as well as of rapes, wife-beatings and desertion. A cultural catalogue of chauvinism would not be hard to compile. The vast cleavages of race and class in this society are paralleled by the equally vast one of sex. The legal system, wages, access to positions of power and authority, are all structural mechanisms whereby a hierarchical, unequal relationship between men and women is perpetuated. Wifehood and motherhood are the supreme female virtues, while cinema advertisements proclaim the necessity for a caricatured machismo on the part of men to complement the sweet-smelling fluffy femininity of the women who wait behind while they finish winning yacht races, rounding up cattle or flying to the moon.

It is the acknowledgement of the existence of a patriarchal system[3] in other societies, or, as Michele Barrett would prefer to call it, 'female oppression', that has been the precondition for the development of Marxist-feminist thought.[4] But having acknowledged its existence, Marxists have considered it their task to go far beyond the descriptive and idealist formulations of the radical feminists. They have questioned the usefulness of the essentially biological rather than social category of 'women' and they have attempted to construct *explanations* for female oppression in materialist and historical terms. They have attempted to discover how female oppression interacts with class exploitation (and in a few cases, with racial oppression).

APPROACHES TO GENDER

This prior demonstration of the existence of female oppression has not been carried out in South African studies – and as a result, no substantial challenges to androcentric tendencies within Marxism have been made. With certain important exceptions, the literature which examines gender relations has instead tended to fall into three categories, none of which, it is suggested, on its own provides adequate theoretical tools to cope with the subtleties which the complex social relations of gender demand.

Many studies, perhaps more in the 'feminist' than the 'Marxist' camp, have adopted what one might call a 'rectificatory' approach. They have undertaken the essential and as yet incomplete task of rectifying the imbalance in history-writing by recovering the hidden history of women and of gender relations. The value of such studies in initiating the discovery of the character of female oppression in South Africa as well as in restoring to women both dignity and pride in their heritage of resistance, is enormous.[5]

However, on their own, such approaches tend not to be based in material factors. It is not clear whether they have fully confronted the question of female oppression as a systematic set of relations nor of its intricate relations with capitalism. Some, for example, assume that the demonstration of the fact of female oppression is on its own a sufficient basis for the explanation of female participation in resistance – failing to acknowledge the subtle variations in ideological and organizational forms of resistance, or to provide a materialist explanation of these ideologies and forms.

Besides those concerned with rectifying past omissions there have been Marxists in South Africa and elsewhere who *have* attempted to provide a material explanation for female oppression. They have tended to place their primary emphasis on the relationship between that oppression, and the capitalist mode of production – they have attempted to show the 'functionality' of female oppression for the capitalist system. This argument, which has taken place over a whole range of issues, carries a certain conviction: female low wages and exclusion from participation in trade unions is a manifestation of capitalist manipulation and division of the working class;[6] the nuclear family, and the isolated unpaid or low-paid labour performed by the woman (wife or domestic servant) within it, serves to lower the cost of reproduction of labour power;[7] the black woman in the reserve economies also functions to lower the cost of reproduction of labour power;[8] women act as a reserve army of labour, to be absorbed and rejected by capitalism in times of economic prosperity and depression respectively,[9] and so on. Female subordination and inferiority do in fact suit the capitalist mode of production in certain crucial ways, and those ways can be demonstrated to great effect.

However, numerous criticisms can be made of this kind of approach and indeed have been made by several analysts although their criticisms have not usually been made in the South African context.[10] The first is that while such analyses explain the points at which female oppression and the capitalist mode of production suit each other, *there are many aspects of female oppression which are not explained by such an emphasis.* The prevalence of rape, for example, or the fact of the exclusion of middle-class white women from positions of power and authority, can be attributed to the machinations of capital only by the most zealous and deterministic of Marxists. This criticism implies the second – which is that such analyses are based upon functionalist assumptions which are unacceptable. The problem of functionalism rests in the fact that descriptions are presented as explanations. Because female oppression performs certain functions for capitalism, this

121

does not mean that it was a pure creation of capitalism. To posit this would be to deny the history of female oppression in other, non-capitalist, societies, and to fail to acknowledge its existence in socialist ones.

The third criticism, originally made by Hartmann,[11] concerns the omission by such explanations of the *sine qua non* of patriarchy – the existence of unequal relations of domination and subordination between *men* and women – not only between *capitalism* and women. The 'functions performed for capitalism' argument deflects concern completely from any consideration of the fact of *male* dominance. The struggle against patriarchy becomes synonymous with the struggle against capitalism.

This collapsing of female oppression into the capitalist mode of production has been the dominant tendency in analyses of women in South Africa today. It is a tendency which has suited the indigenous left, reluctant as it is to consider the implications of its own internal sexism. It appears to be far more comfortable for the left to absorb feminist struggles, or indeed subordinate them, into the general struggle against capitalism, than to begin to consider the vast implications of admitting the relative autonomy of female oppression.

Some have suggested that the culprit in many of these imperfect approaches is Marxism itself. Hartmann, for example, suggests that 'Marxist categories are sex-blind'.[12] Wolpe's approach to the analysis of women in South Africa suffers from precisely these problems. Wolpe's article 'Capitalism and Cheap Labour Power in South Africa'[13] – a structuralist interpretation of the genesis and functions of the 'reserve' economies over the decades since the discovery of gold – has been attractive to many who are interested in analysing the problem of women's oppression. As the demands of the capitalist mode of production for labour increased, he argues, so men were drawn, or forced, off the land, and women were increasingly left behind to maintain the subsistence economies. Men, it is suggested, were drawn into capitalist production, while women performed the function of reproducing, maintaining and sustaining, in times of sickness and old age, the cheap labour force required by the mines. This interpretation has been taken as the theoretical basis for an analysis of the role of black women in South African society.[14] And yet the model itself provides no explanation of the fact that it was *women* who remained behind, and *men* who left. For there is no logic in the fact of proletarianization which determines that men should be first off the land, as historians of nineteenth-century African societies are well aware.[15] In some parts of the world, and indeed in certain pockets of Boer society, young girls have been the first to leave the rural areas; while in others whole families have left from the very beginning. Forces are at work which the blunt concepts of 'reproduction' and 'production' are unable to encapsulate.

It may be suggested that it is the hegemony which structuralism has exerted over South African studies in the past few years, which has made it difficult for feminists to engage with Marxists in any sort of meaningful dialogue. Theories which interpret the family as an 'ideological state apparatus'[16] are unlikely to provide fruitful ground for discourse about the struggles between men and women within it; or the struggles between the family as a social unit, and the wider system in which it is located.

In spite of the existence of some studies which avoid these problems, the system of female oppression in South Africa has not been successfully explained. The purpose of this article is to suggest that an alternative approach to the explanation of gender relations in South Africa can be developed – an approach which draws on a rather different body of literature from that which has prevailed until now.

The approach tentatively put forward here, rather than being based upon the notion of structure, is based upon that of struggle. What is Marxist about this approach is that it retains a materialist, dialectical and historical focus. It posits that social change is based upon the results of contradictory and opposing forces, rooted in material reality, confronting one another, coming to a temporary resolution, and yet further contradictory and opposing forces emerging from that resolution. What is feminist about it is that it posits that the relevant conflicts and contradictory forces for our purposes are located in the 'domestic sphere', and that in certain crucial cases they involve conflicts between certain men and women.

To return to Wolpe, for example, it is clear that his approach does not allow us to ask questions about the sexual division of labour in the 'pre-capitalist modes of production' with which he is concerned, or indeed about other class- and age-based differences either. Like Meillassoux, the writer whose influence upon him is most clearly discernible, Wolpe fails 'to understand or confront the feminist problematic, that is, the fact and implications of women's subordination to men, and of women's struggle against that subordination'.[17] The fact of the subordination of women is taken for granted not only in Wolpe's much criticized work, but in many other examinations of the character of pre-capitalist societies.[18] And yet some understanding of the nature of this subordination is surely important, not only in itself, not only for the sake of making sense of how these social systems operated,[19] but also to clarify our understanding of the path taken by the subordination of those systems to capital, and the disgorging of a labour force, initially male, from them. This is not to suggest that the patriarchal character of pre-capitalist society is the only factor which should be considered in explaining the kinds of migrant labour which it engendered. Beinart and Delius,[20] for example, have shown that age hierarchies and property relationships played an important, indeed central, role in the creation within Pedi and Mpondo society of a young male migrant labour population. However, it may be suggested that a consideration of the possibly more fundamental (and therefore perhaps more invisible) relationships of male domination, of what Wright has called 'Men's control of women's labour',[21] would allow us to ask questions which have not systematically been asked before. Thus, for example, in those societies in which control over cattle in the form of bridewealth constituted a pivotal feature and which facilitated control over women, the entire system must surely be predicated upon the fact that these women were 'able' to be controlled, exchanged and brought into the lineage from the outside. As Jeff Guy has suggested[22] it is the examination of this analytically *prior* process of subordination that must surely underpin an analysis of chiefly power and state formation in Nguni systems.[23]

One of the distinguishing characteristics of the penetration of settler capitalism into South Africa was the difficulty it encountered in destroying (by extermination, for example, as in the case of Australasia, or by full proletarianization, as in western Europe) pre-capitalist societies. In an influential recent article Brenner has argued that the failure of capitalism to destroy noncapitalism should not be attributed, as it had been by 'underdevelopment' theorists, to the particular needs and whims of capital in the Third World, but to the strength of those social and economic systems and the *incapacity* of capitalism to destroy them.[24] The resilience of particular systems and indeed the struggles of the people within them to retain them, are accorded a central place in Brenner's analysis. Where does the power of the pre-capitalist society and economy rest? Surely in its internal relationships, its capacities to resist proletarianization, to retain access to the land and to continue to produce and reproduce, as well as to retain some sort of cultural and social independence.

Thus the reorganization of the male–female division of labour in African societies in South Africa, and in particular the capacities of these societies to sustain themselves for a certain period of time through the use of women's labour, is an issue of central importance. It is not automatic and unproblematic that

> the extended family in the reserves is able to, and does, fulfil 'social security' functions necessary for the reproduction of the migrant work force. By caring for the very young, and very old, the sick, the migrant labourer in periods of 'rest', by educating the young, etc., the reserve families relieve the capitalist sector and its state from the need to expend resources on these necessary functions.[25]

On the contrary, two points can be made about this assumption. The first is that this neat switch, the sudden imposition upon *women*, not 'the family', of full responsibility for the maintenance of a social system under increasing and devastating attack, must surely have involved some conflict, some vast social, moral and ideological reorganization. And the second is that the capacity of the pre-capitalist system to impose these tasks *upon its women*, was quite possibly one of its most potent weapons against the onslaught of capitalism. The question of why women remained on the land and why men migrated, the issue of how and why women were able, for a limited period it is true, to take on the tasks of the absent men, and to sustain the cultural autonomy of rural systems too, these issues are central to the explanation of the fact that South Africa's labour force remained partially proletarianized for so long.

Following Brenner, but injecting his approach with a feminist concern, two forms of struggle need to be identified. The first is struggle *within* the domestic system; the second is struggle *between* the domestic sphere and the capitalist one. Both manifestations of what I have called 'domestic struggle' are important not only in the empirical sense – in that they are important spheres of social interaction whose existence is all too often obscured. This 'rectificatory' aspect of 'domestic struggle' is only the first step to understanding its significance. For the outcome of these 'domestic struggles' may in fact condition and shape the *very form taken by capitalism in that society*. It is not only that 'domestic struggles' are the key to unravelling the evolving subordination of women. It is also that they provide a crucial dimension to our understanding of a whole variety of other factors, ranging from the composition of the labour force, to the form of the state. Male domination and female subordination may be the prevalent form taken by the households emerging from these struggles – but they are not necessarily the outcome of such struggles, even under capitalism, assumed by many to have a necessarily patriarchal character. A further implication of such an approach is that the reification of patriarchy as a single system leaves us with a blunt, static and barely illuminating analytical tool, one which tends to be both ahistorical and idealist. However, if it is true that the outcome of a particular domestic struggle may lead to the establishment of a particular type of female subordination, how are we to characterize that type without the use of this term? For this reason, the term is retained for this article, with one important proviso – that its use be linked to particular historical eras, particular class systems or particular societies.[26] Thus it would seem to be heuristically useful to retain a notion of what one might call 'tribal' or 'chiefly' patriarchy – a term which refers to the particular form taken by the subordination of women within many pre-industrial African societies. If a comparative and historical concept of patriarchy is retained, then it may become a useful device with which to explore further the basis for the emergence of the complex modern patriarchies under capitalism today.

THE 'PATCHWORK QUILT' OF PATRIARCHIES

In order to illustrate how the concepts of 'domestic struggle' and 'types of patriarchy' may be made to work for us, they need to be mobilized in the context of a historical case study. On the basis of the growing secondary literature an attempt will be made here to periodize the development of domestic struggle and patriarchal relations in South Africa; as well as to reveal the ways in which their development is intricately linked with wider social processes at work – such as the penetration of merchant capital, the process of proletarianization, the rise to a position of domination by mining capital, and the overall process of class struggle.

Nineteenth-century South Africa contained not one patriarchy but many, each connected with a particular society. The ultimate origins of these patriarchal forms are largely unknown. However, what is known is that there were important changes inflicted upon patriarchal systems by the penetration of merchant capital and colonial conquest up to and during the nineteenth century. These changes may well have been to the detriment of women. We know that in general merchant capital acts as a force which modifies but does not revolutionize, pre-capitalist forms. In some cases it has been shown to strengthen the power of men over women.[27] If men possess greater physical mobility (by virtue of not being tied to the domestic domain) they are better able to respond to the demands of trade. Mercantile penetration may involve the appropriation by men of craft and other productive activities previously associated with women; or indeed the effects of commodity exchange may be to eliminate crafts altogether. Colonial and missionary activity may, in unintended ways, exacerbate the conditions of female life by drawing off young girls to attend school, thus reducing the amount of help the mother has in the home. These various effects may introduce substantial modifications in male–female relations. And yet merchant capital on its own does not destroy or create uniformity among the systems which it encounters. It results in a 'patchwork quilt' – a system in which forms of patriarchy are sustained, modified and even entrenched in a variety of ways depending on the internal character of the system in the first instance.

Marks and Unterhalter want to emphasize that women were subordinate in a whole variety of ways, in all Bantu-speaking societies. In spite of differences between matrilineal and patrilineal systems, and between systems with and without a central state, they argue that 'in virtually all of these societies women were subject to the tight control of chiefs, headmen and the heads of families'.[28] Their analysis seems to reinforce the need for a term like 'patriarchy'; in its 'chiefly' variant it was indeed rule of fathers over·both sons and daughters. Within this general rubric variations did exist. Since cultivation was the responsibility of the woman of the household; and since a range of prohibitions

127

prevented women owning or being associated in any way with cattle, women were excluded from the primary source of wealth far more effectively in societies which were mainly based on cattle-keeping. Thus John Wright suggests that this prohibition in Zulu society was central to the subordination of women; added to it, he suggests, were ideological controls 'operating largely through the kinship systems, which served to socialize females into accepting a position of inferiority', and material controls, 'as exercised by married men over their wives' and daughters' access to the main means of producing the necessities of life, and to the products of their own labour'.[29]

It would be fruitful to extend analyses such as Wright's into the areas suggested by the notions of internal and external domestic struggle, asking to what extent the encroachments of merchant capital allowed particular occupants of the internal gender hierarchy he has identified to advance their interests. We know that some women seized the opportunity to leave the rural areas when towns began to grow, or that some chiefs used the spread of trade to consolidate their position. But we lack a clear understanding of how each segment of the 'patchwork quilt' responded to the uneven encroachments of merchant capital and thus of how pre-capitalist gender relations were reshaped before the advent of full-blooded migrancy.

What we do know is that by the early twentieth century anthropologists documenting the sexual division of labour in most rural African societies found a markedly distorted pattern. While 'domestic struggles' in earlier times may have been affected, or even shaped by merchant capital, in the era of full-blooded migration, after decades of encroachments by colonial rule on traditionally 'male' spheres of labour (hunting, trading, administration, cattle-herding, fighting), the vast bulk of rural labour had come to be performed by women. Monica Hunter wryly describes the working day of two Mpondo men and two women in the 1930s:

August 16th
Maime: Went hunting badger. Returned with one the size of a mealie cob.
Maime's wife: She still had water left over from the night before, so did not go to the river, but got up and stamped mealies, and put them on to cook. She went to gather fire-

wood and 'imifino'[a] in the fields 2–3 miles distant. She
returned at midday and ate some stamped mealies, her first
food that day. She put the 'imifino' on to cook, ground
mealies to put into the 'imifino'. The 'imifino' eaten by the
women in the evening. She boiled maize and made a milk
dish for the men. At sunset she will go to fetch water.
Cemfu: Went to a beer drink across the 'umTakatyi' (2–3
miles away).
Cemfu's wife: Got up and went to the river to fetch water.
Warmed water and washed her baby of 4 months. Ground
mealies and cooked porridge for breakfast for the men.
Went to fetch firewood and 'imifino' with Maime's wife.
Left her baby with the twins, of 10 years. Returned, helped
Maime's wife to prepare 'imifino'. Remade the surface of
her floor. Sunset, went to fetch water. Then sat and suckled
her baby. Washed baby again in warm water.
N.B. She only fetched water twice on this day but sometimes she goes 4 or 5 times. The 'umzi'[b] is on the road and
travellers call for drinks.[30]

The division of labour was, it is true, not only unequal between
men and women of the same age, but also across age and gender
– for example, grandmothers of a particular 'umzi' did not
labour; while children's labour was clearly divided along sex
lines, with young girls, it seems, being groomed for the heaviest
work of all – that undertaken by young wives and mothers (like
the two cited above) – while young boys herded cattle. But
husbands in the prime of life did not, it seems from Hunter's
detailed account of the division of labour, contribute a significant
amount of labour to this particular economy at this time; while
wives and mothers in the prime of their lives bore the brunt
of agriculture, childcare, cooking, cleaning, housebuilding and
maintenance and a range of other tasks.

Studies such as this one seek to suggest that some change in
the division of labour has taken place in these economies since
the advent of migrant labour, implying that at some earlier stage
the male contribution was more substantial. The assumption is
that migrant labour has brought this change about. But this
assumption needs far more complex and careful elaboration. It
was not simply the men's *absence* that placed the burden of
domestic and agricultural labour on the women; nor is it just

that male tasks had been undermined by the destruction of the African states; it was *also* that these societies possessed a capacity to subordinate women's labour. Indeed, one might even suggest that the giving up of migrant men by these societies partly rested upon their capacity to subordinate women's labour; and that it is in this capacity that the resilience of these systems to 'full proletarianization' may have rested.

The 'struggle' within the domestic economy over the subordination of women's labour cannot be reduced to a struggle between 'men' and 'women', it is true. Perhaps it is more accurately described as a struggle between patriarchal chiefs and women. Evidence of this is adduced by Yawitch, who points to Plaatje's description of the 'drastic measures adopted by chiefs and tribesmen to stop their women from migrating'. Women were prevented from buying bus or train tickets or travelling alone.[31] Beinart, too, has evidence that this type of control took place – strongly supporting the suggestion that some will act as the defenders of the domestic domain and that internal struggles will shape their capacity to do so.[32] 'Chiefly' or 'tribal' patriarchy seems to have been an important foundation for the capacity of precapitalist African societies to survive for as long as they did, while disgorging a permanent, primarily (though not entirely) male migrant labour force.

Important as the contrasts might be between various African systems, a more vivid contrast seems to lie in the distinction between African and non-African societies in the nineteenth century. Boer society seems to have exhibited a different form of patriarchy from that displayed by African distributive lineage or tributary systems. Here the domestic economy seems to have centred on the *pater familias* with his wife and children existing in dependent and subordinate relationships to him, rather than on a wider kinship system with the chief as the controlling male. The patriarchy of Boer society seems to have been semi-feudal in character rather than tribal, with landownership being located in the patriarch, and social reproduction having its focus on the family nucleus and its immediate appendages.[33] While kinship and 'purity' ideologies were used in the African systems to provide an ideological system of control of women, in Afrikaner society Christianity provided the legitimation for their subordination.[34]

It does not seem as if Boer women occupied the central role in agricultural production held by black women. Instead, their labour was (and again the feudal–peasant analogy seems useful) largely located around the household itself.[35] The Carnegie Commission report suggested that in the rural areas the mothers of Boer families on isolated farms (where little community help was available) had to prepare almost all foods from raw materials; to make bread, butter, dripping, soap and candles; slaughter sheep, milk cows or goats and carry water. In addition they undertook the task of helping on the farm at lambing or kidding time; or in some areas taking on total responsibility for goats. The report outlines in a poignant fashion the stories of isolated farm women giving birth to their children in lonely squalor (although the use of midwives appears to have been common); and rearing and educating them themselves. Mention is made at various parts in the report of the fact that daughters helped mothers with domestic labour, although the drawing off of girls into schools may well have deprived the mother of their labour.

The specific position of a woman in Boer society – perhaps one could think of her as being socially more powerful (within patriarchy) than her black counterpart – was an important factor in rendering the Boer systems more brittle than African ones in the face of economic hardship and the development of the cash economy. Instead of undermining *male* labour the spread of commodity exchange relieved the Boer *woman* of certain of her tasks. The report suggests that:

> in homes forming part of any real community . . . the supplies brought by the father are already prepared for use. The animal has already been slaughtered, and the meat is delivered ready to be cooked. The meal is bought ready ground or the bread ready baked; and many other foodstuffs are bought ready for consumption; there is an extensive choice of ready-made clothing or material for clothing.[36]

School and church took on educational functions, while health services became available to mothers giving birth and rearing children.

While the spreading of cash relationships undoubtedly played a similar part in African societies, what relief this may have afforded the black woman was offset by the greater agricultural burden being placed on her at the same time. In the case of the Boer woman, however, the lightening of the domestic load was accompanied by a different form of pressure – that of class formation.

While African societies were of course stratified and inegalitarian, the kind of class formation which Boer society underwent in the late nineteenth century was clearly distinguishable from stratification in the African systems. With property relations, inheritance patterns and cultural norms focusing on the individual family, and in the absence of redistributive mechanisms to inhibit accumulation by some families and not by others, the agricultural crisis of the late nineteenth century and into the twentieth century gave rise to differentiation within the Boer population between well-to-do families and their poorer tenants.[37] Furthermore, the system of primogeniture exacerbated (although did not, as the Carnegie Commission suggests, cause) the process of rural impoverishment of many Boer families, an interesting reflection of the importance of internal domestic relations in shaping responses to capitalism. Once this impoverishment had reached its limits, proletarianization of lower-class Boers began to take place.

The interesting thing about this proletarianization is that it provides both a vindication of our suggestion above that proletarianization is not a uniform process; and a confirmation of the assertion that the 'domestic struggles' within a society are crucial determinants of the pattern taken by its response to economic hardship. (They are, of course, not the only determinants.) For Boers, unlike blacks, did not leave the rural areas through the development of male migrant labour; instead whole families entered the towns from an early date; while in some cases, young Afrikaner women, the daughters of impoverished families on the land, were the first to enter the towns, and indeed in many cases sent back remittances to their families.[38] The Carnegie Commission attributes this early migration by women to the fact that the domestic economy was not making full use of their labour: 'In the country even the daughters of more comfortably situated farmers find little scope for profitable occupation, but in the poor households they can contribute practically nothing towards their own support and that of the family.'[39]

Boer society *lacked* the capacity to subordinate the labour of its women – perhaps a reflection of greater female strength. Thus, they conclude, 'the rural exodus . . . is stronger among women than among men'. By the time of the 1926 Census, there were 58,153 male and 64,057 female 'persons of Dutch South African parentage' in the ten biggest urban centres.[40] This immediate and 'complete' proletarianization was of crucial importance in underpinning the development of urban class consciousness among Afrikaners.

These two examples, of black and Boer domestic relationships and their importance for understanding the origins of the twentieth-century proletariat, could easily be supplemented by a whole range of others. For example, the 'peasantization' thesis put forward by Bundy[41] could and should be recast in the light of questions about the 'domestic struggles' which took place in those societies which became peasantized. Peasantization usually involves the mobilization of family labour in cash crop production; but this process of mobilization of labour should not be taken for granted, as it is by Bundy. The capacity of the (male) head of the peasant family to control and direct the labour of the family towards the end of peasant production is an important consequence, one must assume, of the patriarchal character of African societies; while the destruction of that peasantry through legal redefinitions of land tenure relationships, seems to have involved an attack by the state on the form of these patriarchal relationships, and their substitution by a new form.

A further example may be drawn from black–white relationships on Boer farms. An interesting hint of the significance of male–female relationships in this regard appears in the Carnegie report:

> Farmers give preference to native labour (over bywoners)[c] and advance various reasons for so doing. Many have repeatedly found the poor white disappointing as farm labourer. Besides, the farmer can often avail himself of the services of the native's wife and children to a far larger extent than in the case of a European labourer, whose wife has her own household duties and whose children have to attend school.[42]

While the Carnegie Commission has taken this to mean that the black wife does *not* have her own duties to attend to, we may interpret it as suggesting that the economic and social weakness of the black woman is an important factor in shaping the emerging class relationships on white farms, which needs further exploration.

A final example may be drawn from the sharecropping economy which emerged in turn-of-the-century Transvaal. Again, the contrast between African and Boer patriarchy becomes of central importance to explaining why it was that African household-heads could enter into sharecropping relations, while 'poor white' families could not, being unable to command family labour to the same extent.[43]

To conclude this section, then, we are left with a picture of a variety of systems of female subordination, each in the process of penetration and transformation by economic forces. The emerging irony of the position of women in the 'patchwork quilt of patriarchies' is that in certain crucial cases their weaknesses are turned into strengths and their strengths to weaknesses. Thus a weak and subordinated female population in black societies, upon whom much of the burden of agricultural and domestic labour rests, is ironically protected from proletarianization for longer; while the relatively stronger Boer women, whose position within the household is alleviated by the spread of the cash economy, are torn from the land much more rapidly, and forced to enter the industrial proletariat from the earliest times. In the long run, as we shall see, however, the tables are turned once more.

PATRIARCHY AND MODERN CAPITALISM

These historical foundations for the development of modern patriarchal South Africa are of central analytical importance to the theory being presented here. With the penetration into South Africa of mining capital, the 'patchwork quilt' of societies becomes subordinated to the hegemony of a more powerful and revolutionary form of capital than ever before. While the form taken by the modern South African state may be fragmented on the surface, *one* integrated system of domination and subordination was forged out of the mining revolution.

The forging of modern patriarchy thus must be interpreted as the result of the interplay between the process of state formation on the one hand, and the 'historical givens' of the pre-existing societies in the region on the other. This lends tremendous complexity to the analysis. Tentatively, I wish to suggest that the notion of many patriarchies needs to be retained, with qualifications, for the modern era. While 'patriarchy', like 'racism', has a broad social and ideological manifestation, it would be reductionist and oversimplified to accept this normative side of the phenomenon. For the real workings of patriarchy *on the ground* involve a complex interplay between the 'many patriarchies' of the mercantile era, and the bludgeoning tendencies of modern capitalism. And since it is on the ground that the system is created and reproduced, this is the important arena for analysis.

In this section of the article an attempt will be made to sketch out some of the ways in which the notion of domestic struggle may help us refine our analysis of the emergence of modern capitalism. I have already made such a suggestion in one respect – by showing how the outcome of domestic struggles in African societies may have been one key to unravelling the origins of segregationism. Here, this interpretation is extended by a consideration of the ways in which territorial segregation becomes entrenched, and by asking what the connections are between territorial segregationism and division of the working class into 'black' and 'white' strata.

A key analysis of the origins of the divided working class – that of Davies[44] – argues in a somewhat functionalist manner (and with explicit acknowledgement to Wolpe's own analysis) that at a certain crucial stage, mine-owners rejected whites as unskilled labourers because of their higher necessary means of subsistence. Whites, he argues, were fully proletarianized and blacks were not. Whites, therefore, 'had to be' paid higher wages than blacks. This decision, he suggests, was the foundation for the formation and perpetuation of a structurally divided working class, one of the basic ingredients of the new racist state.

This kind of analysis is deceptive in its simplicity. It avoids consideration of a whole universe of struggle.[45] In the first place it avoids any contemplation of the problems involved in the concept of 'full' proletarianization. For this is indeed something to which gender is central. It is a notion based on the 'black' model of proletarianization: in which males leave the land first, and are thus 'partially' proletarianized; their families may later follow them, in which case they become 'fully' proletarianized. Even for blacks this model leaves room for some considerable doubts. One cannot assume that the later women who leave the land 'belong' to the men who left earlier. But if it is questionable in the case of blacks, it is much more so in the case of whites. For if young daughters leave the land, are they a 'partial' or 'full' proletariat? What if they marry in the towns? Does their class position suddenly change? I am not suggesting that people do not move from being 'partially' to being 'fully' proletarianized. It is rather that the processes involved in such a move are complex, and involve matters such as culture, ideology and family structure; and that of course the assumption that males are always first off the land and always heads of households, is a grossly incorrect one.

The other assumption underlying the Davies model concerns the notion of 'necessary means of subsistence'. His argument is based upon the notion that the 'necessary means of subsistence' of any particular working class is worked out by capitalists, rationally; and that due consideration is given to the needs of workers' families. Furthermore it seems to assume that workers are males whose wives do not earn a wage. Such conceptions remove all notions of struggle from the issue of wages. For what is meant by the 'worker's family'? How many kin does the capitalist take into account in assessing the 'ideal wage' for a particular stratum of the working class? If the worker is single, does he earn less? If he has eight children, does he earn more than if he has two? Powerful and far-seeing as the capitalist class was in South Africa at the turn of the century, Davies and Wolpe seem to attribute to it an omniscience which it did not possess.

This is not to deny that there is a real issue at stake here – which is that different strata of the working class are able to command different wage levels, *on a consistent basis*. This consistency appears to *override* the very factors which Davies cites as its causes. Thus black mineworkers earn less than white *even if* the families of the black men are destitute and living in the towns (as some of them already were in the 1890s); and *even if* the whites concerned are single young men who are also migrants (as in the case of Cornishmen in the 1890s and 1900s). The dubious and unspecified concept of 'full proletarianization' cannot explain consistently different wages on its own, although it may be an important factor.

Stratification in the working class, which Davies quite correctly seeks to explain because of its centrality to the process of state-formation, was not the automatic consequence of differential forms of proletarianization, but was decided in the process of struggle between capitalists and workers. This struggle, I suggest, may be conceptualized as consisting of the programmatic and ideological visions of the dominant class, on the one hand,

and the restraining and shaping capacities of those classes and systems which they seek to dominate, on the other. These 'restraining and shaping capacities' are not quite the same thing as overt resistance on the part of the subordinate. Rather they are themselves the result of internal struggles and the structure of the systems in which the subordinated are enmeshed.

While we know that the mining industry required large numbers of workers at the cheapest possible rates, and that this requirement shaped many of the emerging state structures of the time, what has not been examined in any analytical manner has been the fact that this labour force was a male one. Just as it has too readily been assumed to have been 'natural' and 'automatic' that the first blacks to have left the land would have been men, so it has been assumed 'natural' that the labourers used by the mines should be men. And yet there is nothing 'automatic' about this at all.[46] Certainly the arduousness and unpleasantness of mine labour cannot be cited as the inhibiting factor. Capitalists and mine-owners in other parts of the world have not hesitated to use female and even child labour in the most arduous of jobs, while South African farmers have felt free to use female labourers in heavy farm work. We already know that women in African pre-industrial societies undertook some of the heaviest jobs. There is thus clearly something to be explained here.

The first area of explanation may be sought in the mine-owners' own social vision. Many mine-owners and state officials assumed, it would seem, that male proletarianization was the 'natural' form of proletarianization. Polygamy, they believed, was nothing less than the enslavement of African women by their men; its destruction

> would leave his social fabric a wreck. It would, in the first place, raise the status of women, and would also deprive the man of the cheap labour which now maintains him in idleness . . . but its chief result would be to force the native man to work, and thus habituate him to labour.[47]

Influential mine-managers like Hennen Jennings (whose American background may have influenced his notions of the ideal labour force) assumed, as a matter of course, that male labour was naturally best suited to mining: 'the men of the strongest physique could go to the mines, but the younger and older men and some of the women could work on the farms',[48] he proposed in one of his statements on the ideal future of mining.

Besides the mine-owners themselves, the imperialists under whose aegis the new South African state was forged had themselves been drawn from a Britain in which the state's interest in 'motherhood' and childrearing had become considerable. Imperial ideology was male-centred. In Davin's words: the vocabulary of the time reflected 'the anxiety to build a race of strong *men*, to promote *virility* and so on'.[49] The separation between males (production/war) and females (reproduction/family) was thus part of the social consciousness of the dominant classes, a factor which should not be underestimated in assessing the nature of their visions for the future South Africa. However, this gender-specific vision could only be realized in the case of blacks – whose proletarianization process was *in any case* taking a markedly gender-differentiated pattern. Furthermore it was the weight of the African domestic domain that helped determine that the particular *form* taken by gender division should be that of territorial separation and migrant labour.

In the case of white workers, a similarly complex struggle took place between rulers and the dominated, leading to a somewhat different outcome. Two issues were at stake here: the presence in the towns of wives and children; and the use by the white family of domestic servants. Both of these struggles could be categorized as 'domestic' in the sense in which the term is defined here; and both concern, among other groups, women. In the case of 'wives and children', their presence in the mining areas was partly the result of explicit manipulation by capitalists. As Percy Fitzpatrick said of Rand Mines: 'We recognize that until men can settle in their homes with their families under reasonable conditions as to comfort and cost, a stable and contented mining population is not to be expected.'[50]

Housing policy was self-consciously used by mine-owners to ensure a stable white working class, to reduce its militancy and to ensure its reproduction. And yet this interpretation still begs the prior question – why was the presence of wives and children seen as beneficial to capital in the case of whites, but detrimental to it in the case of blacks? Seeing *all* strategies, even dramatically opposed ones, as serving capitalist interests smacks of functionalism once again. Surely it must be the case that the presence of 'wives and children' was an unavoidable given of the conditions under which a white male working class could be obtained and kept? In the case of English immigrant workers, this may have been a consequence of their own struggles to retain their domestic ties and dictate their own family lives; in the case of the Afrikaner workers we have already examined, it may rather have been a consequence of the inexorable proletarianization of women. The creation of particular family forms was thus the outcome of class and domestic struggles, rather than of simple capitalist manipulation.

The matter of domestic service in white households was also one which can better be understood as the outcome of a complex series of domestic struggles, rather than as an institution designed to serve the interests of capital in an uncomplicated fashion. From the earliest times, many white families were able to build into the cost of their reproduction ('necessary means of subsistence') the price of domestic labour. Many white workers (though by no means all) and particularly white women, were thus able to exact a price from capital in return for their 'stability' and acquiescence – the price of a relatively high standard of living. A middle-class lifestyle was defined as being both attainable and necessary for some sections of the white working class. This was not only a moral victory for parts of the white working-class family 'against' capital, but a victory for the white woman within that family. Through the employment of domestic labour she was able to defend herself against the isolating and un-rewarded labour which her kin would otherwise expect her to perform; and against the double shift. Her victory was at the expense of the subordination and oppression within the white family of the black male domestic worker;[51] and, in later years, of the black female.[52]

How 'functional' the institution of domestic service has been for capitalism is thus debatable. In the early years of mine labour shortage, for example, domestic service drew vital male workers away from the mining industry; throughout this century, white working-class wages have had to include the price, however pitifully low, of one or more servants; some of these servants moreover, perform tasks such as gardening, waiting at table and so on, hardly essential items to the reproduction of the labour force. These 'dysfunctions' are just as important to recognize as are the functions of domestic labour – for in time, it did come to absorb the otherwise unemployable, and thereby act as a

139

mechanism of social control.[53] But its existence must surely also be seen as a victory for the white woman against capitalism's tendency to privatize and trivialize domestic work; and its capacity to burden her with the 'double shift' where necessary.

The gentility of middle-class white home life has an almost pre-capitalist character, akin to the plantation life of white American slave-owners. This pre-capitalist ethos is no accident. For although the domestic sphere is nuclear and apparently a modern capitalist institution as far as formal, kin relationships are concerned (although even here, extended family networks seem to operate more effectively in white society than in, say, the North American equivalent), it is in fact a subsystem within the wider economy with a clearly pre-capitalist character. The domestic labourer has a semi-feudal relationship with her employer, where she is paid partly in kind, and is tied to the employer by a series of obligations, by economic need, and sometimes by law.[54]

To conclude, then, what has been suggested is that struggles both within the domestic sphere, and between that sphere and outside forces, are of some analytical importance in our understanding of modern class and patriarchal relationships. It has been useful to see the white household as a refuge, an arena of defence against capitalism, as much as an institution which serves it; and to see the relative strengths and weaknesses of particular household types, as well as the various strengths of the protagonists in particular household struggles, as having an important influence on the emergence of a privileged white working class, as well as on the places and experiences of men and women respectively.

EDITORS' NOTES

a 'Imifino': a general term for a number of species of wild plants collected and eaten as green vegetables by Xhosa-speaking peoples of the east coast.

b 'Umzi': a Xhosa term for the homestead inhabited by one extended family. Physically, this consisted of a number of huts, traditionally set in a semi-circle around the cattle byre.

c 'Bywoner': the Dutch/Afrikaans term used to describe a white tenant on white-owned farms. As non-propertied rural whites, they were economically vulnerable and the term is often associated with 'poor whites'.

NOTES

* I would like to thank William Beinart, Jacklyn Cock, Peter Delius, Shula Marks, Julie Wells, Marcia Wright and the 'Women in South African History' group for their helpful comments on earlier drafts of this article – but to absolve them from responsibility for the errors and oversimplifications which undoubtedly remain in the present version.

1 Shulamith Firestone, *The Dialectic of Sex* (London, 1971).

2 See Kate Millett, *Sexual Politics* (London, 1969).

3 'Patriarchy' is a controversial term, retained in this discussion only with certain provisos discussed below. For discussions concerning the use of the term see Shelia Rowbotham, 'The Trouble with Patriarchy', and S. Alexander and B. Taylor, 'In Defence of "Patriarchy"', both in R. Samuel (ed.), *Peoples History and Socialist Theory* (London, 1981). See also the discussions by Michele Barrett, *Woman's Oppression Today* (London, 1980), ch. 8; and Gayle Rubin, 'The Traffic in Women' in A.M. Jaggar and P.R. Struhl (eds), *Feminist Frameworks* (New York, 1978).

4 Barrett, *Woman's Oppression*.

5 Women's organized resistance in South African history has been discussed in several recent papers. See C. Kros, 'Urban African Women's Organisations and Protest on the Rand from the Years 1939–1956', BA Honours dissertation (University of the Witwatersrand, 1978); J. Yawitch, 'Natal 1959: The Women's Protests', paper presented to the Conference on the History of Opposition in Southern Africa, 1978; C. Walker, 'The Federation of South African Women', paper presented to the Conference on the History of Opposition in Southern Africa, 1978; B. Kaim, 'The New Surgery: The Illicit Liquor Problem on the Rand, 1920–1945', Sociology III Project, University of the Witwatersrand, 1978; I. Obery, 'Makabongwe Amakosikazi! The FSAW and Mass Struggle in the 50's', *Africa Perspective*, 15 (Autumn, 1980), 36–41; J. Wells, 'Women's Resistance to Passes in Bloemfontein during the Inter-War Period', *Africa Perspective*, 15 (Autumn, 1980), 16–35; J. Yawitch, unpublished essay on the Bafurutse Revolt against passes; J. Wells, 'The Day the Town Stood Still: Women in Resistance in Potchefstroom, 1912–1930', in B. Bozzoli (ed.), *Town and Countryside in the Transvaal* (Johannesburg, 1983); R. de Villiers, 'The Resistance to the Extension of Passes to African Women, 1954–60', unpublished paper; Cherryl Walker, 'Women in Twentieth Century South African Politics: The Federation of South African Women, its Roots, Growth and Decline', MA thesis (University of Cape Town, 1978); and T. Lodge, 'Women's Protest Movements in the 1950s', unpublished ms.

6 C. Stone, 'Industrialisation and Female Labour Force Participation'; and J. Westmore and P. Townsend, 'The African Women Workers in the Textile Industry in Durban', *South African Labour Bulletin*, 2, 4, 1976.

7 See L. Callinicos, 'Domesticating Workers', *South African Labour Bulletin*, 2, 4, 1976, 60–8.

8 J. Yawitch, 'Black Women in South Africa: Capitalism, Employment and Reproduction', BA Honours dissertation (University of the Witwatersrand, 1978); reprinted by *Africa Perspective*, 1980.

9 C. Stone, 'Female Labour Force Participation'.

10 Maxine Molyneux, 'Beyond the Domestic Labour Debate', *New Left Review*, 116 (1979), 3–27; H. Hartmann, 'The Unhappy Marriage of Marxism and Feminism: Towards a More Progressive Union', *Capital and Class*, no. 8 (1979), 1–33; and M. Barrett, *Woman's Oppression*.

11 Hartmann, 'Unhappy Marriage'.

12 Hartmann, 'Unhappy Marriage'.

13 H. Wolpe, 'Capitalism and Cheap Labour Power in South Africa: From Segregation to Apartheid', *Economy and Society*, 1, 4 (1972), 425–56 [this volume, Chapter 3 – Eds].

14 Yawitch, 'Black Women in South Africa'.

15 J. Kimble, 'Concepts in Transition: Labour Migration in Southern Africa c. 1890–1910, with Reference to Basutoland', paper presented to the Seminar on Peasants, Institute of Commonwealth Studies, University of London (1980); and W. Beinart and P. Delius, 'The Family and Early Migrancy in Southern Africa', paper presented to the African History Seminar, School of Oriental and African Studies (1980).

16 L. Althusser, 'Ideology and Ideological State Apparatuses', in *Lenin and Philosophy* (New York, 1971).

17 Maureen Mackintosh, 'Reproduction and Patriarchy: A Critique of Claude Meillassoux, "Femmes, Greniers et Capitaux"', *Capital and Class*, 2 (1977), 119. For further criticisms of the French structuralists see M. Molyneux, 'Androcentrism in Marxist Anthropology', *Critique of Anthropology*, 9 and 10 (1977).

18 See, for example, the collection edited by S. Marks and A. Atmore, *Economy and Society in Pre-Industrial South Africa* (London, 1980).

19 A task which John Wright has set himself in his article 'Men's Control of Women's Labour in the Zulu Kingdom', unpublished seminar paper, Natal University Working Group on Women (1980).

20 W. Beinart and P. Delius, 'The Family'.

21 Wright, 'Women's Labour'.

22 Jeff Guy, 'The Destruction and Reconstruction of Zulu Society', paper presented to the South African History Conference, East Anglia (1980), published in S. Marks and R. Rathbone (eds), *Industrialization and Social Change in South Africa* (London, 1982).

23 As Rubin says, 'We [should] look for the ultimate locus of women's oppression within the traffic in women, rather than within the traffic in merchandise. . . . Women are given in marriage, taken in battle, exchanged for favours, sent as tribute, traded and bought and sold'. The exchange of women, she suggests, 'is a profound perception of a system in which women do not have full rights to themselves'. 'The Traffic', 160–1.

24 R. Brenner, 'The Origins of Capitalist Development: A Critique of Neo-Smithian Marxism', *New Left Review*, 104 (1979), 25–92.

25 Wolpe, 'Capitalism and Cheap Labour Power'.

26 Chris Middleton, for example, uses the term 'patriarchy' in a dynamic and historical manner, in his 'Peasants, Patriarchy and the Feudal Mode of Production in England: A Marxist Appraisal', *Sociological Review*, 29, 1 (1981), 105–54.

27 See Kate Young's brilliantly executed analysis of the effects of mercantile capital on the place of women in a remote Mexican region, 'Modes of Appropriation and the Sexual Division of Labour', in A. Kuhn and A. Wolpe (eds), *Feminism and Materialism* (London, 1980).

28 S. Marks and E. Unterhalter, 'Women and the Migrant Labour System in Southern Africa', unpublished paper (Lusaka, 1978).

29 John Wright, 'Women's Labour'.

30 Monica Hunter, *Reaction to Conquest* (Oxford, 1936), 106–7. See also her 'The Effects of Contact with Europeans on the Status of Pondo Women', *Africa*, VI (1933). See I. Schapera, *Married Life in an African Tribe* (Harmondsworth, 1971), 160 for an even more dramatic depiction of the difference in labour between young men and women.

31 S. Plaatje, *Native Life in South Africa* (London, 1916), quoted in J. Yawitch, 'Black Women'.

32 W. Beinart, *The Political Economy of Pondoland 1860–1930* (Cambridge, 1982), 157.

33 This is based on a conception of 'feudal' patriarchy derived from Middleton, 'Peasants, Patriarchy', C. Middleton, 'The Sexual Division of Labour in Feudal England', *New Left Review*, 113–14 (1979), 147–68 and Roberta Hamilton, *The Liberation of Women* (London, 1978).

34 This is not to suggest that a certain status was not conferred upon Boer women within the patriarchal structure as well.

35 However, the point about the feudal household, and this applies to the 'Boer' one too, was that it was a site of productive activity – in contrast to the modern capitalist one, in which production is socialized and removed from the domestic domain. See E. Zaretsky, *Capitalism, the Family and Personal Life* (London, 1976).

36 The discussion is based upon the Carnegie Commission Report, vol. V(b), *The Mother and the Daughter of the Poor Family* (Stellenbosch, 1932), 169–97.

37 See the Report of the *Transvaal Indigency Commission*, 1906–8 (Pretoria, 1908); and the Carnegie Commission Report, vol. I, *Rural Impoverishment and Rural Exodus*, for the background to this argument.

38 Carnegie Commission Report, vol. I, 214–29; Solly Sachs, *Rebel's Daughters* (London, 1957).

39 Carnegie Commission, vol. I, 215.

40 As note 39.

41 C. Bundy, *The Rise and Fall of the South African Peasantry* (London, 1979).

42 Carnegie Commission Report, vol. II, 60.

43 See P. Delius and S. Trapido, 'Inboekselings and Oorlams: The Creation and Transformation of a Servile Class', and T. Keegan,

'The Sharecropping Economy', both in B. Bozzoli (ed.), *Town and Countryside*.

44 R. Davies, 'Mining Capital, the State and Unskilled White Workers in South Africa, 1901–1913', *Journal of Southern African Studies*, 3, 1 (October, 1976), 41–69.

45 The critique that follows owes much to the work of Charles van Onselen, 'The World the Mine-Owners Made', in *Studies in the Social and Economic History of the Witwatersrand, 1890–1914*, 2 vols (London, 1982), as well as to Maxine Molyneux, 'Beyond the Domestic Labour Debate'.

46 See *Women in South African History*, no. 1 (January, 1981), 25–6.

47 B. Bozzoli, *The Political Nature of a Ruling Class* (London, 1981), 54.

48 Bozzoli, *Ruling Class*, 97.

49 Anna Davin, 'Imperialism and Motherhood', *History Workshop Journal*, 5 (Spring, 1978), 9–66, esp. 12–24.

50 Bozzoli, *Ruling Class*, 96.

51 C. van Onselen, 'The Witches of Suburbia', in *Studies*.

52 C. van Onselen, 'The Witches' discusses the transition from male to female, as does J. Cock, *Maids and Madams* (Johannesburg, 1980).

53 J. Cock, 'Disposable Nannies', African Studies Institute Seminar Paper, University of the Witwatersrand (1981).

54 L. Callinicos, in 'Domesticating Workers'.

THE ELABORATION
OF SEGREGATIONIST
IDEOLOGY

Saul Dubow

Saul Dubow, a South African historian now teaching at the University of Sussex in Britain, has explicitly sought to reintroduce an analysis of segregationist ideology into the debate. His argument is not intended as direct restatement of older liberal views where apartheid was seen as the result of blind racial prejudice. But it does suggest that left analysts placed too much emphasis on the cheap labour system as the driving force of segregation and its ideologies. There were broader white fears, he suggests, relating particularly to black urbanization and proletarianization. Segregation in its early twentieth-century form was conceived by British officials influenced by evolutionist and social Darwinist thought, as well as by South Africans of liberal disposition who used the anthropological notion of cultural relativism as a means of steering a path between 'assimilation' and 'oppression'. The ideology of segregation was primarily expressed as a means to defuse potential class conflict and maintain overall white hegemony. In this account, segregation is viewed as an umbrella ideology which was capable of serving a range of white interest groups, and even some black ones. Its flexibility explains its historical success as an ideology of social and political containment.

* * *

EARLY EXPONENTS OF SEGREGATION

Historians hold a multiplicity of views as regards the historical origins of segregation. Some writers, like Marian Lacey and Richard Parry, trace segregation back to the nineteenth-century Cape and the provisions of Cecil Rhodes's 1894 Glen Grey Act.[1] It has been suggested too that the experience of British rule in

Basutoland provided a model for some of the early theorists of segregation.[2] During the interwar years and beyond there was a widespread assumption (especially among liberal scholars) that the origins of segregation were to be found in the racial attitudes characteristic of the 'frontier tradition' and in the institutions of the nineteenth-century Boer republics. Against this view, David Welsh has claimed that the antecedents of segregation and apartheid are to be found in the Shepstonian policies of colonial Natal. It is in Natal, Welsh argues, that the demarcation of native reserves, the state's use of chiefs for administrative purposes and the recognition of customary law, were pioneered.[3]

The salience of Natal is also highlighted by Shula Marks, who gives the argument a fresh analytical twist. In her study of that region Marks shows that segregation was a means whereby capital and the colonial state came to terms with the 'still pulsating remains of powerful African kingdoms'. Segregationist policies were therefore not simply imposed by an all-powerful state; they emerged out of a complex process of struggle which was 'profoundly shaped' by the 'structures and social relationships of African precapitalist society'.[4] The importance of Natal – which, of all South Africa's regions, most closely resembles a colonial/ settler frontier – is further underlined by the fact that many of the principal advocates of twentieth-century segregation, e.g. Maurice Evans, C.T. Loram, Edgar Brookes and G.H. Nicholls, were closely associated with that province.

There are sound reasons to support all the above claims for the paternity of segregation, and it would therefore be misleading to cite one region to the exclusion of all others. Indeed it was ideologically advantageous to South Africa's early twentieth-century social engineers that segregationist precedents could readily be demonstrated in all the provinces of the Union of South Africa; for, in the context of the centralization of the state after 1910, segregation could be shown to be a consistent feature of the Union's diverse political and constitutional traditions.

At this point it is worth noting that of all the competing explanations for the origins of segregation–apartheid, the theory of Afrikaner nationalist responsibility is perhaps the least convincing. That view is exemplified by such historians as C.W. de Kiewiet and Eric Walker, who portray segregation in terms of the imposition of a retrogressive 'frontier mentality' on the attitudes of the twentieth century, and C.M. Tatz, for whom segregation

146

represents the victory of the racially exclusive north over the liberal traditions of the Cape.[5]

Although now a somewhat discredited view among academic historians, the misleading notion of apartheid as the eccentric creation of racist Afrikaners continues to enjoy wide provenance. In a recent book the BBC radio journalist Graham Leach, for instance, tells us that apartheid 'was a policy steeped in the Afrikaner's 300 years of history' and, even more inaccurately, that 'it was South Africa's first attempt at solving its racial problem'.[6]

This sort of account ignores the fact that the first group of theorists to outline a systematic ideology of segregation were English- rather than Afrikaans-speaking, and that many of them were associated with the interwar tradition of South African liberal thought. Prime Minister Hertzog, who was directly responsible for the passage of the 1936 Native Bills, promoted segregation as a white supremacist rather than an Afrikaner, and he derived most of his ideas from English-speaking thinkers. It is notable that the Afrikaner Broederbond, that powerhouse of twentieth-century Afrikaner nationalist ideological thought, only began to shift its concerns from Anglo–Afrikaner relations to the 'native question' in the mid- to late 1930s, by which time segregationist ideology was already deeply entrenched.[7] The earliest examples of Afrikaner proto-apartheid theory date from the early 1930s, but although they bear the distinctive imprint of Christian-Nationalist thinking and embrace a purist view of total separation, in substance they are largely derivative of already extant segregation and trusteeship ideology.

The first use of the word 'segregation' remains a matter of historical conjecture. Martin Legassick tentatively traced its first occurrence back to around 1908.[8] John Cell considers it 'truly remarkable' that the report of the 1903–5 South African Native Affairs Commission (SANAC) did not actually employ the term, even though it advocated a policy of 'territorial separation'.[9] (In fact, the word 'segregation' *does* occur in paragraph 190 of the report.[10]) Paul Rich recently claimed that 'segregation' was first used in 1903 by the Cape Liberal lawyer Richard Rose Innes 'to rationalize a policy of establishing "native reserves" in order to induce a ready supply of black labour for the mines and farms'.[11] But the word also crops up during the opening of the 1902 Cape parliament, when the Governor-General declared that it was 'necessary for the Government to be endowed with larger powers than they now possess to effectually carry out the policy of segregation . . .'.[12] It may well turn out that 'segregation' was used even earlier than that.

The search for the first use of 'segregation' in South Africa should not obscure the more significant point that segregation became an established political keyword only in the first two decades of the twentieth century. One of the first theorists to outline a reserve-based segregation strategy was J. Howard Pim, who did so in a paper which he delivered at the invitation of Sir Godfrey Lagden to the 1905 meeting of the British Association.[13]

The essence of Pim's argument was that it was preferable for Africans to remain in reserves, rather than their being established in 'locations' surrounding the industrial areas. He explained:

> For a time the location consists of able-bodied people, but they grow older, they become ill, they become disabled – who is to support them? They commit offences – who is to control them? The reserve is a sanatorium where they can recruit; if they are disabled they remain there. Their own tribal system keeps them under discipline, and if they become criminals there is not the slightest difficulty in bringing them to justice. All this absolutely without cost to the white community.[14]

It has been suggested that this quotation furnishes evidence for the validity of the reserve-subsidy theory of segregation as advanced by Harold Wolpe.[15] But when viewed in the context of Pim's paper and his other writings, the emphasis of such an interpretation appears to be misplaced. Pim's advocacy of the reserves occurs as an attempt to refute two prevailing arguments: the first claimed that Africans were occupying land which could be better utilized by whites; while the second contended that the reserves would deprive whites of labour by offering Africans an alternative form of subsistence. Both views therefore implied that Africans should be moved to locations close to large industrial centres where they would be compelled to enter into wage labour.[16]

Pim rejected this analysis (partly on moral grounds) but chiefly because he felt that 'location' Africans would in time constitute an intolerable economic and administrative burden upon white society. The Basutoland precedent apparently demonstrated that, even under 'tribal' conditions, Africans would be compelled – on economic grounds – to enter the labour market.[17] Moreover, experience of the American South in the post-emancipation era supposedly proved that 'the tendency of race feeling is towards segregation' and that 'the greatest benefit each race can confer upon the other is to cease to form part of the other's system'.[18]

On this reading Pim's advocacy of reserve segregation was not in the first instance a manifesto for cheap labour. His primary concern was with the maintenance of social discipline and control, which, he considered, would be most effectively sustained under conditions of rapid industrialization, through the existing 'tribal' system of the reserves. Thus it was Pim's intention to demonstrate that territorial segregation was *compatible* with (rather than *necessary* to) the development of industry, and that such a strategy would help to ensure the preservation of social order.

This interpretation of Pim's reserve policy is consistent with other writings in his private papers.[19] It was 'obviously far easier' to keep Africans 'under some form of discipline' when they lived as 'a native community' than if they were scattered throughout the white population.[20] Yet Pim firmly rejected the notion that 'native policy' should be founded solely in the material interests of whites. It was fallacious to assume that by 'making him of the greatest use to the white man, he will also develop naturally to his own best advantage. . . . I absolutely deny our right to base a native policy on the idea of our making the greatest possible use of the native race'.[21]

Notably, references to social Darwinist and environmental theories are a dominant feature of Pim's early writings on the native question. Thus he took it for granted that physical differences were merely 'outward signs of mental and moral differences', and he cited Africans' alleged 'lack of a sense of responsibility, want of foresight, arrest of mental development and distinctive modes of thought. . . .'[22] Pim also adhered to the common eugenic doctrine that Africans would 'degenerate' morally in the urban environment, thereby constituting a danger to white society. These beliefs reinforced his conviction that Africans should, so far as possible, be excluded from 'white civilization'. Indeed, in evidence to the SANAC Commission, Pim argued that native policy should be predicated on the undeniable fact of racial difference, from which it followed as 'a necessary conclusion that you cannot give the Native his full rights as a citizen of a white State'.[23]

149

In sum, during the period when Pim was an advocate of segregation, he conceived of it as a creative and prudent solution within the art of the politically possible. Given the reality of capitalism's labour requirements, he regarded segregation as a compromise between total separation on the one hand and the danger of unrestrained urbanization on the other hand. This prudence was also informed by a moral position which led Pim to criticize segregation if it was intended for the sole benefit of whites.[24] It is only if we understand Pim in these terms that his later critique of segregation becomes explicable.

Although Pim was one of the original exponents of segregation, his views remained largely outside the public domain, for they were presented in the form of lectures to specialized discussion groups, such as the Fortnightly Club, and diffused silently among Milner's,[a] mandarins.[25] The first thoroughgoing and broadly disseminated theory of segregation was Maurice Evans's *Black and While in South East Africa*, first published in 1911.[26] Evans's book enjoyed a wide circulation and was frequently cited in political debate.[27] Subtitled *A Study in Sociology*, it is noteworthy as one of the first in a tradition of 'expert' writings on the 'native question'. *Black and White* was strongly influenced by Evans's understanding of social conditions in the American South, to which he later devoted an entire study.

According to Evans, segregation was wrongly dismissed by the 'average person' as 'a Utopian chimerical idea' on account of its misassociation with the concept of total segregation. Yet, in a modified form, he believed that it embodied 'a great truth'.[28] Just as the Native Affairs Department was later to argue, Evans portrayed segregation as a natural synthesis of different regional approaches to native administration, each of which contained 'something of value'. By so doing he wished to demonstrate both its practicality and its pedigree.[29] Evans went on to establish three cardinal principles for the government of the native races:

1 The white man must govern.
2 The Parliament elected by the white man must realize that while it is their duty to decide upon the line of policy to be adopted, they must delegate a large measure of power to those especially qualified, and must refrain from undue interference.
3 The main line of policy must be the separation of the

races as far as possible, our aim being to prevent race deterioration, to preserve race integrity, and to give both opportunity to build up and develop their race life.[30]

These three principles resonate strongly with the colonial paternalism of trusteeship ideology, of which segregation was a variant. It will be observed that Evans's positive assertion of white supremacy is mitigated by an acknowledgement that native policy would have to be executed justly, and that considerable devolution of power with adequate mechanisms of consultation would have to be introduced. Like other writers of his time, Evans was strongly informed in his work by the language of eugenics, leading him, for example, to warn against miscegenation and the effects of interracial contact in the industrial sphere. Though not an advocate of total segregation, he believed that it was imperative to '. . . let the roots of the Abantu people remain in the soil of their country', where they would be subject to the wholesome restraints of tribal life and shielded from 'degeneration and despair'.[31]

Just as Afrikaner theorists of apartheid were later to argue, Evans stressed that segregation demanded an important material sacrifice from whites in the form of a generous land settlement. 'We cannot have our cake and also eat it', he warned.[32] In Evans's view segregation was incompatible with rapacious economic greed, and it was therefore not in the long-term interests of whites to submit to immediate calls for cheap African labour.[33] After Evans, the next landmark work on the 'native question' was the publication in 1917 of Charles Templeman Loram's *The Education of the South African Native*.[34] The significance of Loram's work lies in its attempt to articulate a detailed and differential educational policy appropriate to segregation. A number of subthemes already present in Evans's writings are amplified in this work. For instance, Loram is strongly concerned to solve the native question in 'a scientific fashion' by employing the specialist insights of anthropologists, ethnologists and psychologists. In seeking technical solutions to social problems, Loram exhibits a firm belief in the supposedly objective methods of positivist science.

Like Evans, Loram's segregationist proposals bear the strong imprint of the American South, where he had spent fifteen months studying Negro educational institutions. Another important

151

feature of Loram's work is its concentration on the findings of racial science. Although his conclusions about the alleged inferiority of Africans remain ambiguous, Loram devoted considerable sections of *The Education* to an assessment of Africans' actual and potential mental capacities. He conducted a series of intelligence tests in Natal based on similar experiments on American negroes by W.H. Pyle, M.J. Mayo and Louise F. Perring.[35]

Like Evans, Loram is critical of the general indifference towards the 'native problem'. He claimed that only when faced by rebellion, labour scarcity or competition in the cities, did the white man sit up and take notice; and even then such interest was momentary. Loram identified three schools of thought, which he termed the 'Repressionists', the 'Equalists' and the 'Segregationists'. Repressionists, he argued, regarded Africans as being inferior to whites and therefore fit for manual labour alone. Diametrically opposed were the Equalists (Exeter Hall philanthropists and certain European missionaries) who, 'basing their arguments on a common humanity, plead for equality of treatment for White and Black'.

In rejecting both these 'extremes', Loram embraced the Segregationists as a worthy 'midway' party. This school 'would attack the problem in a scientific fashion' and (with reference to Evans's three cardinal principles) 'would endeavour to give the Bantu race every circumstance to develop on the lines of its racial genius'. Strict segregation was, however, impractical in a country 'whose very existence is said to depend on a supply of cheap black labour', and in a situation where the tribal system had suffered irreparable decay.[36]

Finally, we should turn our attention to Edgar Brookes's well-known *History of Native Policy*.[37] This work was originally submitted as a doctoral thesis to the University of South Africa and may be considered to be the first full-length archivally based treatise on the subject of segregation. Brookes's *History* is also significant on account of the controversy it evoked and the wide circulation it achieved among policy-makers. Segregation, he ceaselessly argued, was the

> way out between the Scylla of identity and the Charybdis of subordination. We have seen it in the administrative, in the legal, in the political, in the economic, in the religious and in the social sphere as not merely a plausible or advisable,

152

but as the inevitable, solution. In trying to arrive at a general formula, we are in no doubt that differentiation is the formula to be accepted – differentiation, without any implication of inferiority.[38]

Brookes counterposed complete segregation with what he termed 'Partial' or 'Possessory' segregation. He dismissed complete segregation on the grounds that 'a certain amount of Native labour will always be necessary in South African economic life'.[39] Nevertheless, his sympathies at this stage were with those advocating a white labour policy, and he echoed the idea that Africans were fundamentally unsuited to industrialism.

Brookes's notion of possessory segregation amounts to a thorough statement of liberal-minded practical paternalism. Central to his thinking was the need to preserve the independent existence of the white and black races. He assumed that the natural place of Africans was on the land and affirmed the 'horror' of racial intermarriage. But Brookes felt that it was wrong to institute needless discrimination, such as the horizontal job colour bar. The duty of the white man was 'to civilize as well as control, to develop as well as protect'.[40]

Brookes's *History* is distinctive, both because it was published under the patronage of Hertzog himself, and also because it was the first extensive analysis of segregation. In a sense it was the last, for, with the publication of Hertzog's Native Bills in 1926, segregation came to the fore as declared government policy. Before this date the exponents of segregation were essentially self-appointed experts attempting to influence the content of what was still a vague, undefined theory within white ruling circles. Henceforth most of the literature dealing with segregation was written as commentary or critique, rather than as an explication of its policies.

'CULTURAL ADAPTATION'[41]

The foregoing section has indicated how, in the presentation of segregation as part of a historic compromise, the language of scientific racism, and of eugenics in particular, constituted an important component of its ideological discourse. During the second half of the nineteenth century there was a spectacular explosion of biologically based racial science in the English-speaking world. Evolutionist thought, exemplified by the Darwinian theory of natural selection, came to be applied to the human situation, and to groups rather than individuals. Scientists across a range of disciplines set themselves the task of classifying the world's races according to a 'natural' hierarchy. Biology, notes Greta Jones, helped to 'create the kind of moral universe in which nature reflected society and vice versa'.[42]

By the turn of the century the doctrine of eugenics, founded by Francis Galton, was strongly pervasive in Britain and the United States. This theory was predicated on the idea that social and political objectives could be efficiently achieved through the deliberate manipulation of genetic pools. Eugenics drew strongly on the late nineteenth-century fear of working-class discontent and was infused with an 'air of catastrophism'.[43] According to Galton, western civilization was on the decline; it could only be saved through the adoption of radical measures involving social and biological engineering. Within Britain, eugenics was primarily addressed to the questions of social class. It was viewed (often as not by political progressives) as a means of coping with poverty as well as the physical degeneration and moral 'degradation' of the urban proletariat. Moreover, its language and applications were readily transferred to the colonial domain, where it came to be addressed to questions of race.[44]

The rise of the eugenics movement in the second half of the nineteenth century is indicative of a general decline in confidence about the inevitability of human progress, the Whiggish assumption which so strongly informed the British imperial mission. A similar tendency is discernible in South Africa, where a number of writers have remarked on a distinct ideological shift in the late nineteenth-century Cape. Parry, for example, has demonstrated the manner by which the 'amalgamationist' policies ascribed to Sir George Grey were gradually undermined by the turn of the century: although the rhetoric of 'civilizing the backward races' persisted, the combination of administrative difficulties and the new conditions occasioned by the mineral revolution combined to rob the liberal vision of its practical force.[45]

Similarly, Russell Martin's analysis of the Transkeian administration shows how, particularly after the wars of 1877 and uprisings of 1880–1, officials became ever more sceptical of the potential for success of the Victorian 'civilizing mission'. By slow degrees 'the orthodoxy of Grey who had sought to promote "civilization by mingling" became the heterodoxy of the Transkeian magistrates who set their face against what they called "amalgamation"'.[46] This reassessment of social evolutionary theory appears to have been true of the British Colonial Office as a whole. Thus Hyam, writing of the Liberal government of 1905–8, claims that by this time 'the mid-Victorian objective of turning Africans into black Europeans had long been given up . . . the tendency was towards segregation rather than assimilation'.[47] Notably, Hyam ascribes this change to the historical experience of colonialism, as well as to the teachings of 'pseudo Darwinian science'.[48]

In South Africa the lived relations of paternalism which bound black and white together presented white supremacy as part of the natural order of things. To an extent this assumption obviated the need for an elaboration of explicit theories of racial superiority as evidenced in Britain or the United States. Aside from relatively marginal individuals like Fred Bell, there appears to be a relative absence of virulent scientific racism in early twentieth-century South Africa. This point has recently been made by Paul Rich.[49] In making it, however, Rich has underrated the extent to which scientific racism was an *implicit* component of the political discourse of the time. Indeed it is perhaps by virtue of the fact that racist assumptions were so prevalent in the common-sense thinking of early twentieth-century South Africa that the relative absence of eugenist or social Darwinist theories is to be explained.[50]

The imagery of social Darwinism is clearly discernible in three important areas of political debate: speculation about the relative intelligence of blacks and whites, the almost universally expressed horror of 'miscegenation', and fear of racial 'degeneration' following upon the uncontrolled development of a black and white proletariat in the cities.

In the view of many, Africans were 'naturally' part of the land. Cities were portrayed as an 'alien environment' for which they were supposedly not yet ready. The urban environment was commonly described as the site of vice and immorality, 'influences far too potent for his [the African's] powers of resistance'.[51] The phenomenon of 'poor whiteism' was frequently held up as a perfect illustration of the tendency of civilization to decline. Concern was especially expressed for the physical and moral well-being of Africans in the cities. Notably, urban social welfare became an important area of liberal activity in the 1920s, as

155

attempts were made to prevent 'demoralization' and to defuse the potential for social and industrial conflict.

The language of eugenics is strongly evident in the contemporary obsession with 'miscegenation' and the creation of 'hybrid races' – a preoccupation which was by no means confined to South Africa alone.[52] Miscegenation among the working classes was held to sap the fibre of white civilization and its most vulnerable point. Similarly, 'race fusion' was portrayed in the most apocalyptic terms by such eugenist-inspired catastrophists as Ernest Stubbs and George Heaton Nicholls.[53] Maurice Evans associated himself (as did many white liberal thinkers) with the opinion of the 'average white South African' that the 'admixture in blood of the races is the worst that can happen, at least for the white race, and perhaps for both'.[54] So strong was feeling on this point that African notables took care to distinguish their political claims from the implication that they desired 'social equality' – often as not, a euphemism for miscegenation.

The dangers of miscegenation were powerfully exploited at the hustings. In his speeches on segregation Hertzog warned of the vulnerability of white civilization in the face of the numerical preponderance of Africans, and he frequently equated political rights for Africans with 'swamping'.[55] The full force of these warnings escape us today, as they have eluded those liberal historians who naively attempt to show by means of figures that Hertzog's fears of the rapid expansion in the African franchise were unfounded.[56] But the impact of 'swamping' or of the 'rising tide of colour' is rendered more comprehensible when set in the prevailing mood of the time, with its paranoia about civilization's retrogressive tendencies and its vulnerability in the face of the 'virile' mass of 'barbarians' who were 'flooding' into the cities.

The impact of nineteenth-century racial science also served to confirm the popular justification of white supremacy, which looked to the Bible for its authority. According to this interpretation, which became especially prominent within Afrikaner nationalist thought from the 1930s onwards, Africans were forever destined to be 'hewers of wood and drawers of water' on account of their being descendants of the children of Ham. As de Kiewiet succinctly observes, 'Religion and science each seemed to lend the weight of its peculiar authority to the elevation of one race over another.'[57]

The problem of genetic inheritance provoked three major questions with respect to Africans: their innate as opposed to their potential mental capacities, whether their intellect was 'originative' as well as 'imitative', and whether their mental development was 'arrested' after adolescence.[58] Results of intelligence tests, frequently derived from American models then in vogue, were often invoked in support of arguments for or against segregation.[59]

Speculation about the relative mental capacity of the different races was by no means confined to those who may obviously be considered to be racists. Prominent liberal thinkers, such as J.D. Rheinallt Jones, C.T. Loram and Alfred Hoernlé, all addressed themselves to the question of innate intelligence at one time or another.[60] A.R. Radcliffe-Brown, then professor of social anthropology at the University of Cape Town, was equivocal on the matter. He thought it likely that there were some physiological differences between whites and blacks, but supposed these would not make a vast amount of difference.[61] The general consensus as expressed by the black author S.M. Molema was that 'neither capacity nor incapacity have been shown conclusively to be characteristic of the backward races, or more plainly, of the African race'.[62] A similar conclusion on the indeterminacy of intelligence testing was reached by Werner Eiselen in 1929.[63] Eiselen was then a lecturer in ethnography and Bantu languages at Stellenbosch University, but later served as Secretary of Native Affairs under Hendrik Verwoerd, in which capacity he played a central role in the implementation of apartheid.[64]

If most writers agreed that the matter of biological differences between the races was in doubt, this did not prevent them from making inferences based on their own prejudices and suspicions. For some, innate racial differences were manifestly obvious; the only question which remained was the extent to which Africans could be expected to bridge the intelligence gap. In the case of others, the inconclusive results of scientific research offered hope for the ultimate achievement of liberal ideals. In general, however, to pose the question of biological differentiation in itself presupposed some acceptance of segregation: a policy of 'differentiation', it seemed clear, was the best social laboratory in which the true capacity of Africans could be tested.

South Africa's transition from a mercantile to an industrial economy in the late nineteenth century forms the historical context in which the assumptions of classic liberalism were called into question.[65] But it was only during the first two decades of the twentieth century that the full social implications of capitalist industrialization became apparent. Among its more important manifestations were the growth of urban slums and the emergence of working-class radicalism, as well as a growing awareness of the rapid dissolution of the 'tribal system' and the inadequate agricultural capacity of the reserves. It was with these processes in mind that social theorists began to draw on the brand of liberal reformism and collectivist thought which had been gathering strength overseas.

In this regard it should be observed that the liberalism which developed after the Anglo–Boer War and coalesced on the Witwatersrand during the early 1920s was born in explicit opposition to its Cape forebears. Although in some respects the inheritors of the Cape tradition, the new establishment-liberalism eschewed fundamental tenets of the mid-Victorian project. The writings of Loram and Brookes rejected the policies of identity and assimilation. In their hands 'civilization' was replaced by 'culture', 'progress' became synonymous with 'differentiation', while individualism was subsumed into the collective interests of 'racial groups'. Whereas the racist policies of the nineteenth-century Boer republics were associated with 'repression' and Victorian liberalism with 'identity', segregation came to be portrayed as transcending these opposites. An intellectual organizing principle was required to validate this compromise or synthesis; and the anthropological notion of culture came to serve the purpose admirably.

The study of anthropology in South Africa was institutional-ized during the decade after the First World War.[66] In 1921 A.R. Radcliffe-Brown, one of the acknowledged founders of modern social anthropology, was appointed to the newly estab-lished chair of social anthropology at the University of Cape Town. Within a few years all four teaching universities in the country had departments offering courses in 'Bantu studies' and anthropology, or their equivalents. From the outset anthropology was looked to as a source of applied knowledge. Influential indi-viduals, such as C.T. Loram, J.D. Rheinallt Jones, James Duerden and Jan Smuts, all stressed the role that anthropology could play in providing a solution to the so-called 'native question'.[67] In the words of Radcliffe-Brown, social anthropology was 'not merely of scientific or academic interest, but of immense practi-cal importance . . .'. Given a situation where the economic, social and cultural life of the 'native tribes' was being 'altered daily', Radcliffe-Brown extolled the value of anthropological knowledge in 'finding some social and political system in which the natives and the whites may live together without conflict'.[68]

For a variety of reasons the instrumental effects of anthropology on state policy were limited.[69] But its contribution to the formulation of segregationist ideology was pronounced as a result of claims which made reference to its intellectual authority. For key members of the liberal establishment, a number of whom were strongly influenced by early social anthropology, the nascent theory of 'culture contact' offered new and valuable insights into the 'changing native'. Its recognition of the complexity of African society, and of the distinctive nature of African 'culture', informed their efforts to provide for the differential development of Africans. As an empirical science of a distinctive 'native mentality', anthropology was eagerly seized upon by experts seeking positivist 'solutions' to the 'native question'.[70]

George Stocking, the American historian of anthropology, has convincingly demonstrated how the work of Franz Boas and his students in the period 1900–30 served to 'free the concept of culture from its heritage of evolutionary and racial assumptions, so that it could subsequently become the cornerstone of social scientific disciplines completely independent of biological determinism'.[71] The influence of the Boasian school, explains Stocking, generated a specifically anthropological concept of culture which was distinctly *relativistic*. This was contrasted with the humanist sense of culture, 'which was absolutistic and knew perfection'. Thus, whereas 'Traditional humanist usage distinguishes between degrees of "culture"; for the anthropologist, all men are equally "cultured"'.[72]

As disseminated through Bronislaw Malinowski (and possibly through Franz Boas), a popular notion of 'culture' came to serve as a credible linguistic peg upon which the segregationist compromise was hung. Both the liberal 'civilizing mission' and scientific racism shared the linear assumptions characteristic of evolutionist thought, yet both these theories jarred with those who favoured a form of separate development without repression. The notion of 'culture' offered a way out of these constraints. It did so by incorporating – and transcending – the evolutionist assumptions of liberal assimilationists (who believed in the capacity of the black man 'to rise'), as well as of racist

159

'repressionists' (who based their policies on the assumption that the position of Africans on the evolutionary scale or the 'Great Chain of Being' was fixed at a lower point than whites).

Consideration of the ways in which the term 'culture' was popularly used in the 1920s and 1930s reveals an intriguing diversity in its connotations. 'Culture' was sometimes employed as a synonym for 'civilization', whereby it was seen as a universally transmissible quality on an ascending evolutionary scale. At other times, however, it was employed as a synonym for 'race', in which case it took on an immutable character. Used in the first sense, culture was perfectible, whereas in the latter case it was static in virtue of its being biologically determined. It was out of these contradictory meanings that a distinctive, anthropologically derived notion of culture developed. Though implicitly racist and openly hostile to traditional theories of assimilation, this sense of 'culture' allowed room for a gradual process of racial 'upliftment'.

A paradigmatic example of this mode of thought is evident in General Smuts's celebrated 1929 Oxford lectures in which he outlined his personal view of segregation.[73] Smuts rejected the opinion which saw the 'African as essentially inferior or sub-human, as having no soul, and as being only fit to be a slave'. But he also rejected the converse, whereby the 'African now became a man and a brother'.[74] Although this view had given Africans a semblance of equality with whites, it had destroyed 'the basis of his African system which was his highest good'.[75] Both these policies, according to Smuts, had been harmful: the solution was to be found in a policy of differential development or segregation. 'The new policy', he explained, 'is to foster an indigenous native culture or system of cultures and to cease to force the African into alien European moulds.'[76]

G.P. Lestrade, the government ethnologist, argued similarly that the culturally assimilated and missionary-educated native was somehow fraudulent ('about as original as a glass of skimmed milk') and that it was necessary instead to 'build up a good Bantu future' on the basis of their own culture.[77] In 1931 he informed the Native Economic Commission:

> there is a middle way between tying him [the native] down
> or trying to make of him a black European, between *repres-*
> *sionist* and *assimilationist* schools ... it is possible to adopt

an *adaptationist* attitude which would take out of the Bantu past what was good, and even what was merely neutral, and together with what is good of European culture for the Bantu, build up a Bantu future.[78]

Lestrade's formulation of cultural adaptationism was to become a crucial organizing theme for the Native Economic Commission's advocacy of segregation. Thus in 1932 the Commission 'unhesitatingly affirm[ed]' its adherence to Lestrade's concept of adaptationism, which it considered to be 'not only the most reasonable but also the most economical approach to the native question'.[79]

The concept of 'adaptation', which in biology refers to the manner in which an organism becomes fitted to its environment, was especially suited to the vocabulary of segregation. If differentiation between species was a feature of the natural world, it was (by a process of inference) true of society as well. Thus J.E. Holloway, the Chairman of the NEC, defined adaptation in such a way that it functioned as a biological metaphor for separate development:

> The adaptationist aims at transforming, at giving shape and direction to what is growing, or, to vary the metaphor, at grafting on the existing stock. His view of human beings is essentially evolutionary. They are a part of the conditions which have created them. Their reactions are largely conditioned by their racial past, and are therefore difficult to destroy.[80]

At this point it is necessary to insert a note of caution: although it derived from and was shaped by the emerging discipline of anthropology, the popular notion of 'culture' and of 'cultural adaptation' should not be too closely associated with the modern discipline of social anthropology. Isaac Schapera, for example, was strongly critical of Lestrade's theory of cultural adaptation as adopted by the NEC, since he laid stress on the dynamic qualities of 'culture'. In Schapera's view the penetration of western civilization in the form of 'the missionary, the teacher, the trader, the labour recruiter, and the farmer' was irreversible. Changes in one aspect of culture inevitably reacted upon other aspects, and it was therefore impossible to 'bolster up the Chieftainship and Native legal institutions . . .'.[81]

161

It is clear that Schapera had absorbed W.M. Macmillan's historical insights into his own understanding of anthropology. Macmillan had been bitterly contemptuous of the 'rather doubtful doctrines' of anthropology from as early as 1923, attacking the liberal establishment for its concern with anthropological studies and complaining angrily of the 'paralysing conservatism' of its approach.[82] In Macmillan's view rural poverty and tribal disintegration had 'already gone too far'. It was therefore 'more urgent that we see he [the African] is provided with bread, even without butter, than to embark on the long quest to "understand the Native mind"'.[83]

The concept of 'cultural adaptation' was widely appropriated for use in the political domain. In the hands of George Heaton Nicholls, the Natal politician and prominent segregationist ideologue, it was imperative to recreate a tribally based culture or 'ethos'. The alternative to adaptation was assimilation, which 'substitutes class for race' and would inevitably 'lead to the evolution of a native proletariat inspired by the usual antagonisms of a class war'.[84] Werner Eiselen also emphasized the need to recognize and encourage 'Bantu culture' in order to promote a policy of differentiation. 'The duty of the native', he explained, was 'not to become a black European, but to become a better native, with ideals and a culture of his own.'[85]

The language of cultural adaptation was of distinct advantage in the attempt to associate South African segregation with the wider imperial policies of indirect rule and trusteeship. This linkage constitutes a major theme of Smuts's 1929 Oxford lectures, wherein he sought to demonstrate that the South African policy of differentiation was enshrined in the trusteeship clauses of the League of Nations Covenant.[86] In his keynote statement on the draft Native Bills in 1935 George Heaton Nicholls reinforced this connection, suggesting that the essence of the Bills differs 'in no way in principle from the new conception of native government which is embraced in the word "trusteeship" and translated into administrative action through a policy of "adaptation" in all British States'.[87] The policy of adaptation, he added, was not new to South Africa 'where the people have learnt their anthropology at first hand from actual contact with native life'.[88]

In Britain Lord Lugard's doctrine of indirect rule had likewise been lent theoretical coherence through its association with social anthropology and, in particular, the Malinowskian concept of 'culture contact'. Rich has recently emphasized the intellectual contribution during the 1890s of the writer and traveller Mary Kingsley, who challenged the jingoistic certainties of high-Victorian British imperialism and championed the instrinsic worth of African societies. Kingsley's legacy of 'cultural relativism' may therefore be regarded as having anticipated the theory of indirect rule, as well as providing ammunition for later segregationists.[89]

The South African advocates of segregation sought to accommodate themselves to ideas forwarded by the proponents of indirect rule – a task made considerably easier by the fact that both groups shared the vocabulary of 'culture', 'adaptation' and 'parallelism'. This similarity in discourse was a source of considerable embarrassment during the interwar years to British social anthropologists and commentators, for whom South Africa was increasingly seen as a retrogressive or aberrant member of the Empire.

It is indeed revealing that the attempt to distinguish indirect rule from segregation was somewhat awkwardly accomplished. Margery Perham, in her elaboration and defence of indirect rule, claimed that it was 'strange that segregation and indirect rule should have been confused'.[90] She argued that whereas segregation was characteristic of the 'mixed territories', indirect rule had only been applied in the 'purely native territories'; and she contrasted the doctrinaire artificiality inherent in the strategy of preserving indigenous cultures in South Africa with the essential flexibility characteristic of indirect rule. Perham's arguments were elaborated at greater length by Lucy Mair, for whom indirect rule was not a magic formula whose essence could be deduced theoretically. In the final analysis, Mair contended, the distinction between Nigeria and Tanganyika (where the finest attributes of indirect rule were apparently exemplified) and South Africa (which was based on the selfish preservation of white 'supremacy') could only be judged empirically.[91]

Perham and Mair were undoubtedly correct in their concern to distance indirect rule from segregation – no doubt Kingsley would have wished to do the same. But their manifest difficulty in doing so is testament to the power of the language of cultural adaptation in lending credibility to the ideology of segregation.

163

SEGREGATION AFTER THE FIRST WORLD WAR

Thus far we have considered some of the core elements which went into the creation of segregationist ideology. Yet from the vantage point of someone writing in the early 1920s it was not at all clear that segregation was approved government policy. It is true that significant segregationist legislation was firmly planted (in embryonic form at least) on the statute books by 1920: the 1911 Mines and Works Act, the Native Labour Regulation Act of the same year, the 1913 Natives Land Act and the 1920 Native Affairs Act, are among the most important examples. Together with the pass laws, this legislation laid down job discrimination and territorial separation, as well as mechanisms by which labour could be controlled and coerced. Nevertheless, these measures were seldom interpreted as integral elements of a unified ideological package.

For example, whereas the 1913 Land Act promised segregation, plans for its implementation had in fact been deferred to an unspecified date in the future. The 1916 Beaumont Commission and the 1918 Local Committees, which were intended to finalize the land question, encountered constitutional and political difficulties and were consequently dropped. The 1917 Native Administration Bill, with its key proposals for administrative segregation, was likewise abandoned. Prime Minister Botha's native policy had, in the words of Hancock, 'come to a dead stop'.[92] Or at least it was perceived to have done so. Thus, in 1918 the Native Affairs Department concluded that an Urban Areas Bill would have to 'bide its time' because the policy (of segregation) as expressed by the 1913 Land Act and the 1917 Administration Bill had 'not yet been fully accepted by the country'.[93]

It may therefore be concluded that the legislative and ideological continuity of segregationist policies was severely disrupted during the First World War and its immediate aftermath. Yet, with the introduction and passage of Smuts's Native Affairs Act in 1920, the 'native question' was forced back on the agenda as a matter of urgency. Many observers of a liberal disposition welcomed the 1920 Act, which focused attention on the question of separate political representation for black and white, as an enlightened measure, commending it as 'a great and hopeful step forward'.[94]

The decade of the 1920s witnessed an unprecedented upsurge

in black political radicalism: a volatile, if contradictory, amalgam of working-class militancy, rural populism and Africanist millenarianism. This ferment was intimately related to the declining productivity of the reserves, the development of capitalist agriculture and the quickening pace of proletarianization. And it was largely as a reaction to these social processes that segregationist ideology gathered political momentum, until it became a sort of hegemonic ideology within white South Africa.

The marked change in the political environment after the First World War, a matter which was especially apparent to officials of the Native Affairs Department, was often expressed in terms of an 'awakening of racial consciousness'. . . .

> There has been a growing inclination among Native workers to adopt European methods for the redress of grievances, actual and assumed, and there has been a noticeable, if yet but little successful, attempt of the communist or Bolshevik section to capture and exploit the Native races for the purpose of the subversion of the present form of government. . . . The inevitable development of race-consciousness has begun and is showing itself in the formation of associations for all kinds of purposes – religious, political, industrial and social. These may be at present shortlived and unstable – the product of immature thought – but they indicate how the wind blows and what importance is attached to European example.[95]

E.H. Barrett supported these claims with a detailed account of recent events, mentioning, *inter alia*, agitation in Bloemfontein in 1919 for higher wages and the arrest of H. Selby Msimang; the sanitary workers' strike in Johannesburg; strikes during 1919 at the Natal Collieries, the Messina Mine and the Cape Town Docks; the 1919 deputation of the SANNC to England; the 1920 mineworkers' strike on the Rand; a riot in 1920 at the Lovedale institution; agitation for increased wages and an ensuing riot in 1920 at Port Elizabeth; and the 1921 Bulhoek incident at Queenstown.[96]

Scholars have frequently remarked upon the distinct sharpening in black political awareness during the immediate postwar decade.[97] In recent years these observations have been scrutinized with greater precision. In his perceptive study of the class dynamics of the black population on the Rand between 1917 and 1922, Philip Bonner, for example, draws attention to the intense radicalization of black political leadership during the period 1918–20 as the Transvaal Native Congress confronted a powerful upsurge in working-class agitation.[98] Other recent work has broadened the focus of research to reveal a remarkable degree of militancy in the countryside during the 1920s. Most notably, Helen Bradford's sensitive analysis of the Industrial and Commercial Workers' Union (ICU) provides us with a vivid account of mass-based populist resistance in the rural areas.

The political turbulence of the early 1920s ensured that segregation-talk came to impinge more and more directly on the political agenda. In 1920 the Governor-General remarked (in light of the Native Affairs Act of that year) that the principle of segregation was now generally accepted. But he was forced to add that there was 'some divergence of opinion as to what precisely the term "segregation" should be held to imply'.[99] The ambiguous character of segregation thrived in an environment where there was 'strong demand by the public for a "policy", just as when people are sick they want a pill or mixture that will "cure" the trouble'.[100]

Though General Smuts appeared to endorse segregation in 1920, it was increasingly (if confusedly) associated with J.B.M. Hertzog, who skilfully exploited the desire for a panacea solution to the native question by deliberately leaving the details of segregation obscure. Through the election year of 1924 the pro-SAP[b] *Cape Times* exhibited marked frustration at its inability to pin Hertzog down on the meaning of segregation. It accused him of having 'always been clever enough to leave his meaning entangled in a mass of loosely-spun words, as vague and intangible as a collection of moonbeams'. This expedient, the newspaper noted, afforded Hertzog considerable room for manoeuvre, for he simply claimed to have been deliberately misrepresented or misquoted whenever political opponents chose to put a definite interpretation on his utterances.[101]

In the mid-1920s Hertzog was successfully indulging in a strategy of political kite-flying. The elusive quality with which he invested segregation was its very strength, for it drew differing groups into its discourse, always promising, never quite revealing. In Hancock's words, segregation was 'not a precisely defined programme but a slogan with as many meanings as anyone could want'. Even as the opposition tried to force Hertzog to define what he meant by the term, they might be left 'protesting that they too were segregationists'.[102]

The ideology of segregation was ambiguous but it was not vacuous. At the risk of oversimplification, there were two distinct segregationist traditions, whose distinctive strands coalesced in rough accordance with the fault lines of the major parliamentary parties. They may therefore be loosely associated with Smuts and Hertzog respectively.

On the one hand, Hertzogite segregation maintained strong positions on the abolition of the Cape franchise, the white 'civilized labour' policy, the industrial colour bar and the distribution of farm labour. Its tone was strident, it was racist in character and it emphasized the economic and political exclusion of Africans from a common society.

By contrast, Smutsian segregation drew on the incorporationist and 'protective' elements inherent in liberal segregation and made explicit reference to the paternalist idiom of trusteeship ideology. Unlike the Hertzogite variant, which was often understood as the logical extension of the 'Northern tradition', Smutsian segregation traced its antecedents back to the nineteenth-century Cape. The notion of 'parallel institutions' or 'differentiation' was said to derive from the pragmatic legacy of the 1894 Glen Grey Act. Smutsian segregation celebrated the reputed success of the Transkeian Councils and proclaimed the 1920 Native Affairs Act, which sponsored indirect statutory forms of black political representation, as the basis of a moderate segregationist solution.[103]

The question of the industrial colour bar was probably the issue on which the two segregationist traditions diverged most sharply. In combination with Hertzog's civilized labour policy, the job colour bar was designed to protect white labour against 'unfair' competition from reserve Africans. Liberal opinion was seemingly outraged at this explicit example of discrimination. In a sustained campaign against its introduction the *Cape Times* variously termed the colour bar 'pernicious' and both 'ethically and morally unsound'.[104] The Act was attacked by liberals as an infringement of individual human rights, an example of illegitimate state interference in the market, and a measure whose political and economic effects were bound to be counter-productive.

Much of the opposition mounted against the colour bar represented an alliance between proponents of *laissez faire* economic policies and those more inclined towards the expression of humanitarian sentiment. Yet, in spite of the opposition mounted against statutory job discrimination, it is notable that segregation itself was not under attack at this stage. Indeed some of the most outspoken opposition to the Bill emanated from such liberal paternalists as Brookes, Pim and Loram, who remained supporters of Hertzog. What distressed these individuals in particular was the *principle* of statutory discrimination, which it was feared would arouse unnecessary hostility among the African élite. The colour bar, it was pointed out, had long been a *de facto* feature of South African life and it could effectively be maintained through indirect means – for instance, through manipulation of the Wage Act.[105]

If the two segregationist traditions differed most strongly on the question of the colour bar, on other issues there was a substantial degree of convergence. The 1923 Urban Areas Act serves as a good example. This measure managed to synthesize the findings of the Stallard Commission (which argued that Africans' presence in the urban areas should be restricted to their 'ministering' to the needs of whites) with those of the Godley Commission (which, accepting African urbanization as inevitable, went on to propose measures designed to improve the living conditions of permanently proletarianized Africans). In combining labour control with the 'protection' of Africans the 1923 Act attracted significant support from liberal segregationists, and the manner in which it was debated was portrayed as a vindication of the 'consultative' spirit underlying the 1920 Native Affairs Act.[106]

Common to both strands of segregationist ideology was an unashamed paternalism towards Africans and an unquestioning commitment to the maintenance of white supremacy. There were differences, however, as to what supremacy entailed, as well as the means by which it was to be upheld. By the early 1920s the major white political parties, together with significant elements of African opinion, had come to accept segregation in its broadest terms. This does not mean that there was unanimity about segregationist policies, much less that it was universally welcomed. But arguments about its content tended to revolve around matters of detail and differences in interpretation rather than on the generally accepted principle of consolidating a racially differentiated society.

EDITORS' NOTES

a Sir Alfred Milner: British official who became the High Commissioner in South Africa from 1897 to 1905 during the key period of the South African War (1899–1902) and subsequent reconstruction policies for which he took considerable responsibility.

b SAP: South African Party. Established on a countrywide basis after Union in 1910, it was the ruling party in the all-white South African parliament until 1924 under Generals L. Botha and J.C. Smuts. It was a vehicle for moderate Afrikaner opinion, as well as many English-speakers, anxious to establish conciliation and white unity.

NOTES

1 M. Lacey, *Working for Boroko: The Origins of a Coercive Labour System in South Africa* (Johannesburg, 1981), 14–17; R. Parry, '"In a Sense Citizens, But Not Altogether Citizens ..." Rhodes, Race, and the Ideology of Segregation at the Cape in the Late Nineteenth Century', *Canadian Journal of African Studies*, XVII, 3 (1983), 377–91.

2 See for example Paul B. Rich, *Race and Empire in British Politics* (Cambridge, 1986), 21; E.H. Brookes, *The History of Native Policy in South Africa from 1830 to the Present Day* (Cape Town, 1924), 99–107. Note that the Chairman of the SANAC report was Sir Godfrey Lagden, a former Resident Commissioner of Basutoland. In arguing for segregation Howard Pim (see note 13) often cited the Basutoland precedent.

3 D. Welsh, *The Roots of Segregation: Native Policy in Colonial Natal, 1845–1910* (London and Cape Town, 1971), 322.

4 S. Marks, *The Ambiguities of Dependence in South Africa: Class, Nationalism and the State in Twentieth Century Natal* (Johannesburg, 1986), 5 and ch. 1. See also S. Marks, 'White Supremacy: A Review Article', *Comparative Studies in Society and History*, XXIX, 2 (1987), 385–97.

5 C.W. de Kiewiet, *A History of South Africa, Social and Economic* (Oxford, 1941); E.A. Walker, *The Frontier Tradition in South Africa* (Oxford, 1930); C.M. Tatz, *Shadow and Substance in South Africa: A Study in Land and Franchise Policies Affecting Africans, 1910–1960* (Pietermaritzburg, 1962).

6 G. Leach, *South Africa: No Easy Path to Peace*, 2nd edn (London, 1987), 36, 40.

7 A.N. Pelzer's authorized history of the Afrikaner Broederbond, *Die Afrikaner-Broederbond: Eerste 50 Jaar* (Cape Town, 1979), 163–4.

8 M. Legassick, 'The Making of South African "Native Policy", 1903–1923: The Origins of "Segregation"', seminar paper, Institute of Commonwealth Studies, University of London (1973), 2.

9 J.W. Cell, *The Highest Stage of White Supremacy* (Cambridge, 1982), 211.

10 *South African Native Affairs Commission 1903–5*, vol. I (Cape Town, 1905).

11 Rich, *Race and Empire*, 56.
12 *Cape Argus*, 20 August 1902. Note that the Governor-General was not talking of territorial segregation; he was referring to the creation of special urban 'locations' for Africans in the wake of the bubonic plague. My thanks to Christopher Saunders for this reference.
13 Pim Papers, University of the Witwatersrand Library A881 Hb8.16, 'The Native Problem in South Africa', by J.H. Pim, 1905. J.H. Pim (1862–1934) was born near Dublin and educated at Trinity College, Dublin. He came to South Africa in 1890 as a chartered accountant with Rhodes's British South Africa Company. In 1894 he established his own practice and became an auditor to De Beers Consolidated Mines Ltd. He was a member of Milner's nominated Johannesburg Town Council of 1903. Pim was a committed Quaker, who increasingly devoted himself to a variety of social welfare activities. Through his connection with the Joint Councils and the Institute of Race Relations, he became a prominent figure in liberal circles, and functioned as a theorist, organizer and patron. Various obituaries testify to Pim's humanitarianism and refer to him as a champion of 'native rights'.
14 As note 13, p. 9.
15 P. Rich, 'The Agrarian Counter-Revolution in the Transvaal and the Origins of Segregation: 1902–1913', African Studies seminar paper, University of the Witwatersrand (1975), 15; M. Legassick and D. Innes 'Capital Restructuring and Apartheid: A Critique of Constructive Engagement', in *African Affairs*, vol. 76, issue 305 (1977), 465–6.
16 Pim, 'The Native Problem', 9.
17 Pim, 7, 10.
18 Pim Papers, A881 Fa 3/2, Abstract of paper for British Association, 2. For more on Pim's interpretation of American History see his paper 'The Question of Race', delivered to the Fortnightly Club, 15 November 1906, in Pim Papers, A881 Hb 17.
19 Pim Papers, Fa 1/3, 'A Note on Native Policy', 7.
20 As note 19.
21 As note 19, 7–8.
22 Pim, 'The Question of Race', 2.
23 *South African Native Affairs Commission 1903–5*, vol. I (Cape Town, 1905), 895.
24 Pim Papers, A881 Fa 9/7, 'Memorandum re "Segregation"', (1914), 2.
25 Stanley Trapido has pointed out to me that Pim's ideas about the functions of the reserves appears in Appendix VIII, p. 111 of Cd 7707, *Dominions Royal Commission. Minutes of Evidence Taken in the Union of South Africa in 1914, Part II*.
26 M.S. Evans, *Black and White in South East Africa: A Study in Sociology* (London, 1911). Maurice Smethurst Evans (1854–1920) went to Natal in 1875 and became a member of its Legislative Assembly in 1897. He served on the 1906–7 Natal Native Commission and published a pamphlet, *The Native Problem in Natal* (Durban, 1906). Evans

travelled to the United States, after which he published a second volume, *Black and White in the Southern States: A Study of the Race Problem in the United States from a South African Point of View* (London, 1915).

27 See for example Sarah Gertrude Millin in her *The South Africans* (London, 1926), 279, where she describes Evans as the 'soundest and fairest observer of black and white inter-relationships in South Africa'.

28 Evans, *Black and White in South East Africa*, 276.

29 Evans, 277.

30 Evans, 310.

31 Evans, 153.

32 Evans, 316.

33 Evans, 177. See also 149–50.

34 C.T. Loram, *The Education of the South African Native* (London, 1917). Charles Templeman Loram (1879–1940) was born in Pietermaritzburg and educated at the universities of Cape Town and Cambridge. He completed a doctorate at Columbia University in 1916. Between 1906 and 1920 he worked within the Natal Education Department. He left in 1920 to take up a position on the newly created Native Affairs Commission, in which capacity he served until 1929. In 1930 he rejoined the Natal Education Department as its Superintendent of Education. Loram was part of the Phelps-Stokes Educational Commission to Africa during 1921–4, and played a key role in allocating funds for research projects. He was closely involved in the Joint Council movement and became the first Chairman of the South African Institute of Race Relations in 1929. In 1931 Loram left SA to become Sterling Professor of Education at Yale University. He became Chairman and Director of Studies in the Department of Culture Contacts and Race Relations at Yale in 1933.

35 Loram, chs IX and X.

36 Loram, 17–25.

37 Brookes, *The History of Native Policy in South Africa from 1830 to the Present Day* (Cape Town, 1924).

38 Brookes, 501.

39 Brookes, 343.

40 Brookes, 504.

41 This section is a condensed version of a paper entitled '"Race, Civilisation and Culture": The Elaboration of Segregationist Discourse in the Inter-War Years', in S. Marks and S. Trapido (eds), *The Politics of Race, Class and Nationalism in Twentieth-Century South Africa* (London and New York, 1987).

42 G. Jones, *Social Darwinism and English Thought* (Brighton, 1980), 147.

43 Jones, *Social Darwinism*, 103.

44 Rich, *Race and Empire*.

45 Parry, 'In a Sense Citizens', 384–8.

46 S.J.R. Martin, 'Political and Social Theories of Transkeian Administrators in the Late Nineteenth Century', MA thesis, UCT (1978), 82.

47 R. Hyam, *Elgin and Churchill at the Colonial Office 1905–8* (London, 1968), 539.
48 As note 47.
49 P.B. Rich, *White Power and the Liberal Conscience: Racial Segregation in South Africa and South African Liberalism 1921–60* (Manchester, 1984), 5.
50 On the prevalence (in the pre-Nazi era) of theories of racial superiority in South Africa derived from the biological sciences, see J.M. Coetzee's brilliant essay, 'Blood, Flaw, Taint, Degeneration: The Case of Sarah Gertrude Millin', *English Studies in Africa*, XXIII, 1 (1980).
51 C.T. Loram, *The Education*, 9, 11. See also Brookes, *History*, ch. XVIII. On p. 403 Brookes states that 'The native . . . is not naturally a town-dweller or an industrialist'.
52 See Rich, *Race and Empire*, ch. 6, which investigates the anti-miscegenation movement in interwar Britain, centring on the presence of black seamen in ports like Cardiff and Liverpool.
53 E. Stubbs, *Tightening Coils: An Essay on Segregation* (Pretoria, 1925); G.H. Nicholls, *Bayete!* (London, 1923).
54 M. Evans, *Black and White in South East Africa*, 223.
55 See for example Hertzog's Smithfield and Malmesbury speeches in *The Segregation Problem: General Hertzog's Solution* (Cape Town, nd [1926]).
56 C.M. Tatz, *Shadow and Substance*. On pp. 41–5 Tatz isolates and evaluates the validity of twelve arguments advanced by Hertzog for the removal of the Cape African franchise.
57 De Kiewiet, *A History of South Africa*, 181.
58 See for example J.E. Duerden, 'Genetics and Eugenics in South Africa: Heredity and Environment', *South African Journal of Science* (henceforth *SAJS*), XXII (1925).
59 See for example M.L. Fick, 'Intelligence Test Results of Poor White, Native (Zulu), Coloured and Indian School Children and the Educational and Social Implications', in *SAJS*, XXVI (1929); Loram, *The Education*, chs IX–XI.
60 J.D. Rheinallt Jones, 'The Need for a Scientific Basis for South African Native Policy', *SAJS*, XXIII (1926); Loram, *The Education*; Evidence of Prof. and Mrs Hoernlé to Native Economic Commission (henceforth NEC), 13 June 1931, 9183–5.
61 Union Government, Pretoria, UG (henceforth UG), 14–'26, *Report of the Economic and Wage Commission (1925)*, 326.
62 S.M. Molema, *The Bantu – Past and Present* (Edinburgh, 1920), 328.
63 W. Eiselen, *Die Naturelle Vraagstuk* (Cape Town, 1929), 3–4.
64 On Eiselen's retirement the Bantu Affairs Department's official journal *Bantu*, VII, 8 (1960) devoted an entire issue to him. A lengthy eulogy to Eiselen quoted extensively from the 1929 address cited above. It was represented as a direct antecedent to his views on apartheid.
65 On the material basis of Cape liberalism, see Stanley Trapido's pioneering essay '"The Friends of the Natives": Merchants, Peasants and the Political and Ideological Structure of Liberalism in the Cape,

1854–1910', in S. Marks and A. Atmore (eds), *Economy and Society in Pre-Industrial South Africa* (London, 1980).

66 On the institutionalization of anthropological studies in South Africa and its relationship to segregation see my '"Understanding the Native Mind": Anthropology, Cultural Adaptation and the Elaboration of a Segregationist Discourse in South Africa, c.1920–36', seminar paper, University of Cape Town (1984). For a discussion of the impact of anthropology on liberal thought in the 1920s and 1930s, see Rich, *White Power*, ch. 3.

67 Loram, *The Education*, vii–viii; J.D. Rheinallt Jones, 'Editorial' in *Bantu Studies*, I, 1 (1921), 1; J.E. Duerden, 'Social Anthropology in South Africa: Problems of Nationality', *SAJS*, XVIII (1921), 4–5. According to Adam Kuper, *Anthropologists and Anthropology* (London, 1973), 62, Smuts, in consultation with Haddon of Cambridge, was personally responsible for inviting Radcliffe-Brown to UCT.

68 A.R. Radcliffe-Brown, 'Some Problems of Bantu Sociology', *Bantu Studies*, I, 3 (1922), 5.

69 See my '"Understanding the Native Mind"'.

70 See Rich, *White Power*, ch. 3, especially 54–63; also Rich, *Race and Empire*, ch. 5.

71 G.W. Stocking, *Race, Culture and Evolution: Essays in the History of Anthropology* (New York, 1968). For an assessment of the impact of Boasian thought, see also M. Harris, *The Rise of Anthropological Theory* (London, 1968), chs IX and X.

72 Stocking, *Race, Culture and Evolution*, 199–200. See also the entry on 'culture' in R. Williams's *Keywords: A Vocabulary of Culture and Society* (London, 1976), 78–9.

73 J.C. Smuts, *Africa and Some World Problems* (Oxford, 1930).

74 Smuts, 77.

75 Smuts, 77.

76 Smuts, 84.

77 Evidence of G.P. Lestrade to NEC, Pretoria, 9 June 1931, 8787.

78 Lestrade Papers, University of Cape Town, Jagger Library BC 255 K1. 11, 'Statements in Answer to General Questionnaire Issued by the NEC'.

79 UG 22–'32, *Report of the Native Economic Commission 1930–32*, 31, para. 200. Note that Dr Roberts of the Native Affairs Commission and NEC dissented from this view, adding, 'the way of progress for the Native lies along the path of the Native assimilating as rapidly as possible the European civilization and culture', 31, para. 201.

80 J.E. Holloway, 'The American Negro and the South African Bantu – A Study in Assimilation', *South African Journal of Economics*, I, 4 (1933), 422.

81 Schapera, *Western Civilisation and the Natives of South Africa: Studies in Culture Contact* (London, 1934). See also his 'Changing Life in the Native Reserves', *Race Relations*, I, 1 (1933). See Max Gluckman's paper 'Anthropology and Apartheid: The Work of South African Anthropologists', in M. Fortes and S. Patterson (eds), *Studies in*

African Social Anthropology (London and New York, 1975), 36. Gluckman credits Schapera as the dominant figure in reorientating British anthropology towards the idea that Africans and whites were 'integral parts of a single social system, so that all had to be studied in the same way'.

82 W.M. Macmillan, *My South African Years: An Autobiography* (Cape Town, 1975), 194, 214–19. Macmillan criticized Rheinallt Jones, the Hoernlés and especially Loram for their involvement in anthropological research. For details of his failed attempt to subvert Jones's course on the native law and administration, see Wits. Arts Faculty Minutes, vol. VIII, 38–40b, University of the Witwatersrand Archives, William Cullen Library.

83 W.M. Macmillan, *Complex South Africa: An Economic Footnote to History* (London, 1930), preface, 8.

84 Heaton Nicholls Papers, University of Natal, Killie Campbell Library, KCM 3323, File 3. Handwritten memo on Native Policy, nd, 1.

85 Records of the South African Institute of Race Relations Archives, University of the Witwatersrand Library (henceforth 'SAIRR') AD 843 72. 1. Unmarked newspaper clipping, 10 May 1929 (CPA). For the full Afrikaans version, see Eiselen, *Die Naturelle Vraagstuk*.

86 Smuts, *Africa*, 96.

87 SAIRR Papers, AD 843 B53. 1, *Natal Advertiser*, 15 May 1935.

88 As note 87.

89 Rich, *Race and Empire*, ch. 2.

90 M. Perham, 'A Restatement of Indirect Rule', *Africa*, VII, 3 (1934), 326. See also B. Porter, *The Lion's Share: A Short History of British Imperialism 1850–1983* (London and New York, 1975), 293.

91 L. Mair, *Native Policies in Africa* (London, 1936), 261–9.

92 Hancock, *Smuts*, vol. II, 116.

93 UG 7–'19, *Report of the Native Affairs Department (NAD) for the Years 1913–1918*, 16. This periodization differs from John Cell's, who argues that the essential institutions of segregation were in place by 1924 and that its principal architect was Smuts, not Hertzog. See his *White Supremacy*, 58, 216.

94 See e.g. *The Round Table*, no. 44 (1921), 945; GG (State Archives, Pretoria, Archives of the Governor-General) 1435 50/865, Governor-General Buxton to Viscount Milner, 21 July 1920, 'Native Affairs Bill (Confidential)'; J.H. Hofmeyr, *South Africa* (London, 1931), 170–1.

95 UG 34–'22, *Report of the NAD for the Years 1919–1921*, 4.

96 As note 95, 1–4. See also *Rand Daily Mail*, 21 February 1923.

97 P. Walshe, *The Rise of African Nationalism in South Africa: The African National Congress 1912–1952* (London, 1970), 70–1, 89 and *passim*. See also H.J. and R. Simons, *Class and Colour in South Africa 1850–1950* (Harmondsworth, 1969), ch. 11; E. Roux, *Time Longer than Rope: The Black Man's Struggle for Freedom in South Africa* (London, 1948), 143.

98 P. Bonner, 'The Transvaal Native Congress 1917–1920: The Radicalisation of the Black Petty Bourgeoisie on the Rand', in Marks

and Rathbone (eds), *Industrialisation and Social Change: African Class Formation, Culture and Consciousness, 1870–1930* (London, 1982).

99 GG 1435 50/854, Buxton to Viscount Milner, 3 June 1920, 'Report on the Native Affairs Bill', 1. See also Herbst Papers, University of Cape Town, Jagger Library, BC 79 D24, Memo by E.R. Garthorne on Native Segregation, 7 October 1924. Garthorne said that while segregation was 'freely advocated in general terms, there has as yet been no very precise or authoritative exposition of its implications . . .', 1.

100 *The Round Table*, no. 57 (December, 1924), 192.

101 *Cape Times* (editorial), 3 May 1924. See also 11 and 12 June 1924, 17 September 1924 and 18 October 1924.

102 Hancock, *Smuts*, vol. II, 163.

103 For an account of this lineage, see *Cape Times* (editorial), 22 October 1924; 7 April 1936 (editorial); 1 May 1935 (editorial); 22 August 1936 (editorial). Also Smuts, *Native Policy*, 78–85; Hancock, *Smuts*, vol. II, 227; Hofmeyr, *South Africa*, 313–15.

104 *Cape Times* (editorial) 23 January 1925; 11 May 1926 (editorial); 17 February 1925 (editorial).

105 J.H. Pim, 'General Hertzog's Smithfield Proposals', *The SA Quarterly*, VII, 3–4 (1926), 6. 'I have no quarrel with the native colour bar formed by public opinion' but the proposed legislation 'will have grave reactions upon the relations between Europeans and Natives throughout the Union. It protects the inefficient white against the efficient native'. See also Brookes, *The Colour Problems of South Africa* (Lovedale, 1934), 9.

106 See, e.g. *Cape Times*, 3 April 1922, 29 June 1927 (editorial); UG 36–'23, *Report of the Native Affairs Commission for the Year 1922*, 4–5; *The Round Table*, no. 53 (1923), 174.

7

CHIEFTAINCY AND THE CONCEPT OF ARTICULATION:

South Africa circa 1900–50

William Beinart

This article by William Beinart, a South African-born historian now based at the University of Bristol, was intended to reorient explanations of segregation and apartheid away from metropolitan policy-making and towards the rural African reserves. Taking issue with Wolpe's thesis about the role of the reserves in providing industry with a cheap labour force and the view that segregation/apartheid was tailor-made to the demands of capitalist mine-owners and industrialists, Beinart shows that the migrant labour system was significantly shaped by the dynamics of African societies themselves. Beinart is also concerned to counter the assumption in much liberal and Marxist scholarship that rural Africans were simply available to be reshaped by colonists – either as modernizing Christian peasants or as urban workers. He draws attention to the complex nature of local African politics and the varying forces to which chiefs attempted to respond. As the central state attempted to intervene more and more directly in rural life, some chiefs played critical roles in the defence of communal resources and values and even became the focus of political opposition. Others collaborated with the apartheid government in an attempt to secure their own positions or to preserve some local autonomy for their regions. But the line between resistance and collaboration was seldom impermeable. Segregation was therefore not simply imposed upon rural Africans from 'above' by a state enjoying absolute power; it was constantly negotiated and challenged even as the rise of apartheid led to a steady erosion of the bargaining position of rural Africans.

* * *

176

This note is not primarily concerned with the theoretical standing of, or language surrounding, the concept of articulation. Rather, it explores the metaphor suggested by that term: the idea that two 'modes of production' can coexist, however briefly, during a period of 'transition'. The issue is also approached at something of a tangent by focusing on the survival of chieftaincy in South Africa's African reserves.

Many of those who now hold power in the homelands or Bantustans are descended from, or claim descent from, old chiefly lineages. Yet these areas have undergone far-reaching changes in the last century; their people became deeply dependent on wages even where they retained access to rural plots and stock. Chieftaincy, a political form which recalls pre-colonial society, hardly seems an appropriate institution to represent and govern a migrant labour force, much less those hundreds of thousands, now millions, of people who have been resettled in rural towns.

Confronted with this anomaly, critics of Pretoria's Bantustan policy have often argued that chieftaincy was an imposition. The government resurrected a spent institution as part of its attempt to extend self-government to the reserves. Explanations of the provenance of the policy differ. Scholars are increasingly tracing it back to the 1920s and the heyday of segregationism, rather than just to the early apartheid era of the 1950s.[1] Nevertheless, it is widely recognized that the current form of chieftaincy was entrenched in the latter period when government officials, accompanied by tame anthropologists and black information officers, scoured the rural districts for the remnants of chiefly lineages. 'Tribes' were defined, Tribal and Regional Authorities created and some of the chiefs were installed with much pseudo-traditional ceremony. Chiefs were also given salaries and scope for personal gain. In this way, the state hoped to secure a conservative, or reactionary, rural hierarchy which would help to defuse broader national struggles. Modern chieftaincy, in short, has been seen as a creation of, and creature of, the state.

If this outline caricatures some of the more complex contributions to the debate on the nature of the South African state, it does not entirely misrepresent them. Nor is such a position completely rejected in the equally schematic alternative presented here. What is significant about this line of analysis, for the purposes of the article, is that some of its elements can be related to ideas

WILLIAM BEINART

about the articulation of modes – or at least to the way in which articulation has been applied to South African society. For, out of the materialist and left reinterpretations of the late 1960s and early 1970s, a basic and very influential insight about South African capitalist development emerged: capital and the state – or the 'capitalist mode of production' – did not have to be seen as merely destroying pre-capitalist formations, or African societies.

It was not so much the apparent ability of merchant capital to coexist with and feed off pre-capitalist forms of production that attracted academic attention.[2] Indeed, in some analyses merchant capital was implicitly assigned a very active role as solvent of 'tribal' society.[3] Nor was the crucial point based on the maxim that capital takes labour as it finds it. Rather, industrial capital actively preserved some pre-capitalist forms. This insight allowed those exploring a materialist position to unhook themselves from simple evolutionism in regard to capitalist development and class formation. It seemed to capture, with some precision, the realities of the South African political economy which, especially in the first half of the twentieth century, was characterized to a unique extent by a system of migrant labour.

Various elements of this position have been stressed by different authors; Wolpe's synthesis perhaps came closest to achieving the status of a new paradigm in the mid-1970s.[4] To summarize (and simplify): pre-capitalist forms were partially preserved not to assist in capitalist production but in the reproduction of the labour force. Cheap labour was not only desirable but essential because of the nature of the South African gold-mining industry. Migrant labour was cheap because the workers' families remained behind in the rural areas, thus freeing mine-owners from the expense of paying a wage on which the whole family could subsist. The costs of maintaining workers when away from the industrial areas, and in their old age, were also assigned to the reserve economies. But if a system of migrant labour was to be entrenched, then reserve areas had to be protected, even extended, so that families could continue sub-subsistence production. This policy became the cornerstone of segregation and later apartheid. And within the reserves, as many families as possible had to be guaranteed access to land and resources: this could be facilitated by an insistence on a modified form of communal tenure.

The idea of a partial preservation, and incomplete transforma-

178

tion, of pre-capitalist societies also underlies much of the writing on the political advantages that accrued to the dominant classes from the migrant labour system. Migrancy itself perhaps delayed and diluted the development of class consciousness and working-class organization. The system certainly limited the growth of a potentially dangerous African urban population in the core industrial areas. At the same time, migrancy allowed for the consolidation of a compound system through which the vast mining workforce could be subjected to further physical and psychological controls. Chieftaincy may be seen as the final piece in this complex jigsaw of social control in that it provided the means for bolstering rural attachments and ethnic identities.

A variety of criticisms have been explicitly and implicitly levelled against this position. They include: its inadequacy in dealing with conflicts within 'capital' and the state; its marginal value in explaining social relationships where African societies were more completely dispossessed – in the western and mid-land Cape, on the farms and in the towns; its functionalism in attributing the key social developments to the needs of capital; its failure to come to terms with the specific nature of African society and of class and gender struggles.[5] However, it does not necessarily follow that the heuristic value of a theory should be ignored just because its precision proves, mirage-like, illusory when the object of analysis is approached more closely. Indeed, it could be argued that some of the implications of 'articulation' have not yet been fully explored in South African historiography, and that the concept may still contain some life.

The position outlined has remained persuasive – it certainly is attractive to students approaching materialist analyses of South Africa for the first time – precisely because it does place migrant labour, rather than just the fact that Africans became more dependent on wage labour, at the core of the argument. Second, it provides a means for including the reserves and even the territories beyond South Africa's formal boundaries, in any attempt to define the nature of the state and the political economy as a whole. In this respect it differs from formulations which focus on the character of capital, or which make easy assumptions about class struggle. And third, it raises questions about what is meant by discussing South Africa, at least in the first half of this century, as a single society with a single economy. To address this issue is not to subscribe to a new form of economic dualism nor to

179

suggest that African rural society remained intrinsically 'tribal'. Rather, it focuses attention on the degree to which Africans were incorporated, or needed to be incorporated, or wanted to be incorporated, in a common society.

My own inkling, based on rather localized research in some of the reserve areas of the Cape, is that the metaphor of articulation has some value if it is turned on its head – that is, if the balance of power between articulating forces is reconsidered. (And greater allowance is made for changes in the African communities, and for analysis of politics and consciousness.) The first step in the argument derives from a reinterpretation of the origins of migrant labour, the basic relationship of exploitation on which Wolpe and others focused. (Although Wolpe considered the system in its maturity rather than its origins.) Colonial penetration, needs created through trade, appropriation of land and taxation certainly made it necessary for an increasing majority of African families to secure some wage income. But many of those who went to work did so in such a way as to avoid full incorporation as settled and permanent wage labourers.[6] In certain instances, controls over migrants, usually young men, were exercised by chiefs and homestead heads to ensure that as many as possible returned home with their wages. Even when such controls – through the bridewealth system, regiments or the securing of advance wages – faltered, many individual migrants attempted to balance the need for wages with a concern to consolidate and develop their rural base. It could be suggested, then, that migrancy as a specific form of proletarianization arose out of the dynamics of African societies rather than out of the demands of the mine-owners. The system was, at least initially, a compromise between capital and the peasantry – it reflected the inability of the state to transform African society. That the mining industry came to see this arrangement as in its interests, and increasingly entrenched it, is perhaps the fundamental irony of South African history.

The next step in the argument concerns the nature of the peasantry. There certainly were improving, progressive, sometimes Christian peasant communities, responding to the market by increasing production and enjoying a period of moderate prosperity in some Cape districts. Because of their key position in the political economy of the late nineteenth-century Cape, they achieved considerable prominence as political actors. But a careful reading of Bundy's research, and more especially sub-sequent studies, suggests that they were a relatively small minor-ity. In considerable parts of the Cape reserve areas, especially in the Transkeian Territories, they were less significant than in the eastern Cape proper. And even in the eastern Cape, the Ciskeian districts, the accumulating 'Mfengu' peasant may not have been typical. This is not to suggest that African societies remained unchanged: ploughs and sheep were widely introduced, a lim-ited surplus was produced for the market by the great majority of families. But in many cases this need to extend production was met through cautious shifts within the parameters of pre-existing social relationships rather than an unfettered 'market response' which presaged rapid accumulation and individualization of productive resources. There was a significant reaction when accumulation by individuals or communities threatened more general access to rural resources. And when the state was seen to intervene in favour of 'progressives', loyals or accumulators, rural defensiveness was cemented.

This suggestion feeds into an understanding of local political authority in the reserves.[7] The formal administrative arrange-ments made after annexation appeared to be simple and regular in that magistrates were to rule through government-appointed headmen. However, in practice they were rather more varied. In certain areas, paramount chiefs were left with some influence, recognized informally, not least over the selection of headmen. Those selected for headmanships were often from leading branches of chiefly lineages. But where chiefs had led rebellions, they could be completely displaced in favour of the political representatives of progressive, Christian or immigrant commun-ities. Disputes over headmanships, and more generally over local political authority, were frequent during the early decades of the twentieth century, when Cape colonial and then South African rule had been firmly entrenched; they are extensively recorded in the archives of the Native Affairs Department. It is not always easy to detect general trends in the mass of detail about districts in which rather different political arrangements had been made. But there do seem to have been significant patterns of change. First, different branches of the various chiefly lineages in a wide variety of areas staged a tenacious battle for recognition, and for control over appointments to headmanships. Second, where immigrant or progressive headmen had been imposed on traditionalist communities, there was a strong reaction. Popular movements arose which favoured the restoration of some form of chieftaincy, not least of those chiefly families associated with opposition to colonial rule during the period of conquest. And third, there were political fissures within the Christian communities which had become economically threatened. Some moved out of the mission churches around the turn of the century and espoused an Ethiopianism which had political as well as religious implications. They attempted to build bridges, initially without much success, to the traditionalists by mobilizing popular opposition on issues such as the council system, new taxation and cattle dipping. By the 1920s, some Christian political leaders from the old 'collaborating' communities began to explore radical Africanist thinking. This could include support for chieftaincy and the entrenchment of communal tenure; the potential for creating popular movements across the cleavages brought into being by colonial rule was greatly increased.

The thrust of this argument – if it can be generalized from what remain a limited number of case studies in one part of the country – is that the persistence of certain pre-capitalist forms resulted not least from struggles within the rural communities and the way in which rural people fought to retain access to resources. Chieftaincy provided the kind of institution, and set of symbols, behind which rural people could unite at a local level and stake claims to land and communal rights. Such political and social expressions were of course traditionalist, rather than 'traditional'; their content was constantly shifting. Although rural consciousness took some of its referents from the past, it was shaped by, and sensitive to, the new context of colonial rule and industrialization. Those advocating the restoration of chiefs, for example, were not seeking to re-establish pre-colonial forms of tributary authority. Rather, they hoped to install a political process which would allow popular participation in decision-making and popular control over the bounded world of the districts. They saw this as an alternative to 'puppet' headmen and councils under the direct control of the administration. It was not an inappropriate response for communities increasingly involved in migrant labour. For if migrancy, as a form of proletarianization, is seen to result not least from an attempt by rural people to defend themselves against full incorporation into the capitalist economy, then it is not surprising that the political struggles of rural Africans were geared to a defence of their rural base.

In a sense, then, rural communities offered up their chiefs – or those chiefs and headmen who were seen to be sensitive to popular demands – to the administration. Officials were not insensitive to the political shifts that underlay the complex genealogical disputes through which claims to legitimacy were often put forward. Nor were they averse to defusing local political crises and conflicts by incorporating some of the chiefs and headmen who were seen to have popular support. The administration did not want men with legitimacy for quite the same reason as the people; indeed sometimes it backed members of chiefly lineages who were not particularly popular. And the shifts in official practice and policy took place largely within the established system of administration through headmen and councils. But the important point in the context of this argument is that chieftaincy and the position of headmanship continued to be, perhaps increasingly became, the political arena within which local political struggles were fought.

Chiefs and headmen were not, of course, all of one ilk. Some, particularly the more senior chiefs, were by now educated in mission institutions and shared some of the values of the progressive élite in salaried posts in the rural districts. Some remained staunchly traditionalist. Some were not averse to using their position to accumulate; others fulfilled popular expectations in providing scope for political participation. It is perhaps possible to suggest two general features of the political compromises that had been reached. Most chiefs and headmen backed the system of 'communal' land tenure even if they sought advantage for themselves, and their immediate supporters, within that system. Many had an increasing material interest in the payments that could be derived from the allotment of lands. This, along with the political compromises reached in the first few decades of the century, had important implications in subsequent years.

For a time, especially in the 1930s it seems, many chiefs and traditionalist headmen were able to balance the variety of roles that they were called upon to play. They understood rural popular thinking and were able to act as spokesmen and defend rural rights. At the same time, the administration – at the height of the segregationist era – was less active in attempting to restructure rural life. But from the late 1930s officials formulated, and began

183

to implement, a new series of initiatives designed to reform rural production. The concerns, among both officials and ruling groups, which gave rise to these overarching betterment or rehabilitation policies were various and cannot be elaborated here. At the very least, the schemes envisaged extensive reorganization of settlement patterns and land use in the reserves, as well as cattle culling, so that agriculture could be 'developed' and soil erosion controlled. There was, however some lack of clarity among policy-makers as to whether the schemes should go further. Some, including technical officers, aimed to concentrate resources in the hands of a minority of rural Africans on 'economic' units. This would necessitate pushing many off the land. Others seemed content with technical solutions where all those with claims to land would receive plots in the newly rehabilitated locations.

My own reading of the limited material available on the actual implementation of the schemes in a few Transkeian districts suggests that little attempt was made to differentiate plot sizes and that grazing land remained open to all. (Although there was not always sufficient land to meet all claims.) In part this outcome was a result of government reluctance to face the consequences of 'economic' units; the decentralized industries which might absorb those thrown off the land were still largely figments of the imagination of planners. But it also seems that local officials were responding to the very real demand for general access to land from the communities they 'planned'. In short, the administration was not keen to face the political consequences of any radical concentration of land-holding. If this argument is correct, then it suggests that rural communalism remained an important political force through to the 1950s – and a force that had perhaps been bolstered by the administrative arrangements made over the previous few decades.

There was, nevertheless, deep suspicion about the administration's plans for intervention. Opposition to the culling of stock and to resettlement was widespread. This placed chiefs and headmen in a difficult position. On the one hand, they were called upon by officials to help implement the schemes – or at least to secure acquiescence from the areas under their authority; on the other, they were pushed from below to articulate popular feelings. The difficulty became acute when, in the early 1950s, the new Nationalist government sought to bolster and increase the power of chiefs through the Bantu Authorities programme. Some of the educated chiefs and headmen accepted the logic behind the schemes; others thought they might benefit from co-operating with the government. Many, however, tried to sit on the fence, only to find that the pressures forced them to topple into the government's camp. (A few actually led opposition to the state.) It was these issues, not least, which lay behind the widespread popular protest movements, even rebellions, of the period from the late 1940s to the early 1960s. These were years of great turbulence in the Cape reserve districts (and elsewhere); the target of popular movements were often those who had co-operated with the state.

But it would be wrong to assume that the rejection of some chiefs and headmen in these years meant that the institution of chieftaincy was no longer of importance in the rural areas. Popular movements sometimes bypassed the issues of chieftaincy, but in a number of cases they also focused on demands for the reinstatement or elevation of certain members of chiefly lineages: Sabata Dalindyebo rather than Kaiser Matanzima; Nelson rather than Botha Sigcau in Pondoland. Bantu Authorities were opposed because they seemed to deliver chiefs into the hands of the government rather than because they involved chiefs. Nationalist movements did succeed, sometimes belatedly, in linking up with this phase of rural struggle, but it is questionable as to whether they were able to install new ideologies which rejected both the state and the older forms of rural authority. The rebellions were crushed by force where necessary and the state entrenched the Bantu Authorities, thus accelerating the decentralization of political power. But even the new political order of the Bantustans, while highly repressive in some ways, could provide for some popular demands. For example, stock culling was stopped in the Transkei when limited self-government was introduced in 1963; the idea of the economic unit was not resurrected until recently. And chiefs could still play on communalist ideology, and old symbols, while dispensing new patronage. The rural political order, in short, depended – at least till this time – not just on repression and coercive archaic institutions, but at least partly on the ambiguities of rural thinking.

It is of course true that the process of accumulation in South Africa involved the concentration of wealth and power in the hands of a racially defined minority and the dispossession of some of the indigenous inhabitants. The contrast between South Africa and most of the rest of subsaharan Africa, where relatively few of the indigenous inhabitants were separated from the means of production, is stark. It is also possible to conceive of a different outcome to accumulation in South Africa where, if agrarian capital and settler colonialism had remained the dominant forces, all land might have been declared private property. But the ability to conquer is not synonymous with the capacity to dispossess. Even where land was alienated to settlers, long struggles were involved before African peasants could be made to labour with regularity and it took even longer to deny them rights to land on farms. (The suggestions made here about the trajectory of rural struggles in the early decades of the twentieth century may have relevance to some farming districts.) And at every stage of dispossession, the social and political costs had to be counted. Even in so coercive an environment as South Africa, the patterns of domination were constrained – in part by fear of the consequences of other routes and in part by the defensive responses of the dominated. Certainly, capital and the state – and these were not uniform categories – had only limited power to shape social relationships in those areas which were left under African occupation.

The fact that a majority of Africans in the country retained a base in the reserve districts at this time has bedevilled analyses of class formation. The vast majority of reserve-based families depended in varying degrees on both wages and rural production. There has been a healthy reaction in the literature to the notion that migrants were tribal target workers: wage income was a necessity. But the fact that a migrant works for a wage, even for a number of years, does not necessarily determine the totality of his, much less his family's, class position and consciousness. The importance of defensive struggles in the rural areas, among communities which included seasoned migrants, has generally been underestimated; class struggle has been conflated with conflict in the urban industrial world or on the farms.

Moreover, the content and character of rural political responses remains ill-understood. Reserve dwellers have been seen as passive, or their will has been induced from the outward or statistical manifestations of their poverty. But poverty and oppression do not in themselves determine the content of political struggles. It has of course been important, in a political world shaped by segregation and apartheid, to stress the need for political unity. But it cannot be assumed that rural people in the earlier decades of this century saw this as the paramount aim. The evidence suggests that their political responses were often particularist and even separatist. Though aware of the system which gave rise to their grievances, they tried to establish local autonomy rather than to challenge and capture the state. They were not necessarily available for nationalist struggles, or class alliances which sought equal rights within the country as a whole. (Although such alliances were sometimes possible.) The pattern of rural politics may have differed if a more incorporative political system had been established in the country, but the great majority of reserve dwellers had little experience of such a system, even in the late nineteenth-century 'liberal' moment.

To explore the strength of rural traditionalism in Africa's most industrialized country is not to subscribe to the notion – which has had such influence with South Africa's rulers – that Africans, whatever else they may be, are members of tribes and that tribes must have chiefs. But the result of such an exploration might indicate that chieftaincy has been seen in too static a light. 'Legitimate' chieftaincy did not necessarily die with the conquest of the great African polities of the nineteenth century. The political processes surrounding the institution had always offered some scope for the articulation of popular demands. In the twentieth century, it may be argued, when chiefs had been stripped of many of their tributary powers, there may have been particular scope for the development of popular and representative forms of chieftaincy. Chiefs could be, and have been, used as instruments of control, but at various times the institution has also been seen by rural people as a focus for the defence of their rights.

Whether the concept of articulation is the most fruitful means of capturing the balance of forces in the country in the first half of this century is open to question. It certainly needs to be infused with a more dynamic content, [8] and with ideas about politics and consciousness, if it is to be deployed. However, it has been one of the influences in the formulation of the above analysis. And it may provide further scope for a re-examination of the South African political economy – and the peculiar blend of coercion, economic incorporation and political exclusion, that characterized it. Segregation was in some senses a route which followed the line of least resistance. For it seemed to promise a limited local autonomy to Africans.

NOTES

* [Footnotes changed from original Harvard system – Eds.]
1 S. Marks, 'Natal, the Zulu Royal Family and the Ideology of Segregation', *Journal of Southern African Studies* 4, 2 (1978), 172–94.
2 G. Kay, *Development and Underdevelopment: A Marxist Analysis* (London, 1975).
3 C. Bundy, *The Rise and Fall of the South African Peasantry* (London, 1979).
4 H. Wolpe, 'Capitalism and Cheap Labour Power in South Africa: From Segregation to Apartheid', *Economy and Society*, 1 (1972), 425–56. [See this volume, Chapter 3.]
5 B. Bozzoli, 'Marxism, Feminism and South African Studies', *Journal of Southern African Studies*, 9, 2 (1983), 139–71; J. Lewis, 'The Rise and Fall of the South African Peasantry: A Critique and Reassessment', *Journal of Southern African Studies*, 11, 1 (1984), 1–24.
6 W. Beinart, *The Political Economy of Pondoland, 1860–1930* (Cambridge, 1982); P. Harries, 'Kinship, Ideology and the Nature of Pre-Colonial Labour Migration', in S. Marks and R. Rathbone (eds), *Industrialization and Social Change in South Africa* (London, 1982); P. Delius, *The Land Belongs to Us: The Pedi Polity, the Boers and the British in the Nineteenth-Century Transvaal* (Johannesburg, 1983).
7 W. Beinart and C. Bundy, *Hidden Struggles in Rural South Africa* (London, 1987).
8 H. Wolpe (ed.), *The Articulation of Modes of Production* (London, 1980).

8

THE GROWTH OF AFRIKANER IDENTITY

Hermann Giliomee

*Hermann Giliomee is a liberal Afrikaner historian and respected politi-
cal commentator formerly based at the University of Stellenbosch and
now teaching at the University of Cape Town. This extract first
appeared as a chapter in a book jointly authored with the Canadian-
based sociologist Heribert Adam. Giliomee was responding in part to a
much mythologized interpretation of Afrikaner history which suggested
that apartheid was the consequence of the racism of Afrikaners as well
as their stubborn commitment to doctrinaire neo-Calvinist thought.
Giliomee was also reacting to an alternative Marxist interpretation of
South African history which located the rise of Afrikaner nationalism as
an expression of class interests. Giliomee's outline of the development of
Afrikaner identity rests instead on the idea of 'ethnic mobilization' and
he argues that Afrikaner identity has undergone constant redefinition
in response to different historical circumstances. He recognizes that the
rise of modern Afrikaner nationalism in the first half of the twentieth
century was shaped by the desire to secure collective economic advantage, in particular to 'uplift' Afrikaans-speaking 'poor whites'. But it
also had a vital psychological and cultural dimension, affording a sense
of collective security and solidarity. In the post-1948 period Afrikaner
identity was powerfully asserted through apartheid ideology.
Underlying Afrikaners' insistence on protecting their political and
economic supremacy were lingering fears of their vulnerability.
According to Giliomee, apartheid was not a sacrosanct ideology. It was
first and foremost a means of securing group survival. From this it
followed that if the insistence on Afrikaner exclusivity was no longer
perceived to be in their own interests – as was increasingly apparent
from the mid-1970s – Afrikaners would be prepared to engage in a
painful process of personal redefinition and political reform.*

* * *

HERMANN GILIOMEE

Like the trim outline of Table Mountain seen from afar, Afrikaner identity appears to be a well-defined feature of the South African political landscape. Yet a look at history shows that this identity was much more blurred than this appearance suggests; indeed its boundaries were often adjusted in order to fit historical circumstances and social contexts. Even now, Afrikaner identity may be going through a decisive phase of redefinition and change.

It is not predictable how a group of people existing within a common cultural and kinship network will formulate its political identity and goals.[1] Ethnic groups require leaders who inspire them to think and act collectively in politics. Such leaders in turn depend on favourable social conditions in which men could be persuaded to shelve their individual and class differences for the sake of group mobilization. Ethnic identification occurs most strongly where a collection of individuals come to consider themselves communally deprived and believe that mobilization as a group would improve their position or where persons seek to protect the privileges they share with others against those who do not have them or whom they are exploiting collectively. The Afrikaners have known all these: the gradual awakening of ethnic consciousness, the leaders who fostered or fragmented it, the bitterness of being a despised minority, and, at present, the challenges to the privileges they enjoy as the dominant group in a deeply divided society.

The main contention of this chapter is that South Africa's institutionalized racism (the policies that distribute power, wealth and privileges unequally on a racial basis) can best be understood as the product of the Afrikaners' conception of their distinct place in the social structure. They have come to regard 'group-belongingness', group mobilization and the defence of the group position as positive responses that occur universally. Discrimination and prejudice are seldom justified as ends in themselves but as the inevitable consequence of the maintenance of ethnic rights and interests. In such a context discrimination and prejudice often rest more on the construction of group rights than on fear or scorn of an out-group.

This analysis attempts to outline the development of the Afrikaners' conception of themselves, with emphasis on the political self-conception. For this reason, considerable weight has been attached to the pronouncements of political leaders who sought to stimulate group concepts and articulate the group's

190

characteristics, rights and ideals. It is a survey of how Afrikaner identity has been shaped by both these conscious self-definitions and the social matrix of South Africa.

AFRIKANER IDENTITY IN THE TWENTIETH CENTURY

Different contexts shaped Afrikaner identity during the first half of the twentieth century. First there was the new political framework of the Union of South Africa, a member of the British Empire. The force of rapid industrialization left a deep imprint on Afrikaners who increasingly were being drawn or pushed to the cities. At the beginning of the century only 10 per cent of the Afrikaners lived in cities and villages; in 1911 this figure had risen to 29 per cent; in 1926 to 41 per cent; and in 1960 to 75 per cent.[2] The new industrial context called for new strategies: some Afrikaners abandoned their ethnic identity, others chose to underemphasize it, while still others decided that the assertion of Afrikaner identity would be the most advantageous course.

The Union of South Africa was a compromise between the determination of English-speaking whites to maintain the 'British connection' (the link with the Empire) and the deep desire of the vanquished republican Afrikaners for independence. The South African Party, which held power from 1910 to 1924, and the United Party, which ruled from 1934 to 1948, were imbued with this spirit of compromise. Although the background, interests and outlook of their members were highly diverse, these parties tried to integrate the white population into a nation consisting of the two white language groups. They were prepared to de-emphasize distinctions between these groups and strove towards greater homogeneity and mutual understanding. Their leaders, Generals Botha and Smuts, saw Afrikaners and English-speaking whites as flowing together in 'one stream'. Botha wished to 'create from all present elements a nationality; whoever had chosen South Africa as a home should regard themselves as children of one family and be known as South Africans'.[3] For some 'Sap-Afrikaners', as they were called, the new political order meant only accepting the British monarch as sovereign, for others it even meant the abandonment of parochial sentiments and loyalties in favour of membership in a magnificent world-wide civilization. Thus a Dr Niemeyer proclaimed at the time of

Union: 'We are all Britishers alike now. We have all accepted the British, and the majority of us ... wish to form one nation with you, to the glory of the British Empire.'[4]

A growing group of nationalists led by General Hertzog and Dr Malan rejected these strategies. Unlike the participants in the rebellion of 1914, Hertzog recognized the legitimacy of the new South African state. However, he insisted that it should develop a separate and independent political identity within the British Empire. And within the South African polity the Afrikaners should retain their unique 'nationality'. In stressing separateness, Hertzog staked a historical claim: he described the Afrikaners as pioneers of the 'South African civilization'. Because this group had played such a special role he was not prepared to have it assimilated, along with new arrivals and with those who had a double identity through their ties with England.[5] A minister of the Dutch Reformed Church, Malan was inclined to appeal to metaphysical notions. He viewed the continued existence of the Afrikaners as a separate entity, as part of a divine dispensation. In 1915 he stated: 'Ask the nation to lose itself in some other existing or as yet non-existent nation, and it will answer: by God's honour, never.'[6] He argued that the Afrikaner had a full right to cling to his nationality as something upheld by God through the years. National unity dared not be emphasized at the expense of a duality of the white population.[7]

Hertzog and Malan proposed that the streams of English and Afrikaner nationality should flow apart until the Afrikaner stream developed to the level of the English. There was also a white and black stream. Hertzog saw the differences in terms of civilization: the whites were the bearers of civilization; the blacks stood only on the first rungs of the 'civilized ladder'. It was the duty of the white to protect 'civilization' through the so-called civilized labour policies, while at the same time helping the 'natives' to make the 'transition between semi-barbarism and that of civilization'.[8] Hertzog regarded the Cape coloureds as already part of the white nation, politically and economically, although not socially.[9]

Hertzog and Malan from an early stage employed language as a mobilizing tool. In 1908 Malan stated: 'Raise the Afrikaans language to a written language, let it become the vehicle for our culture, our history, our national ideals, and you will also raise the people who speak it. . . . The Afrikaans Language Movement is nothing less than an awakening of our nation to self-awareness and to the vocation of adopting a more worthy position in world civilization.'[10] After the founding of the National Party in 1914 the Botha government came under frequent attack for having failed, for the sake of conciliation with the English, to press for equality of rights for Afrikaans. Through Botha's one-stream policy, it was alleged, the tender plant of Afrikaans culture would be swamped by the all-powerful English world culture. Only by keeping the cultural lives of the Afrikaners and English in two separate streams would Afrikaner nationality be maintained and developed.

The Nationalists also appealed to the psychological needs that ethnic identification met. For many Afrikaners there could be no question of conciliation with the English while the memories of conquest in war and concentration camps were still fresh in their minds. For Afrikaner Nationalists the alienation, anxiety and insecurity of the new order could only be reduced within the womb of ethnic collectivity. Only by stressing their ethnic identity could the humiliation of defeat and the cultural chauvinism of the English be overcome.

Ethnic identification, then, sought to attain political and cultural goals and meet diverse psychological needs. It was more than a struggle for material rewards, but the outcome of the Afrikaners' struggle in the economic field would be decisive in determining whether they would see themselves primarily as an ethnic group or as a class. In the twentieth century, Afrikaners who had been forced to migrate to the cities often entered the job market on the lowest rungs, hardly any higher than the equally unskilled black labour force and far beneath the skilled English worker. Viewed from a Nationalist perspective, the dominant feature of the South African economy was the vast gap between Afrikaner and English wealth (the ratio of the per capita incomes of the Afrikaner and English is estimated to have been as high as 100:300 in 1910).[11] But from a class perspective the obvious characteristic was the cleavage between the capitalists and workers in a system that exploited the largely unskilled and proletarianized Afrikaner and black labour.

For various reasons the Afrikaner workers ultimately assumed an ethnic rather than a class identity. The racial values formed in the eighteenth and nineteenth centuries militated against a class coalition across racial lines. However, more important than abstract racism was the existence of a split labour market in which whites, who were expected to maintain a distinctive standard of living, had to compete with blacks, who did not have to meet such expectations. Afrikaners objected to competition with blacks not so much because they were black but because they were offering their labour at a cheaper rate than whites could socially afford. For instance, in the cities blacks were prepared to do unskilled manual labour for two shillings a day during the period 1900–40; competing white workers were unwilling to accept a daily wage of less than three shillings and six pence, or sometimes five shillings.[12] When blacks in the 1930s and 1940s entered the semi-skilled ranks in industry at rates lower than those established for white workers, the same objections against cheap labour were raised. In denying that this amounted to racial discrimination, Malan argued that 'the white is really discriminated against in the labour market when he comes into competition with the non-white. The white man, because he is white, is expected – whatever his chances in the labour market – to maintain a white standard of living . . . you can understand that in the circumstances the competition for the white man is killing'.[13]

The political order formed another obstacle to a class identity. In 1910 every white male was given a vote. Most Afrikaner workers looked to political action to promote their material interests. They did not identify from the outset with the Nationalist movement and its attempt to establish separate Christian-National trade unions. Many joined the English-speaking white workers in the trade union movement and the Labour Party. However, they gradually lost their tenuous identification with the white working-class movement as they came to regard the Labour Party as an ally of British imperialism and the trade union movement as being led by foreigners who in some cases concluded agreements with management against the workers' interests.[14]

In 1937 out of 118 trade union organizations about 100 had non-Afrikaner secretaries although the majority of members were Afrikaners. These trade union leaders fatally underrated the force of ethnic sentiments. One of the few who did realize this was E.B. Sachs, a well-known English trade union leader who was most successful in fostering a class consciousness among Afrikaner workers that transcended racial cleavages. He stated:

The workers' organizations looked upon the Afrikaner people with an air of disdain. . . . The Labour Movement . . . failed almost entirely to try to appreciate fully the development, tradition, sentiments and aspirations of the masses of Afrikaners . . . as a people which suffered cultural, economic and political oppression. People of a ruling race, including even class conscious workers, usually fail to understand the feelings of a conquered nation, of an oppressed people.[15]

In the 1930s the Afrikaner's quest for identity entered a new stage when the United Party was established, fusing Hertzog's National Party with the pro-Empire South African Party of Jan Smuts. Equally significant was the vast influx of Afrikaners in the 1920s and 1930s into industry in semi-skilled operative positions. For the followers of Malan's 'purified' National Party, fusion constituted a material threat. They anticipated that big capital, especially mining capital, would become predominant in the United Party. This would split the whites into a capitalist and working class and would enable the capitalists to replace un- or semi-skilled Afrikaner workers by cheaper black labour. Moreover, South Africa's almost neo-colonial economic dependence on the British Empire would increase and would make a mockery of formal political independence. The attack on the joint enemies of imperialism and capitalism was led by a group of men usually labelled in a class analysis as 'petty bourgeois': Afrikaans lawyers, teachers, professors and lower-level civil servants whose career opportunities were limited by the increasing influence of the English language and imperialist values under United Party rule. Especially in the Transvaal this group was politically isolated because farming capital in the north supported the capitalist United Party. This left the white workers as the only potential political ally. For the petty bourgeoisie, fusion posed the threat of the Afrikaner workers becoming denationalized in the process of mobilizing themselves on a class base. Should this happen, there was no hope of an Afrikaner party winning power and using the state to promote the interests of the Afrikaners at large and those of the petty bourgeoisie in particular.[16]

An orthodox class analysis, however, does not provide an adequate answer to the question of why the 'purified' version of Afrikaner nationalism became a driving force in such a comparatively short time. As important as material interests were cultural and psychosocial fears and needs to which a strategy of ethnic mobilization could address itself. Fusion presupposed competition on an equal footing of the young and fragile Afrikaans culture with the rich British world culture. The purified Nationalists claimed that this would end in the Afrikaans culture being swamped. Fusion also embodied reconciliation with English-speaking South Africa. The Nationalists argued that this was a chimera before the Afrikaners had asserted themselves economically and culturally against the richer and more worldly-wise section of the white population. Lastly, fusion represented the strengthening of the political ties with Britain and an entrenchment of the duality of national and imperial symbols. For the Nationalists these imperial symbols did not evoke a sense of pride in membership in the British Empire but reminded them on the contrary that their nation had not yet taken its place in the row of independent nations of the world.

To understand these Afrikaner goals and sentiments, they should be viewed within the context of the deep psychosocial fears and resentments that many Afrikaners experienced in the 1930s and 1940s. The dislocation of rapid urbanization at a comparatively late stage instilled in them a deep sense of insecurity. In a society in which urban and capitalist values predominated, the Afrikaners not only were from a rural origin and the poorest white group but also were perceived as culturally backward and lacking in sophistication. It was middle-class Afrikaners, particularly educators and clergy, who were most attracted to a strategy of ethnic mobilization to overcome the deep feelings of insecurity and social inferiority that plagued Afrikaners. It was they who disseminated the ethnic gospel that self-realization and human worth could only come through group identification and assertion. It was because the 1930s was such a traumatic period for these Afrikaners that they would be so attracted to the radical 'solution' of apartheid.

Both Hertzog and Malan tried to mobilize the electorate by exploiting the concept of Afrikanerdom and both defined it in ways that suited their political strategies. Hertzog, in attempting to build a cross-ethnic middle-class base, wished to make the term an inclusive political concept. He proclaimed the rise of a 'new Afrikanerdom' consisting of Afrikaans and English-speaking whites – 'equal Afrikaners'[17] – who subscribed to the

196

principles of South Africa First, and of full equality between the two white groups. In contrast, Malan's political strategy was to unify politically the Afrikaners who constituted more than 50 per cent of the electorate. For the Cape Nationalists, who dominated the party, an Afrikaner was someone whose home language was Afrikaans. Religion and political views were not qualifying factors.[18]

Malan's Purified National Party hoped to mobilize the Afrikaners by staking group claims based on the notion that Afrikaners occupied a special place in the South African society. Politically it rejected the compromise of Fusion and called for republican independence. It argued that until a republic had been established justice would not have been done to the Afrikaners. National unity was only possible if the English-speaking section became part of the new South African nation of whom the indigenous Afrikaner people was the core. In the economic field the Afrikaners were urged to unite as an interest group to close the gap between Afrikaner and English wealth and to protect the poor white from competition with blacks, which could lead to the disintegration of the white race and 'semi-barbarism'. Culturally, the party demanded a two-stream approach entailing mother-tongue education and separate educational, student, cultural and religious societies in order to restore the Afrikaners' self-confidence and liberate them from their sense of inferiority.[19]

The most significant achievement of the National Party in the 1930s was to rally most of the intellectual élite of the Afrikaners behind its cause. These men were 'cultural enterpreneurs'[20] who made extensive use of the Afrikaner Broederbond to ideologize Afrikaner identity and history. This northern-controlled secret organization with extensive influence in Afrikaner educational institutions believed that only by imbuing the Afrikaners with the sense that they were members of an exclusive *volk* could they be mobilized to pursue the National Party goals aimed at safeguarding the future of Afrikanerdom. The Broederbond spread the doctrine of Christian-Nationalism, which held that nations were products of a Divine Will, each with a diversity of allotted tasks and distinguished from each other by their separate culture. From this followed that certain political, cultural and spiritual values were a prerequisite for membership in the Afrikaner ethnic group. These were predominantly bourgeois values with little appeal for workers. Concerned with winning their support, Broederbond thinkers such as Nico Diederichs and Piet Meyer defined the *volk* almost in pre-industrial terms: the Afrikaners were an organic unity in which workers and capitalists had an assigned place and function with corresponding rights and duties. To these thinkers true Afrikaners would never exploit a fellow Afrikaner but would protect and support him.[21]

The cultural entrepreneurs also ideologized Afrikaner history. A recent study by Dunbar Moodie points out how central events in the Afrikaners' history such as Blood River, the Wars of Independence and the concentration camps were woven together in a 'sacred history' in which God had repeatedly revealed Himself to the Afrikaners as a chosen people. Moodie argues that the sacred history constituted a civil religion and that after the emotion-charged commemoration of the Great Trek in 1938 the ordinary Afrikaner had made the main themes of the civil religion part of his own emotional identity. Indeed by 1938 'most Afrikaners believed that they belonged to an elect People'.[22]

Moodie's work is the most sophisticated on Afrikaner ideology yet, but it is difficult to imagine the majority of Afrikaners at this stage conceiving of themselves as an elect people with a sacred history. Cultural entrepreneurs may spice their speeches with such notions but for an audience it was enough to be told that they were a separate people with particular interests that could best be promoted through mobilization. By 1938 the feeling of belonging to a distinct political entity had grown considerably but it only made a major breakthrough after 1939 when a rival political identity was crippled. This was Hertzog's concept of an Afrikaans- and English-speaking *volk* united in a new Afrikanerdom which was shattered in 1939 when the Smuts faction of the United Party took South Africa into the Second World War on the side of Britain. It rekindled all the old anti-British and anti-imperialist sentiments and was ultimately decisive in persuading the majority of the Afrikaners to go it alone politically.[23] Afrikaners now more readily accepted civil religion as part of their identity, but even leaders did not subscribe as faithfully to its tenets as historians imagine. Malan, leader and prophet of the Purified Nationalists, remarked by 1946 that the Afrikaners did not, as outsiders alleged, consider themselves as a uniquely chosen people.

The truth is that the Afrikaner ... generally speaking retained his sense of religion. As a natural consequence his nationhood is rooted in religious grounds: in his personal fate, as in that of his people, he sees the hand of God. ... But that he claims this as his exclusive right and thus raises his people above others as God's special favourite is a false and slanderous allegation.[24]

In 1948 the Afrikaners won exclusive political power. In the standard literature the common assumption is that they could only do so by exploiting the Afrikaners' racist sentiments. From this perspective the election of 1948 was clinched by the ideology of apartheid. There are serious problems with this interpretation. In the political campaign preceding this election, Nationalists often suggested that racial policies should not be allowed to become a political issue between the two parties. Some argued that the only hope South Africa had of solving its racial problem lay in taking the issue out of political contention.[25] The electoral victory was in fact ensured by a decisive measure of Afrikaner unity. The appeal of the apartheid platform to classes such as the workers and the farmers was no doubt an important factor in attracting support for the National Party, but equally important were the party's demands for South African national independence, its promotion of Afrikaner business interests, and its championing of the Afrikaans culture. Or to put it differently, apart from 'putting the Kaffer in his place', 1948 also meant to the Afrikaners – particularly the professionals, educators and civil servants – 'getting *our* country back' or 'feeling at home once again in *our* country'.

With single-minded vigour the National Party set out after its victory to entrench its political control. In its endeavour to make the country safe for Afrikanerdom it set up a bulwark of restrictive racial legislation. However, no laws could ultimately prevent the growing dependence on a voteless labour force and the consequences flowing from that. This realization only gradually penetrated. Twenty years after the electoral victory an Afrikaans paper editorialized: 'Every white person will have to be made to recognize that there is a race problem in South Africa. How this knowledge can be brought to the whites is a problem nobody has as yet solved.'[26]

POWER, UNITY AND IDENTITY, 1948–78

After 1948 Afrikaner political power and ethnic unity gradually reinforced and consolidated each other.[27] It has often been assumed that the cohesiveness of the National Party should be ascribed to a rigid adherence to the ideology of apartheid. However, central to the party's concerns was not so much the apartheid ideology but the need to maintain Afrikaner unity as a prerequisite for the promotion of Afrikaner interests. If there was any dominant ideology it was one that stressed the values of *volkseenheid* (folk unity), which transcended class or regional (the North–South antagonism) differences, and *volksverbondenheid*, the notion that the realization of the full human potential comes not from individual self-assertion but through identification with and service of the *volk* (people).[28] The indispensable support English-speaking whites provided in maintaining the racial order worked against advocating Afrikaner hegemony too openly. But the same purpose was served by espousing Afrikaner unity. The policy of apartheid should be seen as an instrument that structures the South African polity in such a way that it fosters and conceals Afrikaner hegemony.[29] However, it is unity that is of decisive importance rather than the official policy that is not considered untouchable.

To ensure that a sense of ethnic identity remains the major determinant of political behaviour in a changing world, the values of the group and its attitudes towards other groups are constantly redefined. Such redefinitions draw on new insights into the causes of past conflicts and future challenges to the Afrikaner power structure. In the thirty years that the Afrikaners have held exclusive power their ethnic identifications have remained constant. None the less in different times different aspects of their identity were stressed. During the period 1948–59 the central theme in the Afrikaners' self-concept was the paradox of an insecure white people in need of legislation to ensure its survival. Their thinking was racist to the extent that miscegenation was considered an evil that would lead to the degeneration of their race. Absent, however, was the belief that the superior will naturally prevail over the inferior. The Afrikaner politicians of 1948–58 were a rising middle class who feared their English and black adversaries as much as they distrusted their own lower class to maintain separateness and purity of race. They had to be educated in a proper sense of colour to maintain proper behaviour; and they had to be instructed along the paths of apartheid to ensure that the white man would remain master. To allow social intercourse would be to allow familiarity to breed, blurring the sense of colour distinctions. Legal lines had to be drawn in order to establish white as well as black in their 'proper' place in society.

In the legislation two considerations were inextricably linked: without a privileged position the Afrikaners could not survive as a separate people; without safeguarding the racial separateness of the people a privileged position could not be maintained. The words of J.G. Strijdom illustrate this connection:

> If the European [white] loses his colour sense, he cannot remain a white man. . . . On the basis of unity you cannot retain your sense of colour if there is no *apartheid* in the everyday social life, in the political sphere or whatever sphere it may be, and if there is no residential separation . . . South Africa can only remain a white country if we continue to see that the Europeans remain the dominant nation; and we can only remain the dominant nation if we have the power to govern the country and if the Europeans, by means of their efforts, remain the dominant section.[30]

The outcome of these views was the 1949 Mixed Marriages Act and 1950 Immorality Act, which prohibit sexual intercourse across racial lines; the 1950 Population Registration Act, which compels every citizen to have an identity certificate showing his 'race'; and the 1953 Reservation of Separate Amenities Act, which segregates post offices, stations, trains, park benches, hospitals, beaches and swimming pools. The Group Areas Act provided for separate residential areas for lower-class Afrikaners unable to 'buy their apartheid'. Political power was safeguarded by removing the coloureds from the existing voting rolls, thus forestalling a coloured–English coalition, which in theory was strong enough to end Afrikaner rule.

Verwoerd's term as Prime Minister (1958–66) saw a shift in attitudes. With the colour lines firmly drawn, the Afrikaners, who had gained full political independence with the establishment of the Republic (1961), now emphasized their separate nationhood rather than their separateness as a race. In line with the universal rejection of racism, government spokesmen did not view blacks as innately inferior. Rather than different races they were considered different nations even if they did not agree with the official definition of their identity. Like the Afrikaners, they simply had to accept the values of ethnic identity and ethnic identification in evolving towards a separate nationhood. The unspoken assumption was, however, that their historical and cultural heritage made them unprepared to exercise political power too soon. Because of these differences, contact between the various peoples had to be restricted to the minimum since it would deter the non-white peoples from evolving along their own lines. Bedazzled by Verwoerd, many Afrikaner intellectuals for a decade believed with some fervour that apartheid was the restructuring of South Africa according to a vision of justice, all with a view to lasting peace, progress, and prosperity. For this brief period there was indeed a sense of purpose, dedication, and destiny.[31]

Under Vorster there has been a further shift. Having made great material progress, the Afrikaners of the 1970s increasingly see themselves as a politically based class with vested interests. There was little to fear of the deracializing and denationalizing influences that haunted them in the 1950s. Their ethnicity was now expressed in identification with the South African state and the symbols of the state which had become fully Afrikanerized.[32] At the same time they no longer believed the rhetoric of the 1960s that apartheid will bring about the social harmony of 'separate freedoms'. It has become much clearer that apartheid maintains white power, wealth and privileges – usually subsumed under the code words 'white identity'. Economic discrimination is no longer justified in ideological terms but in terms of the 'economic' or 'political realities' that do not allow the gap between black and white wealth to be narrowed more rapidly. Racist rhetoric is seldom heard in the public life, nor is the unspoken assumption of Verwoerd that the historical differences of blacks will impede their progress. Instead Vorster has emphasized that differences do not constitute inferiority. He frequently states that 'the policy of separate development was conceived not because we considered ourselves better than others ... we created the policy of separate development because we maintained that we were different from others and valued that difference, and we are not prepared to sacrifice that difference'.[33]

No longer is there a biological justification of white domination; instead history is called in to legitimize group claims.

Whereas during the first half of the century whites argued that in view of their superior civilization they had the right to rule over all of South Africa, Vorster claimed that whites have the *historical* right to maintain their sovereignty in 'white' South Africa: 'We have our land and we alone will have the say over that land. We have our Parliament and in that Parliament we and we alone will be represented.'[34]

Afrikaner Nationalists can now criticize the apartheid policy in a forthright way without being considered disloyal as long as the criticism is considered to serve the purpose of internal peace and prosperity. A leading editor could write with reference to the failures of apartheid: 'Human plans are not sacrosanct. If they do not work they must be changed and refurbished. To elevate them to the status of untouchable truths and eternally valid slogans, might be politically expedient in the short run but would be nationally harmful and disastrous in the long run.'[35] Gerrit Viljoen, head of the Afrikaner Broederbond, stated: 'Apartheid is not an ideology nor a dogma. It is a method, a road along which we are moving and is subject to fundamental reassessment.'[36]

NOTES

1 My theoretical understanding of group identification has been influenced most by Herbert Blumer, 'Race Prejudice as a Sense of Group Position', in J. Musuoka and P. Valien (eds), *Race Relations: Problems and Theory* (Chapel Hill: University of North Carolina Press, 1964); Heribert Adam, *Modernizing Racial Domination* (Berkeley: University of California Press, 1971); and Nathan Glazer and Daniel P. Moynihan, *Ethnicity: Theory and Experience* (Cambridge, MA: Harvard University Press, 1976).
2 F.A. van Jaarsveld, *Stedelike Geskiedenis as Navorsingsveld vir die Suid-Afrikaanse Historikus* (Johannesburg: Randse Afrikaanse Universiteit, 1973), 16.
3 C.P. Mulder and W.A. Cruywagen, *Die Eerste Skof van die Nasionale Party in Transvaal, 1914–1964* (Johannesburg: Voortrekkerpers, 1964), 13; W.K. Hancock, *Smuts*, vol. 1, *The Sanguine Years* (Cambridge, 1962), 361.
4 Sheila Patterson, *The Last Trek: A Study of the Boer People and the Afrikaner Nation* (London: Routledge and Kegan Paul, 1957), 97.
5 C.M. van den Heever, *Generaal J.B.M. Hertzog* (Johannesburg: APB, 1943), 301–11.
6 *Glo in u Volk: Dr. D.F. Malan as Redenaar, 1908–1954*, edited by S.W. Pienaar (Cape Town: Tafelberg, 1964), 16.
7 A.H. Marais, 'Die Politieke Uitwerking van die Verhouding van die

Afrikaanssprekende tot die Engelssprekende, 1910–1915', PhD dissertation, University of the Orange Free State (1972), 588.

8 *Gedenkboek Generaal J.B.M. Hertzog*, edited by P.J. Nienaber (Johannesburg: APB, 1965), 233–42.

9 C.M. Tatz, *Shadow and Substance in South Africa: A Study in Land and Franchise Policies Affecting Africans 1910–1960* (Pietermaritzburg: University of Natal Press, 1962), 46.

10 Pienaar, *Glo in u Volk*, 175.

11 Personal communication, J.L. Sadie.

12 J. Lever, 'White Strategies in a Divided Society: The Development of South African Labour Policy', unpublished paper, 3.

13 Union of South Africa, House of Assembly Debates (1939), col. 5524.

14 Dan O'Meara, 'Analysing Afrikaner Nationalism: The "Christian-National" Assault on White Trade Unionism in South Africa, 1934–1948', *African Affairs*, vol. 77, issue 306 (January, 1978), 45–72.

15 *Forward*, 15 July 1938.

16 This paragraph and the preceding one are based on two excellent studies by O'Meara, 'Analysing Afrikaner Nationalism', and 'The Afrikaner Broederbond 1927–1948: Class Vanguard of Afrikaner Nationalism', *Journal of Southern African Studies*, 3, 2 (1977), 156–86. It will be seen that my analysis differs from O'Meara in that I attach separate weight to the factors of ethnicity and class.

17 For an analysis of statements such as these see D.J. Kriek, 'Generaal J.B.M. Hertzog se Opvattings oor die Afrikaans-en Engelssprekendes na Uniewording', PhD dissertation, University of Pretoria (1971).

18 Phil Weber, *Republiek en Nasionale Eenheid*, Hertzog Memorial Lecture, University of Stellenbosch (1973).

19 See Malan's series of articles entitled 'Op die Wagtoring', published in *Die Burger*, particularly the articles published on 16 and 23 December 1933.

20 The term is used by Crawford Young, *The Politics of Cultural Pluralism* (Madison: University of Wisconsin Press, 1976), 45.

21 O'Meara, 'Analysing Afrikaner Nationalism'.

22 T. Dunbar Moodie, *The Rise of Afrikanerdom* (Berkeley: University of California Press, 1975).

23 See the argument of Newell M. Stultz, *The Nationalists in Opposition, 1934–1948* (Cape Town: Human and Rousseau, 1974).

24 See his unpublished manuscript 'Op die Wagtoring', c.1946, D.F. Malan collection, Carnegie Library, University of Stellenbosch.

25 Stultz, *The Nationalists in Opposition*, 136–43.

26 *Die Transvaler* cited by William R. Frye, *In Whitest Africa* (Englewood Cliffs, NJ: Prentice-Hall, 1968), 104.

27 F. van Zyl Slabbert, 'Afrikaner Nationalism, White Politics, and Political Change in South Africa', in Leonard Thompson and Jeffrey Butler (eds), *Change in Contemporary South Africa* (Berkeley: University of California Press, 1975), 3–19. This short piece is the best analysis of the sociology of Afrikaner nationalism.

28 For a further analysis see A. James Gregor, *Contemporary Racial Ideologies* (New York, 1968), 221–76. Gregor gives a succinct account,

based on primary sources, of the ideology of apartheid. My analysis differs from his in that I do not consider separate development as the dominant ideology.

29 André du Toit, 'Ideological Change, Afrikaner Nationalism and Pragmatic Racial Domination in South Africa', in *Change in Contemporary South Africa*, 37.
30 Tatz, *Shadow and Substance*, 133.
31 W.A. de Klerk, *The Puritans in Africa* (Harmondsworth: Penguin, 1975).
32 Stanley J. Morse, J.W. Mann and Elizabeth Nel, 'National Identity in a "Multi-National" State: A Comparison of Afrikaners and English-Speaking South Africans', *Canadian Review of Studies in Nationalism*, 2, 2 (1977), 225–46.
33 Hermann Giliomee, 'The Development of the Afrikaner's Self-Concept', in H.W. van der Merwe (ed.), *Looking at the Afrikaner Today* (Cape Town: Tafelberg, 1975), 27. The Minister of Justice, Mr Kruger, told Chief Gatsha Buthelezi recently: 'I accept you as my brother. I accept the black man of Africa as my black brother. . . . But he's a different nation and this is the whole point and that nobody can go against history', *The Star*, 3 December 1977.
34 Giliomee, 'Development', 28.
35 *Die Burger*, 25 September 1972.
36 John de St. Jorre, *A House Divided* (New York: Carnegie Endowment, 1977), 13.

9

THE MEANING OF APARTHEID BEFORE 1948:

Conflicting interests and forces within the Afrikaner Nationalist alliance

Deborah Posel

In this contribution, Deborah Posel, a Witwatersrand University sociologist, questions two views of apartheid that were common until the mid-1980s: on the one hand, the perception of liberal critics that apartheid was a seamless 'grand design' created and implemented by Afrikaner zealots; on the other hand, a Marxist interpretation that sought to explain apartheid ideology in terms of the competing interests of different 'fractions of capital'. By carefully disentangling the different elements which comprised the Afrikaner nationalist alliance in the 1940s, Posel argues that the meaning and intent of apartheid was strongly contested from within. Posel stresses the tensions between those idealists who believed in 'total' apartheid (a position that implied dispensing with African labour and creating wholly self-sufficient African 'homelands') and the pragmatists who sought to implement apartheid without abandoning the migrant labour system. She shows how this competing conception of apartheid was reflected in the landmark Sauer Commission Report of 1947 which played an important role in articulating the apartheid vision. In view of these incompatible positions, Posel concludes that the Sauer Report was unable to develop a logically coherent blueprint for apartheid and that it remained ambiguous on crucial issues – most notably, the continuation of migrant labour. The historiographical significance of Posel's contribution lies both in her re-evaluation of the relationship between ideological and material factors, and also in her rejection of theories that see apartheid as the working out of a long-term grand plan.

* * *

206

In 1948, an alliance of Afrikaner nationalist groupings, rallying together under the shared ideological slogan of 'apartheid', brought the Herenigde Nasionale Party (HNP) into power in South Africa. What was it about the notion of apartheid that won the support of Afrikaners from businessmen, farmers and workers, to teachers, academics, lawyers and journalists?[1] Several studies of apartheid[2] attribute the power and appeal of the term to the fact that it accommodated the distinct interests of each member of the Afrikaner nationalist alliance within a single policy blueprint. The substance of this blueprint, it is argued, was outlined in the Sauer Report commissioned by the HNP to develop wide-ranging solutions to the country's 'colour problems'. Moreover, this Report equipped the newly elected Nationalist government with the 'grand plan' which informed the substance of apartheid policies from 1948 onwards.[3]

This article disputes such a view of the meaning of apartheid before 1948 and its implications for the nature of policy-making after 1948. It is argued that while Afrikaner nationalists shared a single (albeit rudimentary) ideological discourse on apartheid and a basic commitment to white supremacy, they had conflicting ideas about how white supremacy was best preserved. Incompatible versions of the apartheid blueprint thus emerged. The term apartheid won the support of Afrikaner nationalists across the board because it successfully described and legitimized the Afrikaner cause in an ideological discourse sufficiently ambiguous to accommodate these conflicting versions of apartheid policy. Furthermore, the Sauer Report reproduced rather than resolved these divisions, in the form of an internally contradictory blueprint. The significance of this discussion of apartheid pre-1948 then lies in refuting the popular view that policy-making after 1948 consisted in the systematic implementation of a ready-made blueprint. Indeed, it is suggested in conclusion that explanations of state policy in the 1950s must go beyond simply the interests of the Afrikaner nationalist alliance, to include various non-Afrikaner interests and powers – notably English-speaking capitalist lobbies and the African 'struggle from below'.

Dan O'Meara's important and pioneering study of Afrikaner nationalism, Volkskapitalisme, includes an analysis of the development of the 'apartheid idea' during the 1940s which has strongly influenced subsequent scholarship. The discussion following is therefore developed by way of a critique of O'Meara's position on this issue.

Debunking the myth of monolithic Afrikanerdom, O'Meara explains the growth of the Afrikaner nationalist movement as a class alliance, 'based on Transvaal, Cape and Orange Free State farmers, specific categories of white labour, the Afrikaner petty-bourgeoisie', Afrikaner industrialists and financiers.[4] Organized and co-ordinated by the Broederbond, this alliance was spearheaded by the 'economic movement' in the drive to advance Afrikaner economic prospects, and by 1948 was championed politically by the National Party under D.F. Malan. He argues that this party political alliance was associated with an overall Afrikaner nationalist consensus concerning the policies for which the National Party stood – namely, apartheid, because it simultaneously accommodated the class interests of each class grouping within the alliance. In O'Meara's words, by 1948 apartheid, although still 'a vague concept', nevertheless already

> crystallized and condensed the responses of various class forces to . . . the social transformations wrought by capitalist development during the war [of 1939–45]. . . . It reflected the farmers' concern over their declining labour supply and inability to compete for labour against the higher wages paid in industry and commerce. It encompassed the concern of emerging Afrikaner business for a cheap labour policy to ensure their own accumulation. And it pandered to the fears of specific strata of white workers at being displaced in the new industrial division of labour by cheaper African labour.[5]

O'Meara argues, moreover, that the development of this 'apartheid idea' was bound up first and foremost with the economic movement, in deference to the economic priorities of Afrikaner capital: '[The] emerging emphasis [during the 1940s] on the "Native question" concerned itself with the conditions of accumulation for a fledgling capitalist class'.[6] The meaning of apartheid which then emerged was an expression of the ideological hegemony of Afrikaner capital within the economic movement and the Nationalist alliance as a whole.[7] Thus by 1948, claims O'Meara, 'the ideology of Afrikaner capital formed the core component of Nationalist ideology'.[8]

As evidence of the hegemony of Afrikaner capital in the formulation of apartheid, O'Meara cites the fact that the notion of apartheid as a 'total segregation' was never taken seriously, since such a system would have disrupted the process of capitalist accumulation by prescribing the withdrawal of African labour from white areas.

> Except for a few intellectual visionaries locked in the Afrikaner ivory towers, apartheid . . . was never intended to imply the total economic segregation of the races. It was designed to secure and control the supply of labour for all capitalists, not to deprive any employer of it.[9]

He thus dismisses the 'total segregation' blueprint as an impotent and closeted academic vision which never featured as a serious or popular option on the agenda of Afrikaner politics during the decade.

O'Meara argues, furthermore, that within Afrikaner capital, agriculture was the dominant fraction. The class interests of Afrikaner financiers and industrialists were tied to those of the farmers, since the mobilization of farmers' capital within the economic movement fuelled the advance of Afrikaner business. The concept of apartheid was thus first and foremost a solution to the problems of farmers within the Nationalist alliance. In O'Meara's words, 'apartheid sought primarily to secure a stable labour supply for agriculture'; the 'most important' principle governing the formulation of apartheid 'was the need to secure the labour supply of agriculture in the face of the massive movement of labour from the rural to the industrial areas'.[10]

This article takes issue with O'Meara on several counts. It is argued that by 1948, incompatible conceptions of apartheid co-existed within Afrikanerdom. Notwithstanding their common ideological ground, these versions of apartheid differed over a basic question: the relationship between 'political segregation' and the 'economic integration' of Africans in 'white' areas. Furthermore, the version of apartheid expounded by Afrikaner capital was neither hegemonic nor uncontested within the Nationalist alliance. Indeed, the Sauer Report, accepted by O'Meara as an expression of that hegemony, was a symptom of exactly its absence.

All versions of apartheid developed from a common starting point – a shared perception of the need to protect white supremacy and preserve the 'purity of the white race'.[11]

Ideologically this premise was articulated and defended in the language of 'separate development'. 'Separate development' referred to the road out of the country's present 'quagmire' of interracial mixing, by allocating the different races territorially separate 'homes', in which each could maintain its cultural distinctiveness, exercise political rights and acquire wealth and education separately from one another.[12]

Neither the dedication to white supremacy nor the notion of 'separate development' were new or unique to the Afrikaners. But both were expressed in a novel and distinctive way, as constituting the Afrikaners' divine mission, the service entrusted by God to the Afrikaner nation (*volk*) acting on behalf of the white race.[13] As the vanguard of white supremacy, the Afrikaner *volk* simultaneously fulfilled its 'natural' role as 'trustee' (*voog*) of the African peoples, by undertaking to protect their distinct ethnic and cultural identities.[14]

By the late 1940s, Afrikaner nationalists shared the view that the preservation of white supremacy required new forms of state intervention. The rapid expansion of manufacturing during the war years had increased the urban demand for African labour. This, coupled with widespread rural impoverishment, had stimulated a massive increase in the size of the urban African proletariat. Their burdens of poverty and overcrowding, coupled with rising political expectations, accounted for mounting disaffection and militancy in the townships and on the shop floor.

Afrikaner nationalists were divided, however, in their views on the lengths to which the state would have to go in order to arrest the threat of further more powerful and aggressive mass resistance, and protect a system of 'political segregation'. One faction remained confident that the problem was simply one of control, produced by a weak United Party government. Threats to the political and economic order could be quashed without the state having to evict Africans from 'white' South Africa and its economic structure. The opposing faction, however, perceived the political turbulence of the late 1940s as a symptom of the ultimate incompatibility between a system of political segregation and continuing white dependence on African labour. In their view, since this 'economic integration' of Africans in 'white' South Africa lay at the root of the problem, measures to extricate African labour from the 'white' areas would be indispensable.

The following discussion shows briefly how different

Afrikaner class interests were largely responsible for their conflicting responses to the issue of Africans' 'economic integration'. It was precisely because the Afrikaner nationalist alliance comprised an alliance of class groupings that consensus was *not* reached over the meaning of apartheid. The subsequent section then examines the political significance and manifestations of this division.

THE SOUTH AFRICAN BUREAU OF RACIAL AFFAIRS' (SABRA'S) CONCEPTION OF APARTHEID

SABRA was created in 1947, at the instigation of the Broederbond, in order to undertake 'the scientific study of the country's racial problem [and] the promotion of sound racial policy'.[15]

Taking an unconditional commitment to white economic and political supremacy as its starting point, SABRA developed its concept of apartheid as 'total segregation' through a critique of the 'logic' of 'economic integration'. The greater the whites' economic dependence on African labour, argued SABRA, the greater the powers of the African working class to endanger white economic prosperity by withholding its labour power. In SABRA's eyes, the 1940s had demonstrated the already substantial powers of African trade unionism. It would be both unfair and impossible, it was argued, to withhold full trade union rights from Africans indefinitely, and once they were conferred, the privileged position of the white worker would be toppled.[16] Unless white dependence on African labour was systematically diminished, political rights for Africans in 'white' areas were likewise a matter of time. For, argued SABRA, 'economic integration' entailed that Africans were *de facto* a permanent part of the country's population, in their capacity as workers in residence. The denial of the vote to these Africans was not only 'immoral'; it would also become increasingly the target of more vociferous and powerful African opposition. As the economic bargaining strengths, standards of living and levels of education of urban Africans grew, so too would their political expectations and powers. The edifice of white supremacy was thus destined to fall as long as it was premised on 'economic integration'.[17]

For SABRA, then, apartheid, as a recipe for the preservation

of white supremacy, necessitated segregation on all fronts –
economic, as well as political, territorial, social, cultural and
educational. There could be no half-measures in which whites
enjoyed political supremacy without forgoing access to an abundant supply of African labour.

As SABRA was well aware, by the 1940s white farmers, businessmen and mining companies alike had become increasingly
dependent on African labour in a growing number and variety of
jobs. The extrication of African labour from the white economy
would therefore be a difficult and slow process. Yet, argued
SABRA, it was possible to achieve this goal without bringing the
economy to its knees. It was a 'major fallacy' to assume that 'if
Native labour were withdrawn from farms, industries and
domestic service, the whole economy would be dislocated and the
country would tumble to ruin'.[18] Besides, said SABRA, African
workers were less of an economic asset than customarily claimed.
Their productivity was low, and the high turnover of African
labour was costly for white employers.[19]

Still, SABRA was careful to emphasize, nevertheless, that it did
not advocate the immediate and wholesale withdrawal of all
African labour from the white economy. Rather, the process
would be slow and controlled, to minimize the economic inconvenience. It was conceded, however, that some measure of
economic disruption would probably be inescapable. But then,
for SABRA, white supremacy necessitated economic sacrifices for
the sake of a higher political and moral good.[20]

Progress towards 'economic segregation' would be slow, but
immediate steps could be taken. The size of the existing urban
African workforce could be pared considerably by improving
productivity: 'Gradual withdrawal of Native labour should . . .
be correlated with substitution of even more efficient European
and mechanized labour.'[21] Such economic strategies should be
accompanied by the ongoing removal of African families from
the urban areas, so as gradually to reverse the process of urbanization. The influx of African families into the urban areas also
had to be stopped. Only migrant workers (in declining numbers)
should be permitted into the urban areas, to meet diminishing
white needs for African labour during the transition to complete
segregation.[22] SABRA stressed that the use of migrant labour
should only be a temporary expedient. In principle, the system
had a destructive effect on both family life and agricultural

productivity in the reserves, since male breadwinners were absent for long periods.[23]

SABRA insisted that each of these onslaughts on 'economic integration' only made sense in the context of an immediate, vigorous effort to 'develop' the reserves, to the point where they could ultimately absorb the returning urbanized African population. The reserves ought to become self-sufficient economic units in their own right, as opposed to being merely reservoirs of labour for white industries and agriculture. This, SABRA conceded, might well require the extension of the reserve land – the immediate interests of white farmers notwithstanding.[24]

APARTHEID AS SEEN WITHIN THE FEDERATION OF AFRIKAANS CULTURAL ORGANIZATIONS (FAK)

At least one of the members of the FAK, the Instituut Vir Volkswelstand, shared SABRA's vision of apartheid as a blueprint for 'total segregation' on all fronts, economic included. This Institute explained its position on the subject in its submission to the Fagan Commission in 1946, on which the following discussion is based.

The basis of the Institute's memorandum was its conviction that

the urbanization of Africans conflicts with the accepted policy of segregation, and therefore the state must institute all possible controls on the influx of natives into the cities, until whites can satisfy the demand for labour from within their own ranks, after which complete segregation must be implemented.[25]

Both migrant African labour and an urbanized African labour supply were deemed undesirable, albeit for different reasons. The migrant labour system was pernicious because it made for the unproductive use of cheap African labour and caused 'detribalization', which in turn eroded tribal authority and culture.[26] But the prospect of an urbanized African workforce was even less appealing because it signified the permanent integration of Africans into the 'white' areas and economic life of the country.[27] Better, they argued, to refrain from using African labour altogether and find an alternative labour supply instead.

213

The memorandum proposed a number of means to this end. The country should be divided into 'labour districts'. The number of Africans presently employed in each area should be frozen. This would then constitute the maximum quota of African labour to which employers in these districts would be entitled in the future. This strategy would force employers to look elsewhere for labour, so that gradually their dependence on African labour would decline. The Institute also called on the state to initiate a concerted white immigration policy to enlarge the country's supply of white labour. For the same reason, white South Africans should be encouraged to produce larger families. Then, in order to encourage employers to make more use of white labour, the state should institute 'a policy of civilized labour and a system of subsidizing industries in order to enable them to employ whites'.[28] The cost of higher wages paid to white workers as compared with Africans would thus be borne by the state.

A combination of these sorts of measures, argued the Institute, constituted an essential part of the apartheid blueprint, by providing for 'the systematic and progressive reduction of migrant workers, stretching over a long period, coupled with the augmentation and increase in the number of white workers. All natives must be brought home systematically to the native areas'.[29]

The Instituut vir Volkswelstand was one among many members of the FAK, and obviously cannot be taken as a mouthpiece for the Federation as a whole. Nevertheless, its memorandum does indicate one strand of thinking within the FAK, in which the concept of apartheid was thought through in a relatively thorough and detailed manner as a blueprint for 'total segregation'.

THE AFRIKAANSE HANDELSINSTITUUT'S (AHI'S) CONCEPTION OF APARTHEID

The AHI was launched by the Broederbond in 1942 as one of the instruments of the economic movement. It was an organization dedicated specifically to the cause of Afrikaner business – both the small-scale businessmen concentrated in the north and the more prosperous financiers and industrialists in the south of the country. The immediate interests of small and large Afrikaner businesses did not always coincide, but they had little reason to disagree over fundamental features of an apartheid blueprint.

For both, profitability was inescapably dependent on uninter-rupted access to an abundant supply of cheap African labour. The alternatives to African labour urged by the 'total segrega-tionists' – such as accelerated mechanization and a proportion-ately larger (and more expensive) white workforce – were wholly unpalatable, since they entailed vastly increased capital and labour costs. Afrikaner businessmen, then, expressed little if any discomfort at their deepening economic dependence on African labour. In the words of *Volkshandel*, the AHI's journal, in 1948,

> No, a person must be practical. It must be acknowledged that the non-white worker already constitutes an integral part of our economic structure, that he is now so enmeshed in the spheres of our economic life that for the first fifty to one hundred years (if not even longer), total segregation is pure wishful thinking. Any government which disregards this irrefutable fact will soon discover that it is no longer in a position to govern.[30]

The AHI stressed, therefore, that it conceived of apartheid in essentially 'practical' terms, confident that renewed 'economic integration' was not fundamentally irreconcilable with white political and economic supremacy. On the contrary, apartheid was seen as a means of *expediting* whites' access to African labour in the urban and rural areas alike. The AHI acknowledged the plight of Afrikaner farmers in being unable to compete with urban industries for African labour. Their blueprint for 'practical apartheid' therefore included a system of state control over the allocation of African labour, by means of which surpluses of labour from the urban areas (that is, the urban unemployed or 'workshy') would be redistributed to the rural areas where farm labour was in short supply.

The principle of influx control was upheld; Africans' access to the urban areas would be strictly controlled according to the labour requirements of white employers within those areas. But the AHI refused to accept artificial, political restrictions on the scale of urban African employment – such as fixed labour quotas.[31]

The AHI also opposed the call by 'total segregationists' for an immediate and complete freeze on the process of African urban-ization. The continuing growth of an urbanized African popula-tion in the 'white' areas was favoured, provided it was regulated according to white economic need. That is, Africans from rural areas who were taking jobs with white employers in the towns ought to be permitted to settle there, accompanied by their families, if they so wished: 'Fundamentally, we are against migratory labour. . . . Where you have an established industrial community such as you have on the Rand, such labour must be drawn from permanent residents and not from migratory labour.'[32]

However, the AHI also opposed the sudden or drastic reduction of the flow of migrant labour into the cities to meet labour demands which were not satisfied by the local African population. Like SABRA and the Instituut vir Volkswelstand, the AHI foresaw a declining demand for migrant labour. But this drop would be effected not by the imposition of economically artificial restrictions but by the continuing growth of the urbanized population. As more and more Africans taking up employment in the cities settled there permanently, a progressively greater proportion of local labour needs would be met by urbanized workers.

THE SOUTH AFRICAN AGRICULTURAL UNION'S (SAAU'S) CONCEPTION OF APARTHEID

As an organization created to represent the interests of English- and Afrikaans-speaking farmers, the SAAU was not drawn directly into the Afrikaner nationalist crusade. Indeed, before 1939 the political leanings of the country's farming community tended towards the United Party's 'Fusion' government and away from the HNP. However, during the 1940s, as the overall farm labour shortage worsened and the United Party government failed to remedy the problem, white farmers threw their weight increasingly behind the HNP. By 1948 the SAAU was the most prominent, although not wholly representative, vehicle of Afrikaner agricultural interests.[33]

It was the promise of apartheid which won the HNP the backing of Afrikaner farmers. They identified it with the SAAU's blueprint for 'separate development', presented in 1944 to the Minister of Native Affairs as a solution to the labour shortages troubling white farmers. Reiterated in 1952 in evidence to the Tomlinson Commission, this memorandum thus establishes the meaning of apartheid as understood by the SAAU.

As the urban African workforce expanded during the 1940s, white farmers complained increasingly of labour shortages caused by the loss of would-be farm labour to the towns. Farmers, along with much of the white population at large, believed that the result of this townwards migration was the creation of a massive labour 'surplus' in the urban areas, alongside worsening labour shortages in many of the 'white' rural areas. White farmers were therefore drawn to the idea of apartheid as a system whereby state control over the allocation of labour would correct this alleged 'maldistribution' of African labour. Apartheid promised farmers an adequate supply of African labour without their having to compete with the manufacturing sector in an open labour market.

The 1944 memorandum on separate development set out the SAAU's ideas on how this system of labour allocation should function. Its aim should be 'to encourage and to develop the division of the native population into two main groups: agricultural or rural; and industrial or urban'.[34] Labour bureaux could fence this divide by enforcing regulations prohibiting an African worker from switching camps. Farmworkers should not be permitted to accept urban industrial employment, irrespective of the jobs available. Strict influx and efflux controls would be essential to enforce these regulations. In this way, farmers would stop losing their African labour to the towns and would gain the services of urban Africans 'surplus' to the requirements of urban industries. An additional guarantee of sufficient farm labour would come with the abolition of African labour-tenancy, transforming farmworkers into full-time wage labourers.[35]

However, the SAAU did not oppose the principle of deepening urban industrial dependence on African labour and therefore did not share the conviction, current in other Afrikaner circles, of the need to freeze and ultimately reduce the number of Africans employed in urban industries. Rather, the continuing presence of Africans in urban areas was seen as an economic necessity, and condition of – rather than a barrier to – the protection of white economic supremacy. Asked by the Tomlinson Commission whether he envisaged 'all the Natives ultimately in the reserves', the SAAU spokesman answered, 'No, we regard that as totally impossible. You will completely dislocate the country's economy if you do that.'[36]

Contrary to the conventional wisdom,[37] the SAAU accepted continuing African urbanization as a necessary concomitant of the country's economic development, provided its rate was strictly controlled according to urban economic need. A permanent, indispensable, urbanized workforce, enlarged by Africans from the reserves migrating on a permanent basis, was preferable to the continual drift of Africans from the farms to the towns as migrant workers. Thus, the SAAU did not oppose the urban settlement of the families of workers from the reserves, provided accommodation was available.[38] This position, reiterated during the SAAU's evidence to the Tomlinson Commission, disconcerted Tomlinson and prompted him to ask, 'Are you not afraid of the social complications deriving from the [urban] settlement [of workers' families]?'[39] The SAAU's answer was 'No'.

Another reason for farmers' preparedness to accept the fact of continuing African urbanization in the 'white' areas was their vested interest in the limited development of the reserves. The 'total segregationists' stressed that if the reserves were to absorb the African population currently settled in 'white' urban areas, vigorous agricultural development programmes were essential. Furthermore, the reserves would ultimately have to be enlarged in size. The SAAU vehemently opposed both ideas. Farmers were reluctant to foster competition from thriving African farms in the reserves. Moreover, some of the reserves bordered on areas which held valuable water sources. Intent on ensuring white control of this resource, the SAAU preferred the prospect of an enlarging African proletariat in the 'white' urban areas to the development and extension of the reserves necessitated by programmes of urban population removals.[40]

This brief survey of the policy preferences of selected Afrikaner organizations establishes the following picture of the meaning of apartheid within the Afrikaner nationalist alliance. All members of the alliance agreed that white political supremacy depended upon the political exclusion of Africans from the white polity. Africans were to exercise political rights in their 'true' spiritual 'home' in the reserves (irrespective of whether or not they in fact resided there). The alliance was divided, however, over the conditions on which this 'political segregation' depended. The exponents of 'total segregation' saw renewed 'economic integration' as a fundamental and irreversible threat, whereas the supporters of a more 'practical' conception of apartheid insisted upon the economic and political advantages of 'economic integration'. White political and economic supremacy pre-supposed a stable and flourishing economy, built on the back of a predominantly African workforce. Moreover, tampering with processes of 'economic integration' would damage the strength of the economic movement which spearheaded the Afrikaners' drive for economic and political power.

These competing conceptions of apartheid were therefore associated with different blueprints for the country's economic development. 'Total segregation' entailed a long slow haul towards 'economic segregation', in which some sacrifice of short-term profitability was necessary for the sake of a higher good. Short-term strategies such as the imposition of labour quotas, accelerated mechanization and decentralization, an immigration drive to boost the white labour supply, and state subsidization of white wages, would effectively reorient the path of economic development so that renewed profitability ceased to depend upon African labour. Afrikaner capitalists, on the other hand, had no reason to abandon the existing trajectory of capitalist development, provided strict state controls were instituted to channel the indispensable African workforce 'rationally' between the economic sectors.

Supporters of the competing conceptions of apartheid therefore also adopted different attitudes towards Africans in urban areas. For the purists, the mere presence of Africans in urban areas was undesirable, since it violated the principle of 'total segregation'. African urbanization was wholly inimical to the long-term design of apartheid, and had therefore to be dismantled, in a slow but systematic fashion. As the process of 'economic segregation' advanced, so displaced workers together with their families settled in the urban areas should be removed to the reserves. For the exponents of 'practical' apartheid, however, the continuing presence of an urban African population was, and would remain, an economic necessity. Both the AHI and SAAU accepted that, in the interests of a stabilized urban workforce, African urbanization should continue, subject to economic need. For Afrikaner capital, the goal of apartheid would be to control the status and powers of Africans in urban areas, rather than progressively to eradicate their presence there.

An account of how and why these divergent approaches to apartheid emerged surely devolves largely on the different class interests associated with each position. It is not surprising that the exponents of 'total segregation' should have been drawn primarily – although not exclusively – from the ranks of the Afrikaans petty bourgeoisie and working class. It was their class interests alone which were served by the purists' calls for quotas restricting white dependence on African labour, state subsidies of white wages, the development and extension of the reserves, etc. Obversely, Afrikaner industrialists, financiers and farmers were profoundly threatened by the sorts of proposals germane to the 'total segregation' position. Their 'practical' version of apartheid reflected an attempt to reconcile their class interests with their political defence of white supremacy and nationalistic support for the cause of the *volk*. This is not to deny the relevance of other political and ideological factors in determining Afrikaners' allegiances to one or other conception of apartheid. Indeed, some capitalist organizations, such as the Stellenbosch Chamber of Commerce, endorsed SABRA's blueprint for 'total segregation'.[41] Nor was support of the 'practical' position restricted to the Afrikaner bourgeoisie. My point is rather that a fundamental source of the unresolved division over the meaning of apartheid was the divergent class interests accommodated within the Afrikaner nationalist alliance. Whereas O'Meara sees Afrikaners' distinct class interests as having united them in support of a single, hegemonic concept of apartheid, I have argued that these class interests underlie precisely its absence.

Although this discussion has stressed the differences between the purist and practical conceptions of apartheid, it is important too to point out a significant consensus regarding the migrant labour system. Both factions disapproved of the migrant labour system 'in principle', albeit on different grounds, and proposed that industrialists' recourse to migrant labour ought to diminish over time.

Dan O'Meara's analysis dismissed the 'total segregation' blueprint as politically irrelevant. But his grounds are slim and unconvincing. Having stated his hypothesis that the notion of 'practical' apartheid was hegemonic within the nationalist alliance by 1948, he cites an editorial in *Volkshandel* (journal of the AHI) as proof.[42] This passage, quoted above,[43] makes the AHI's case that the withdrawal of African labour would bring the state to its knees. But this surely begs the very question at issue, namely, the hegemonic power of Afrikaner capital to speak for the Nationalist alliance as a whole. O'Meara fails to argue for the hegemony of Afrikaner capital. He simply asserts it as a fact, and then deduces from it that the 'total segregation' blueprint can simply be relegated to the academic ivory tower.

A closer look at the development of the 'apartheid idea' reveals that the faction espousing the 'total segregation' position was larger and more powerful than O'Meara's assertion recognized. He sought the origins of apartheid in the economic movement; 'the emerging emphasis on "the native question"'during the 1940s, he argued, 'concerned itself with the conditions of accumulation for a fledgling capitalist class'.[44] In fact, however, 'the Native question' together with the concept of apartheid were widely discussed in a variety of Afrikaner circles with different perspectives and priorities. Prominent and important among these were earnest and intensive debates among Afrikaner intellectuals, lawyers, journalists and clergy. Willem de Klerk describes how from 1941, in the Cape, young intellectuals – 'mainly lawyers, journalists from Die Burger and professional politicians' – met with D.F. Malan, leader of the HNP, to discuss the 'racial issue'. In the Transvaal too, academic explorations of apartheid made their mark on Afrikaner thinking via the oratory and publications of leading intellectuals such as Dr N. Diederichs, P.J. Meyer and Professor G.A. Cronjé.[45]

Yet in these intellectual circles, 'the changing conditions of accumulation' were often of little interest or importance. Cronjé, for example, was an outspoken and influential critic of 'economic integration', in the name of a higher moral and political cause. His first book, 'n Tuiste Vir Die Nageslag, published in 1945, rallied in defence of a future based on 'complete racial separation' – including economic segregation. Afrikaners were called on to follow this 'radical solution' to the country's problems 'as their Christian duty'.[46] His third book, Voogdyskap en Apartheid ('Trusteeship and Apartheid'), published in 1948, was written specifically to rebut the 'practical' version of apartheid. Cronjé recognized that 'the labour question (namely, the extraction of non-white labour from the white economic system) can be regarded as the key issue in the segregation of the . . . races',[47] and provided a lengthy account of how and why African labour was not indispensable in the manner claimed by some Afrikaners. O'Meara paid little attention to Cronjé's mode of argument, but according to De Klerk and Du Toit,[48] Cronjé's books set the agenda for much of the debate about apartheid, and exerted a

221

profound influence on its course in certain circles. Cronjé's first book in particular, according to De Klerk, 'formed the subject of intense discussion within the Broederbond. In the cells, Cronjé's facts and figures were thoroughly dissected, critically weighed and basically accepted'.[49]

A similar input into Broederbond thinking came from SABRA. Although not a Broederbond puppet, SABRA nevertheless had one foot firmly planted in the organization. Its executive members were all prominent Broeders, and therefore well placed to ensure a serious hearing for the 'total segregation' position within the Broederbond. Contrary to O'Meara's view then, the Broederbond, which played a crucial role in organizing and mobilizing the nationalist alliance, was itself host to a faction favouring 'total segregation'.

Cronjé's enthusiasm for 'total segregation' was shared within the FAK too, another organization well placed to influence Afrikaner thinking on the subject of apartheid. As an affiliate of the FAK, the Instituut vir Volkswelstand set out to foster a sense of Afrikaner identity by publicizing the Afrikaner nationalist cause within local Afrikaner communities and then further afield. One index of the Instituut's political influence is the fact that the Pretoria City Council's evidence to the Fagan Commission was a near verbatim copy of that presented by the Instituut, both being a vigorous defence of 'total segregation'.[50] The 'total segregationist' blueprint also commanded support in the columns of the Afrikaans press and within the Dutch Reformed Church,[51] both powerful vehicles of, and influences over, Afrikaner thinking beyond the confines of the academic ivory tower.

All in all, therefore, O'Meara's case for the hegemony of a 'practical' conception of apartheid underestimated the influence and profile of the concept of 'total segregation' within the higher echelons of the Afrikaner nationalist alliance, as well as among its rank-and-file. There is little reason to assume, as he does, that before 1948 the 'practical conception of apartheid' had won the largely unanimous support of the Afrikaner nationalist alliance. It comes as no surprise, then, that the Sauer Report, endorsed by the HNP as a statement of its principles and objectives, was not simply a blueprint for 'practical politics' in the manner assumed by O'Meara and others. Indeed, being a curious hybrid of the two competing blueprints, the Report illustrates precisely the absence of a hegemonic conception of apartheid before 1948.

THE SAUER REPORT

The unresolved conflict between the competing conceptions of apartheid was reproduced in the Sauer Report in two ways: in its declaration of the long-term objectives of apartheid and, more conspicuously, in its proposals concerning the means by which these objectives would be achieved.

The Report began by advocating 'total apartheid between whites and natives' as the 'eventual ideal and goal'.[52] Hence the assertion, wholly at odds with the 'practical' conception of apartheid, that

> the ideal which must be focused on is the gradual extraction of Natives from industries in white areas, although it is recognized that this can only be achieved in the course of many years. In the meantime, there are certain guidelines which must be observed in the use of Native labour in white areas so that it does not endanger the preservation of the white race and Western civilization in South Africa.[53]

Again in line with the 'total segregationist' rather than the 'practical' position, the Report also advocated the ultimate removal of urbanized African communities from 'white' areas, on the grounds that 'the urbanization of Natives conflicts with the policy of apartheid'.[54]

Yet the Sauer Report also acknowledged the importance of 'practical' considerations, stressing that the implementation of apartheid would 'as far as it was practically possible, be pursued gradually, always taking into account the national needs and interests and with the necessary care to avoid the disruption of the country's agriculture, industries and general interests'.[55]

A similarly ambiguous combination of purist and practical recommendations informed the Report's proposals for the immediate steps necessary to embark on the apartheid road. On the one hand, it took a leaf out of SABRA's book, in calling for 'a plan for the gradual reduction of the number of detribalized Natives in the urban areas by making other arrangements for them'. The Report also recommended the imposition of labour quotas within the 'white' areas, to fix a maximum ratio of African to white workers.[56] An even stricter approach was called for in the case of 'foreign' Africans (that is, those born outside the Union). Those already in employment in the 'white' cities would not have their contracts renewed, and no further foreign workers would be permitted access to the cities – notwithstanding the fact that secondary industries, particularly on the Witwatersrand, drew heavily on a foreign African labour supply.[57]

Yet, other short-term measures prescribed by the Report bore the marks of the competing 'practical' blueprint. Thus the call for labour quotas was vague, even hesitant. Quotas were to be imposed 'wherever practical and desirable'[58] rather than as a rule in all areas and industries. Also, despite having decried the deepening integration of Africans into the country's economy, the Report nevertheless insisted that 'everything possible must be done to deter the exodus of natives from the (white) farms'.[59] It further recommended the institution of a labour bureaux system, premised on an acceptance that continued economic growth necessitated continuing 'economic integration'. The labour bureaux system's principal objective should be to harness sufficient numbers of African workers to meet the growing demands of white rural and urban employers alike. This process would in turn foster the growth (rather than a contraction) in the size of urban African communities. Clearly, therefore, the Sauer Report's recommendations on the subject of labour bureaux did not square with other recommendations aimed at the gradual reduction in the size of the African workforce and population in the urban areas. Although proffered ideologically as part of the 'transition' to 'total segregation', the labour bureaux system would in fact take the country increasingly further from this goal.

However, the Sauer Report's acceptance of the continuing growth of the urban African workforce and population at large was not wholly in line with the Afrikaner capitalist position on African urbanization. The AHI and SAAU had recommended that in order to 'stabilize' the urban workforce, rural Africans entering urban employment be permitted to settle permanently in the cities with their families. But the Sauer Report went along with SABRA in calling for an immediate freeze on further urbanization, insisting that African workers recruited from the rural areas remain temporary residents of the cities, unaccompanied by their families.[60]

The combination of its 'practical' commitment to an expanding urban African workforce and its purist call for a freeze on further urbanization then led the Sauer Report into a position on the migrant labour system which *neither* of the competing conceptions of apartheid shared. Both factions opposed the expansion of the migrant labour system as the basis of the state's influx control policy. Albeit for different reasons, both the purist and 'practical' blueprints for apartheid called for a gradual phasing out of the use of migrant labour in the 'white' areas. Yet the Sauer Report proposed that urban employers make *increasing* use of migrant labour, so as to meet their labour needs without incurring the cost of further urbanization.

The Sauer Report, then, did not bear the imprints of a single hegemonic conception of apartheid. It was rather an internally contradictory and ambiguous document – contradictory, because it wove together strands from mutually exclusive conceptions of apartheid; and ambiguous, because it did not finally choose between them. Furthermore, its combination of these competing conceptions of apartheid distanced the Sauer Report from both, in its proposals for the extension of the migrant labour system in the 'white' urban areas.

In conclusion, it remains to draw out some of the implications of this analysis of conflicts over apartheid before 1948, for an understanding of both Afrikaner nationalism and state policy-making during the 1950s.

First, this article has drawn attention to what proved to be persistent sources of conflict and division within Afrikaner ranks throughout the 1950s. The 'total segregationist' cause continued to find support within the National Party, the Afrikaans press, the Dutch Reformed Church and the Broederbond. Nor were its exponents politically unimportant. SABRA members, for example, were among the supporters of 'total segregation' who won prominent and influential positions within the state apparatuses soon after the Nationalists' election victory. For example, Daan De Wet Nel, a founder member of SABRA, was appointed to the Native Affairs Commission, a body briefed to monitor and advise on the implementation of 'native' policy. W.M. Eiselen, a university professor, also a founder member of SABRA, was appointed Secretary of Native Affairs in 1951, over the heads of more experienced, long-serving officers of the Native Affairs Department (NAD). When Verwoerd, as Minister of Native Affairs, created a departmental research division to advise him on policy matters, he intended it to incorporate SABRA members. I have argued elsewhere that the architects of the state's apartheid policies distanced themselves from the 'total segregation' position in key respects.[61] The presence of SABRA members within the state therefore partly reflects an effort to co-opt their support for state policies, so as to pre-empt division and opposition. But then the pursuit of this sort of strategy is testimony in itself to the seriousness with which SABRA's views were regarded. Furthermore, their incorporation into the state afforded the exponents of 'total segregation' some opportunities to influence the agenda of state policy-making (more than the substance of these policies) during the 1950s. For example, according to Nic Olivier, a founder member of SABRA, the appointment of the Tomlinson Commission to investigate the prospects for developing the reserves was at SABRA's initiative. Although its proposals were largely rejected by Verwoerd, the Commission played an important ideological role in legitimizing the state's claims as the vanguard of 'separate development'. By the late 1950s, moreover, the SABRA position on 'total segregation' made a key contribution to the ideology of 'ethnic self-determination', which marked the inauguration of the state's new Bantustan self-government policy.

In short, therefore, although the state's apartheid policies were strongly influenced by the 'practical' proposals endorsed by Afrikaner capital, it would be a mistake to ignore the political influence and ideological import of intra-Afrikaner struggles over the meaning of apartheid during the 1950s.

Second, this article has also removed one plank from the popular explanation of the state's apartheid policies during the 1950s as simply the pursuit of a readymade 'grand plan'. It can no longer be argued that 'the National Party [having] fully adopted the recommendations of the Sauer Commission ... immediately set about implementing them after 1948'.[62] For the Sauer Report, having straddled mutually exclusive sets of strategies, clearly could not have provided this sort of simple 'recipe' for state policy-making. The fact that the state, pursuing its own version of 'practical politics', implemented some of the Report's proposals but rejected others, will therefore require further explanation. The substance of this explanation is beyond the scope of the present article; but, having disputed the depiction of apartheid policy-making during the 1950s as simply the implementation of a pre-existing long-term blueprint, this paper opens the way to a recognition that the apartheid policies of the 1950s were, in some respects, *ad hoc* reactions to immediate problems and priorities.[63]

O'Meara, Hindson and others conflated the Sauer Report, the alleged source of the state's 'grand plan', with the Afrikaner capitalist blueprint for apartheid. Having exposed the difference between the two, it therefore remains to ask whether the capitalists' 'practical' blueprint fulfilled the role commonly attributed to the Sauer Report. Afrikaner capitalist interests did play a crucial role in determining the nature of apartheid in the 1950s. It is partly the power of Afrikaner capital which explains the state's acceptance of an expanding African workforce in 'white' areas as economically necessary and politically inescapable. However, the state also set out to impose a freeze on further African urbanization and entrench the migrant labour system as the basis of rural Africans' access to urban employment in the future – both measures which the AHI had specifically rejected. This is but one illustration among many of the need to examine policy-making during the 1950s more closely so as to take into account a wider range of interests, constraints and struggles.

NOTES

1 This is not to presuppose that the concept of apartheid was decisive in the election. Whether or not this was the case, apartheid had nevertheless become a summary slogan for the views of diverse Afrikaner groupings. My question is why?

2 For example, W.A. de Klerk, *The Puritans in Africa* (London, 1975); D. O'Meara, *Volkskapitalisme* (Cambridge, 1983); D. Hindson, 'The Pass System and the Formation of An Urban African Proletariat: A Critique of the Cheap Labour-Power Thesis', PhD thesis, University of Sussex (1983).

3 For example, D. Hindson, 'The Pass System', 188; D. Welsh, 'The Growth of Towns', in M. Wilson and L.M. Thompson (eds), *The Oxford History of South Africa*, vol. II (London, 1971), 191; B. Bunting, *The Rise of the South African Reich* (Harmondsworth, 1967), 132; R. Horwitz, *The Political Economy of South Africa* (London, 1967), 2.

4 O'Meara, *Volkskapitalisme*, 243.

5 O'Meara, 173

6 O'Meara, 175.

7 O'Meara, 176.

8 O'Meara, 145.

9 O'Meara, 175.

10 O'Meara, 177.

11 *Verslag van die Kleurvraagstuk kommissie van die Herenigde Nasionale Party* (1947) (henceforth the *Sauer Report*), 1.

12 *Sauer Report*, 1–2.

13 See De Klerk, *Puritans in Africa*, ch. 9.
14 See for example G. Cronjé, *Voogdyskap en Apartheid* (Pretoria, 1948).
15 *Journal of Racial Affairs*, 1, 1 (September, 1949), 2–3.
16 See for example SABRA's pamphlet, *Integration or Separate Development* (Stellenbosch, 1952), 12.
17 SABRA, *Integration or Separate Development*, 13.
18 This case was argued by W.W.M. Eiselen, for example, a founder member of SABRA, in 'The Meaning of Apartheid', *Race Relations*, XV, 3 (1948), 79.
19 This case was argued strongly in 1946 by H.B. Thom, B. van Eeden and others, a group of academics at Stellenbosch University, in their memorandum 'Naturelle in Stedelike Gebiede', presented to the Native Laws Commission of Enquiry (hereafter the Fagan Commission). See the unsorted evidence to the Fagan Commission in the South African Institute of Race Relations (SAIRR) collection, University of the Witwatersrand (Wits).
20 SABRA, *Integration or Separate Development*, 4.
21 Wits, SAIRR, Fagan Commission Evidence, W. Malherbe, B. van Eeden and others, 'Reply to Mr Justice Fagan's Defence', 4.
22 Archive of University of South Africa (UNISA), Record of Evidence to the Commission on the Socio-Economic Development of the Native Areas Within the Union of South Africa (hereafter the Tomlinson Commission), vol. 4, 14/5/52, 282.
23 Wits, SAIRR, Fagan Commission Evidence, Thom *et al.* 'Naturelle in Stedelike Gebiede', 5.
24 As note 23, 2. Also UNISA, Tomlinson Commission Evidence, vol. 2, 13/5/52, 85.
25 Wits, SAIRR, Fagan Commission Evidence, Instituut Vir Volkswelstand, 'Naturelle in Stedelike Gebiede: Getuienis Voorgelê aan die Kommissie van Ondersoek Insake Wette op Naturelle in Stedelike Gebiede' (undated), Question 1, para. 2(d). (The memorandum comprises a series of answers to a questionnaire circulated by the Fagan Commission.)
26 As note 25, 24(a) (ii) (1).
27 As note 25, 24(a) (i) (d).
28 As note 25, 24(b), paras 3(d), (b) and (g).
29 As note 25, para 3(i), p. 44.
30 Cited in O'Meara, *Volkskapitalisme*, 175.
31 See for example the AHI's evidence to the Tomlinson Commission, in UNISA, Tomlinson Commission Evidence, vol. 87, 13/2/53, 8010–11.
32 UNISA, Tomlinson Commission Evidence, vol. 87, 8006.
33 No doubt these interests differed according to the type, scale and area of farming undertaken. However, in order to make the point about the presence of varying blueprints for apartheid within Afrikanerdom, it is not necessary to canvass Afrikaner agricultural interests in their entirety.
34 Wits, SAIRR, Fagan Commission Evidence, 'List of Recommendations For Discussion With The Minister of Native

Affairs By The Conference of Representatives Of The Affiliations of the Union, on 15 September 1944'. See also UNISA, Tomlinson Commission Evidence, vol. 10, 19/5/52, 560(a).

35 Wits, SAIRR, Fagan Commission Evidence, SAAU, 'List Of Recommendations', 1–2.
36 UNISA, Tomlinson Commission Evidence, vol. 10, 549.
37 Many scholars share M. Legassick's view that 'both farming and gold-mining retained an interest in limiting or preventing permanent African urbanisation'. See his 'Legislation, Ideology and Economy in Post-1948 South Africa', in M. Murray (ed.), *South African Capitalism and Black Political Opposition* (Massachusetts, 1982), 479.
38 UNISA, Tomlinson Commission Evidence, vol. 10, 538.
39 UNISA, vol. 10, 539.
40 UNISA, vol. 10, 551–4.
41 See Stellenbosch Chamber of Commerce's memorandum to the Fagan Commission in Wits, SAIRR.
42 O'Meara, *Volkskapitalisme*, 175.
43 See above.
44 O'Meara, *Volkskapitalisme*, 175.
45 De Klerk, *Puritans in Africa*, 202–3.
46 De Klerk, 216–17.
47 G. Cronjé, *Voogdyskap en Apartheid*, 62.
48 A. Du Toit, 'Ideological Change, Afrikaner Nationalism and Pragmatic Racial Domination in South Africa', in L. Thompson and J. Butler (eds), *Change in Contemporary South Africa* (Stanford, CA, 1975), 40.
49 De Klerk, *Puritans in Africa*, 219.
50 See Wits, SAIRR, Fagan Commission Evidence, Pretoria City Council, 'Getuienis Voorgelê aan die Kommissie van Ondersoek Insake Wette op Naturelle in Stedelike Gebiede'.
51 See SAIRR, *The Economic Development of the Reserves*, Fact paper no. 3 (1959), 4.
52 *Sauer Report*, 3.
53 *Sauer Report*, 11.
54 As note 53.
55 *Sauer Report*, 3.
56 *Sauer Report*, 10–11.
57 The Tomlinson Commission heard evidence from the SAIRR that by 1952, 58 per cent of the Witwatersrand's African workforce (inclusive of mining) was foreign. UNISA, Tomlinson Commission Evidence, vol. 1, 60.
58 *Sauer Report*, 11.
59 *Sauer Report*, 9.
60 *Sauer Report*, 10.
61 D. Posel, 'Doing Business with the Pass Laws: Influx Control Policy and the Interests of Manufacturing and Commerce in South Africa in the 1950s', paper presented to Institute of Commonwealth Studies, London (27 February 1987).

62 Hindson, 'The Pass System', 188.
63 These points are expanded in my Oxford University doctoral thesis on 'Influx Control and the Construction of Apartheid in South Africa, 1948–1961' [published as *The Making of Apartheid 1948–1961* (Oxford, 1991) Eds].

10

DISPLACED URBANIZATION:
South Africa's rural slums*
Colin Murray

Colin Murray, a British anthropologist, has done extensive research on rural social conditions in the Orange Free State/Lesotho region. When he wrote this article in 1987, South Africa was experiencing a state of heightened social crisis and seeming political deadlock. On the one hand, apartheid was manifestly beginning to unravel in the face of massive popular resistance and unsustainable internal contradictions. On the other hand, the imposition of a draconian State of Emergency in June 1986 suggested that the apartheid state was determined to resist loss of power with all the means at its disposal. Murray begins by drawing attention to the repeal of the pass laws in 1986 and their replacement by an inchoate strategy of 'orderly urbanization'. In the light of this confusion over the government's intentions, Murray draws attention to the phenomenon of 'displaced urbanization', a phrase that neatly captures the contradictory effects of apartheid policies in respect to continued white reliance on African labour within the context of the development of notionally independent African 'Bantustans'. In his case study examination of two rural population concentrations in the Orange Free State and the Transvaal, Murray demonstrates how African urbanization has been diverted from the white cities, leading to the rapid creation of massive rural slums in the countryside. Of the economically active inhabitants of these ghettoes, most spend a great deal of time and money commuting daily to jobs in the white metropolitan areas; but the majority of the population are unemployed and live a marginal existence, having been evicted from white farms and cities on the grounds that they are surplus to economic requirements. Murray's article powerfully captures the endemic confusions and contradictions characteristic of late apartheid. And, in the case of KwaNdebele, he highlights the volatile politics of popular resistance

231

*directed against the Bantustan authorities responsible for its adminis-
tration.*

* * *

The pass laws were formally repealed in July 1986. They have
been regarded for decades as a lynch-pin of the system of
apartheid, since they comprised the discriminatory legislative
framework, the cumbersome bureaucratic apparatus and the
vicious daily harassment through which access for black South
Africans to jobs and housing in the 'white' urban areas was
rigidly circumscribed. Their abolition was accordingly welcomed
in many quarters as a significant step along the road to reform.

The pass laws were replaced, however, by a strategy of 'orderly
urbanization', elaborated in the President's Council report of
September 1985 and a White Paper of April 1986. There is still
much confusion about what this implies in practice, for a number
of reasons. First, influx control now depends primarily on access
to jobs and housing. It is administered in terms of legislation
nominally passed for other purposes, such as the Slums Act and
the Prevention of Illegal Squatting Act. It is to be regulated by the
'local state' and the 'market' rather than by the central state. One
consequence is that influx control is differently administered in
different regions of the country. Housing shortages are more or
less acute. People experience variable combinations of direct and
indirect pressures to live in designated residential zones at
greater or lesser distances from the main urban centres. Second,
what is meant by the 'local state' in this context remains obscure.
The White Paper of April 1986 explicitly connected the management of 'orderly urbanization' with a proposed third tier of
government, that of the Regional Services Councils. But their
political constitution and strategic responsibilities have never
been clearly defined. Indeed, this whole reformist initiative has
run into the ground, it appears, since the declaration of the
present Emergency in June 1986. Third, while the freedom of
movement of black South Africans is constrained in practice by
their lack of access to employment and accommodation, people
already identified as citizens of the four 'independent' Bantustans
(Transkei, Bophuthatswana, Venda and Ciskei, TBVC) remain
aliens and are therefore formally precluded from a *right* of access
to jobs and housing in 'white' South Africa. South African citizen-

ship is to be restored only by a complex formula of administrative concession to TBVC citizen who were 'permanent residents' of 'white' South Africa in July 1986 – an estimated 1.75 million out of a total of approximately nine million TBVC citizens. The political boundaries between these Bantustans and 'South Africa' (in the reduced sense used by Pretoria to exclude the TBVC states) are therefore extremely important formal barriers to the freedom of movement of many millions of people who consider themselves to be South African.[1]

This article suggests that the key to understanding the confusion lies in an analysis of the phenomenon of 'displaced urbanization'. The phrase refers to the concentration of black South Africans, over the last ten to fifteen years in particular, in huge rural slums which are politically in the Bantustans and economically on the peripheries of the established metropolitan labour markets. Two such cases are examined here. One is the huge slum of Onverwacht/Botshabelo in the heart of the eastern Orange Free State (see Map 10.1). The other is a string of slums comprising the newest Bantustan, KwaNdebele, in the central Transvaal to the north-east of Pretoria (see Map 10.2).

Onverwacht/Botshabelo was bare veld in 1979.[2] Now it accommodates perhaps half a million people. It is the largest relocation slum in the country, or the second largest black township (after Soweto). Its population is predominantly Southern Sotho, since most people who have been moved there since 1979 have come from the northern, central and eastern districts of the Orange Free State. But Onverwacht/Botshabelo is physically adjacent to the Thaba'Nchu district of Bophuthatswana, part of the 'independent' Tswana Bantustan; and it is a long way from QwaQwa, the 'non-independent' Southern Sotho Bantustan on the boundary of Natal, the Orange Free State and Lesotho. The original establishment of Onverwacht as a site for Southern Sotho refugees from Thaba'Nchu, within commuting range of Bloemfontein but at a great distance from QwaQwa, the other pole of physical concentration of the Southern Sotho population, obviously contradicts the ethno-national/territorial logic of the Bantustan strategy. Such contradictions, reflecting some of the injustices, the failures and the absurdities of the original strategy, were acknowledged in President Botha's formulation of an alternative strategy of regional development in 1982.[3] Nine Development Regions have been identified. They are supposed to transcend the political and economic boundaries of grand apartheid under which South Africa was divided into ten Bantustans on the one hand and 'white' urban and rural areas on the other. Onverwacht/Botshabelo is the core of Development Region C which embraces both the provincial capital of Bloemfontein, with its own black townships in 'white' South Africa, and also the Thaba'Nchu district of Bophuthatswana. The burgeoning slum was explicitly adopted as a prime site of experiment for the pragmatic modernizers within the state, committed to technocratic reform of apartheid 'from above'.[4] Accordingly, one of the critics of 'regional development' has recently analysed Onverwacht/Botshabelo as a test case for the strategy of 'orderly urbanization'.[5]

By contrast with the relative political passivity of Botshabelo, KwaNdebele[a] has been a seething cauldron of violent confrontation. There are two main reasons for looking at KwaNdebele in some detail. First, it represents an extreme case of displaced urbanization. Second, it was a prime site of popular struggle throughout 1986 against the implementation of Bantustan 'independence'. It illustrates the complexity of factional conflicts which are transposed to the Bantustans from the sites of direct confrontation between the people and the state in the black townships of 'white' South Africa. Although they are politically transposed in this way, I would argue that the outcomes of such conflicts are of fundamental and by no means peripheral importance to the outcome of the larger struggle in the country as a whole.

DISPLACED URBANIZATION AND REGIONAL DEVELOPMENT

There are three important elements of the phenomenon of displaced urbanization. They are, first, the relative concentration of population in the Bantustans over the last three decades; second, the diversion of state expenditure on housing to the Bantustans, albeit on a grotesquely inadequate scale, with a corresponding deliberate freeze on black housing in the 'white' urban areas; and, third, the widespread commuterization of the black labour force. The simplest evidence of the first trend is Charles Simkins's estimates of the distribution of the black population of South Africa at decennial intervals between 1960 and 1980. He calculated that, while 39.1 per cent (of a total black population of 11.5 million) were living in the black reserves or Bantustans in 1960, 52.7 per cent (of a total black population of 21 million) were in the Bantustans in 1980. While there was an absolute increase in the numbers of Africans living in both urban and rural areas of 'white' South Africa over the period, there was a slight *relative* decline in urban areas from 29.6 per cent in 1960 to 26.7 per cent in 1980, and a very substantial relative decline in rural areas from 31.3 per cent in 1960 to 20.6 per cent in 1980.[6] This redistribution of the black population reflects overwhelming state pressure against the tide of black urbanization that would otherwise have occurred in 'white' South Africa, consistently with deepening poverty in the black rural areas, with rapidly rising black structural unemployment in white capitalist agriculture, and with rates of urbanization prevalent elsewhere in the Third World.

What *has* happened, in summary, is massive 'urbanization' in the Bantustans, in terms of the sheer density of population now concentrated there. One recent estimate is that 56 per cent of the population of the Bantustans are now 'urbanized'.[7] Several million people have been relocated from white farms, from 'black spots', from small town locations and from the metropolitan areas.[8] In addition, some densely populated zones have been formally incorporated into the Bantustans by the redrawing of boundaries on the map. Some of the concentration has taken place in 'proclaimed' (officially planned) towns in the Bantustans, whose population was 33,500 in 1960, 595,000 in 1970 and 1.5 million by 1981.[9] But most of the concentration has taken place in huge rural slums which are 'urban' in respect of their population densities but 'rural' in respect of the absence of proper urban infrastructure or services.

Most housing in the rural slums is self-built. For many years central and local government authorities have used the acute shortage of black housing as an administrative arm of influx control. The 'orderly urbanization' strategy which has replaced the pass laws has merely made this more explicit. In many townships new building has been frozen as a deliberate tactic to enforce 'voluntary' removal to new towns or closer settlements in the Bantustans. Estimates and projections of housing shortage differ widely, of course, depending on premises and methods of calculation. One official source in 1984 estimated that the backlog of housing for Africans in 'white' areas was a staggering 420,000 units, contradicting the then Minister of Co-operation and Development's claim of less than half that number. Only 11,902 houses were built for Africans in 1984.[10] Irrespective of formal repeal of the pass laws, it is clear that, despite small increases in the rate of construction in recent years, the continuing acute shortage of housing affords an administrative barrier to black urbanization in 'white' South Africa which state officials at various levels have repeatedly exploited.[11]

Associated with the trend of rapid 'urbanization' in the Bantustans is an increase in the numbers of frontier commuters, defined as people who live in a Bantustan and commute daily or weekly to work in a 'white' area. Official figures record 615,000 in 1978 and 773,000 commuters in 1982; while the total number of migrants from the Bantustans officially recorded in 1982 was 1.395 million.[12] Thus there are still substantially more migrants than commuters but, taking into account unofficial estimates from different areas and booming bus transport in the early 1980s on certain key routes, it is evident that commuters represent an increasing proportion of the black labour force as a whole. A particularly stark indication of this development was recorded by Joe Lelyveld in his excellent book *Move Your Shadow*. The number of daily buses running between the desolate slums of KwaNdebele and the Pretoria region, operated by the major private bus company Putco but heavily subsidized by central government, was 2 in 1979, 66 in 1980, 105 in 1981, 148 in 1982, 220 in 1983 and 263 in 1984. Lelyveld commented: 'In a period in which South Africa is alleged to be changing and phasing out apartheid, the expansion of Putco into . . . the homeland provides as accurate a measure as can be found of the real thrust of change.'[13]

The significance of this trend is that the black labour force is no longer simply divided (as in the Riekert philosophy of 1979) into relatively privileged urban 'insiders' with Section 10 (1)(a)(b)(c) rights to live and work in 'white' South Africa, on the one hand; and disadvantaged 'outsiders' from the Bantustans and from foreign labour reserves who have no such rights and must seek work in the 'white' areas as temporary migrants, on the other hand. Rather, frontier commuters from the slums of KwaNdebele, for example, or from those of the Moretele-Odi block of Bophuthatswana to the north-west of Pretoria, are effectively integrated into the metropolitan labour market, in terms of their access to and dependence on wage incomes in the industrial region of Pretoria–Rosslyn–Brits. But housing is not available for them in those industrial centres, and they and their families must find a place to live in the fragments of this or that Bantustan which are not wholly beyond the reach of the Putco buses.

Corresponding, then, to the state's refusal to accommodate blacks residentially within 'white' South Africa is a strategy of industrial decentralization intended to disperse productive activities to the metropolitan fringes, away from the established industrial cores.[14] This strategy depends on generous wage and transport subsidies and tax incentives. Thus, in the eastern Free State, for example, Bloemfontein was identified in 1982 as an Industrial Development Point (IDP) along with Botshabelo outside Thaba'Nchu and Selosesha inside Thaba'Nchu. Now rising on the veld beside the Bloemfontein–Thaba'Nchu main road, and one-third of the way along it, is a site called Bloemdustria which is intended to develop in relative proximity both to Bloemfontein and to the vast pool of potential labour concentrated at Botshabelo. Writing recently of Botshabelo and Ekangala, another IDP in the central Transvaal which is supposed to be incorporated into KwaNdebele, William Cobbett has pointed out that they show

> how far labour provision has moved from the simple traditional division between urban workers and long-distance migrants. Peripheral labour pools form part of extended urban labour markets, by complementing controlled residential exclusion with labour market inclusion.[15]

This is what 'orderly urbanization' is all about: partial labour market inclusion and controlled residential exclusion. On the one hand, the rapidly 'urbanized' inhabitants of the rural slums have been integrated, to a degree, into metropolitan labour markets. On the other hand, they are kept at arm's length, as it were, from the major 'white' industrial and residential areas.

The constitutional corollary to these 'regional development' initiatives is that frameworks have to be devised to administer the distribution of local services. Accordingly, elaborate and ingenious proposals have been put forward for Regional Services Councils (RSCs), on which all communities will be represented in proportion to their consumption of services provided. Since white municipalities have a much greater capacity to consume services than black townships, it may be inferred that the RSCs are intended to manage the putative incorporation of the rural slums into a loosely federal political framework without making any concession to the demand of black South Africans for a unitary democratic state. This 'solution' is sponsored by reformists within the state who acknowledge, apparently, that the Bantustans will eventually be reincorporated but who are anxious to retain the substance of white power. The implementation of RSCs has been substantially delayed, however, for the obvious reason that, in the wake of the demise of the black local authorities, they are fatally deficient in political credibility. They also conflict with, and are opposed by, the established administrative authorities of the Bantustans.

Thus struggles in the rural slums of South Africa today relate above all to the terms and to the degree of their economic 'integration' into the principal metropolitan labour markets, and of their political 'integration' as black South Africans within a single state. There is much uncertainty over the outcomes of such struggles, partly because of confusion and contradiction within the state and partly because of the scale and momentum of popular resistance. Onverwacht/Botshabelo is analysed here as a case study of confusion and contradiction within the state. KwaNdebele is analysed as a case study of protracted and partially successful popular struggle against the imposition of Bantustan 'independence'.

In seeking to identify strategic lessons for the future in the experience of the inhabitants of the rural slums, it is vital to be clear about the criteria of 'urbanization' which are deployed in the argument. In the past the term has been used to refer to the scale of the movement that has taken place into the 'prescribed' (urban) areas of 'white' South Africa, as a result of conflict between two opposing forces: the overwhelming pressure of poverty in the rural areas, on the one hand, and the remorseless effort of the state to push people back to the black reserves, on the other hand. The terms of the debate have shifted now, in response to the tidal wave of urbanization displaced to the Bantustans. The term 'urbanized' is used now in the sense of daily access to or effective integration into or functional dependence on the urban labour market. But integration into and dependence on are very much matters of degree. A criterion of functional dependence on the urban labour market may be

238

sensibly applied to incorporate the 'urbanized' population of the Bantustans in an analysis of contemporary trends in the political economy of apartheid. But it should *not* be used to imply either, on the one hand, that recognizably rural households beyond commuting range of the metropolitan areas are not primarily dependent on an urban wage for their livelihoods, through migrant household members; or, on the other hand, that people who live in the slums no longer aspire, ultimately, to recover a past livelihood on the land.

ONVERWACHT/BOTSHABELO

Onverwacht began as a 'place of refuge' for nearly 40,000 'illegal squatters' living at Kromdraai within Thaba'Nchu who were repeatedly harassed by Bophuthatswana police after 'independence'

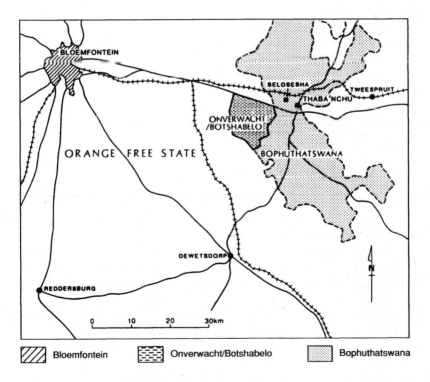

Map 10.1 Onverwacht/Botshabelo

239

in 1977.[16] They were all removed to Onverwacht in the second half of 1979 and Kromdraai was razed to the ground. Onverwacht was also planned as a site for the relocation of 'surplus' population from Mangaung, the black residential area of Bloemfontein; and for the concentration of people removed from small town locations and white farms all over the Free State. The population has massively expanded from a figure of 64,000 by the end of 1979 to an unofficial estimate of 500,000 in 1985. By the end of 1984 the labour force domiciled in Botshabelo included some 23,000 daily commuters to Bloemfontein and 30,000 migrants to the Free State gold fields.[17] Initially the residents of Onverwacht complained bitterly of repeated harassment under the pass laws. Not only was it extremely difficult to find a job; it was also extremely difficult to get a work-seeker's permit – the *soekwerk* stamp – so that anyone who took the initiative of looking for work in Bloemfontein was immediately 'endorsed out' back to Onverwacht. This situation was later eased somewhat by an act of administrative discretion. From 1982 commuters from Onverwacht to Bloemfontein were given Section 10(1)(d) rights to compete on equal terms with urban 'insiders' who had Section 10(1)(a)(b)(c) rights.[18]

This is the basis of Cobbett's diagnosis of the 'integration' of Botshabelo within the regional labour market. But there must be two crucial qualifications, in my view, of this diagnosis. First, while it is true that the number of daily commuter buses between Onverwacht/Botshabelo and Bloemfontein has steadily increased, partly in response to the administrative concession above, it must also be true that the number of commuters *relative* to the total population of the slum has declined. Unemployment has escalated much faster, in other words, than employment. Second, we must remember that the rural slums not only have a future but also a past. The overwhelming statistical fact about Onverwacht/Botshabelo and many other rural slums which have sprung up in the last ten to fifteen years is that they represent concentrations of ex-farmworkers and their families, who have been decisively dis-integrated, so to speak, from the agricultural labour market. They carry with them, in their desperate search for urban employment, the enduring disadvantages of very little education, relative illiteracy and the non-transferability of limited skills.

Another obvious statistical feature of households in Botshabelo as in other rural slums is the extent to which family life is managed by women. The circumstances of one family may be briefly described.[19] In October 1979 it was evicted with seventeen other families at 24 hours' notice from a white farm south of Tweespruit and dumped in Onverwacht without food, money or means of livelihood. In July 1986 the husband-father, a former tractor-driver, was effectively retired, having been unable to find any regular job. Two adult daughters with young children in the household were themselves domestic servants, respectively in Johannesburg and Bloemfontein. Another daughter remained at home where the only possibility of employment was in the local chicken farm where wages were appallingly low. Their mother, on whose broad shoulders rested the immediate responsibility for feeding and clothing this large household, entered the informal sector with vigour and desperation but initially with very low returns from long hours invested. She bought sheep on credit from the local butcher and then hawked the meat around Onverwacht. She graduated, in due course, to the most lucrative part of that sector: the concentrated weekend booze.[b] But it is a risky business, and often violent and sordid as well.

This household encapsulates the structural disadvantages in the labour market experienced by ex-farm families and specifically by women. They have three options only: domestic service under conditions of extreme exploitation by white employers beyond the reach of daily commuting; residual employment at very low wages in a Bantustan or 'border' industry established to take advantage of an unlimited local supply of cheap labour; or an informal sector at home subject to strong competition and official harassment. A question mark should be placed, then, against the meaning of 'integration' in practice; and analysis of state strategy at the macro-level must be complemented by empirical study of the extent and the manner of that 'integration' in the experience of individual households.

It is this labour force which is described by the technocrats of state reformism, in their blandly enthusiastic advocacy of regional co-operation and regional development, as 'highly motivated and responsible'.[20] 'Highly motivated' in effect means extremely poor and desperate for any kind of employment; 'responsible' in effect means unorganized. Regional co-operation is recognized, however, as a 'delicate bloom'. This is also a coded phrase and acknowledges the fact that conflict between different agencies pervades the implementation of regional development.

Bloemfontein IDP and Bloemdustria are administered by the Bloemfontein City Council and, prospectively, by the RSC. Botshabelo is on land owned by the South African Development Trust (SADT), the state agency responsible for purchasing land for black occupation under the terms of the Trust and Land Act 1936, and is administered by the Department of Development Aid, the rump of the old Department of Co-operation and Development. Selosesha IDP falls under the Bophuthatswana National Development Corporation (BNDC) and the Bophuthatswana government.

Such bureaucratic proliferation greatly compounds the difficulties of planning and implementing regional development initiatives. On 9 July 1986 it was announced that Botshabelo would become part of QwaQwa, which represented a setback for the reformist technocrats since their strategy is based in part on the erosion of the political boundaries of the Bantustans. Despite official denials and strong opposition from within Botshabelo, its incorporation into QwaQwa[c] was judged in March 1987 to be 'imminent'. The logic of this can only be to push QwaQwa into 'independence' alongside the TBVC states.[21] Meanwhile the political boundary between Thaba'Nchu and 'South Africa' was reinforced by the official refusal of Bophuthatswana to allow dual citizenship. On 12 July 1986 big men from Mafikeng, the capital of Bophuthatswana, held a public meeting in Thaba'Nchu and threatened the people that, if they applied for the new (allegedly uniform) South African identity documents which are replacing the hated *dompas* but which remain a condition of employment in 'South Africa', they would forfeit all rights in Bophuthatswana, including citizenship and residence permits. If this is a serious threat, several hundred thousand commuters from Moretele-Odi to the Pretoria region and from Thaba'Nchu to Bloemfontein face the appalling dilemma of whether to give up a job in 'white' South Africa or a place to live in Bophuthatswana. The people were confused and angry. 'Negotiations' are taking place, allegedly, to resolve this problem.

It is a story of confusion and contradiction at both economic and political levels. Regional development, the new reformism, is supposed to transcend the boundaries of Bantustans. But the prospective incorporation of Botshabelo into QwaQwa and President Mangope's[d] aggressive insistence on the exclusive integrity of citizenship of Bophuthatswana represent a 'hardening', not a 'softening', of the boundaries.

KWANDEBELE

KwaNdebele is a belated afterthought in the grand design of 'separate development'.[22] Until the mid-1970s there was no provision in land or administrative authority for the Ndebele people, scattered throughout the Transvaal on white farms and in different sections of Bophuthatswana and Lebowa.[e] Representations from various Ndebele tribal chiefs led to the establishment of two regional authorities in 1974 and 1977. These arrangements incorporated three Ndebele groups living in the Moretele 1 district of Bophuthatswana, but excluded North Ndebele groups living in Lebowa, despite some agitation in the late 1970s from followers of one chief to secede from Lebowa and join the incipient South Ndebele Bantustan. The (South) Ndebele territorial authority was constituted late in 1977. It became a legislative assembly in October 1979, consisting of forty-six nominated members. Self-governing status was granted in 1981. The Chief Minister Simon Skosana (a former lorry-driver with a Standard 4 pass) announced in 1982 that KwaNdebele would opt for 'independence' as soon as it had its own capital, industrial infrastructure and more land. Meanwhile it was reported that all the territory's liquor licences were held by government ministers and most new businesses were owned by them or by senior officials. Loans from the Corporation for Economic Development were apparently monopolized in the same way. Minister of the Interior Piet Ntuli, for example, who became the 'strongman' of the KwaNdebele government and the vigilante organization Mbokhoto, had a supermarket at the capital Siyabuswa and a similar complex of shops and liquor outlets at Vlaklaagte, another of the new slums.[23]

In view of the paucity and inconsistency of the reports available, it is very difficult to reconstruct the process by which the land area identified as KwaNdebele has been expanded and partially consolidated at various stages over the last ten years. In 1976 KwaNdebele apparently consisted of about 75,000 hectares of land,[24] made up of 'black spots' scattered between Moretele 2 district of Bophuthatswana and Moutse 1, 2 and 3 districts of Lebowa, and a block of Trust farms to the south-west (see Map

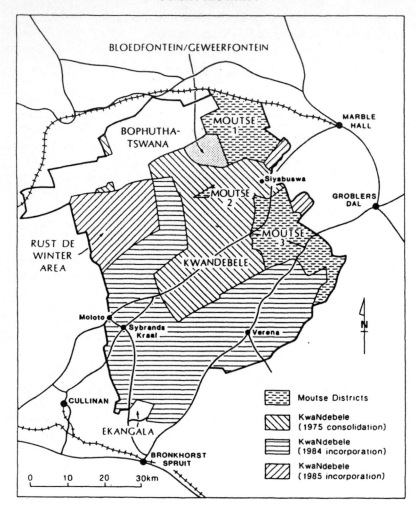

Map 10.2 KwaNdebele

10.2). These Trust farms now contain a series of sprawling slums which straddle the road between Cullinan and Groblersdal. New consolidation plans were announced in February 1983, which would increase KwaNdebele's size from 98,000 to 341,000 hectares. They embraced a large block of white farms in the Moloto region north of Cullinan and Bronkhorstspruit, part of the Ekandustria growth point and the Ekangala residential area, the Moutse districts (which had been excised from Lebowa in

1980), and eleven farms on the southern edge of Lebowa. Incorporation of the latter two areas was strongly resisted by the Moutse people themselves and by the Lebowa authorities; and the issue of Moutse in particular reached stalemate. Some white farmers protested that they would receive inadequate compensation and that the value of border farms would drop. Others anticipated that compulsory purchase would save them from drought-induced bankruptcy.[25]

It may seem that KwaNdebele's constitutional progress from bits and pieces of tribal authority in the mid-1970s to prospective 'independence' by the end of 1986 was an unseemly scramble. It may seem that its projected appropriation of fragments of Bophuthatswana and Lebowa was a blatant contradiction of the ideological rationale of 'separate development' and a cynical inducement to KwaNdebele's businessmen-thugs-politicians to take 'independence'. But a full sense of the absurdity and the sinister reality of KwaNdebele as an extreme case of displaced urbanization emerges only by asking the question: where have its inhabitants come from?

An estimated 90 per cent are recent immigrants, relocated since the late 1970s in a dozen slums stretching from Tweefontein and Gemsbokfontein in the south-west to Siyabuswa in the northeast. Probably not more than half of them are ethnically Ndebele. Even official estimates acknowledged an increase of population from 51,000 in 1975 to 166,000 in 1980. In March 1983 a joint statement from Pretoria and the Chief Minister's office said that more than 111,000 people had settled in KwaNdebele over the previous twelve to eighteen months. In 1982 a survey carried out by the Human Sciences Research Council found that 55.4 per cent of the immigrants had come from white farms in the Delmas, Witbank and Middelburg districts to the south; 29 per cent had come from Bophuthatswana; and 8.5 per cent had come from 'white' urban areas.[26] There were also removals from 'black spots' elsewhere in the region. No one knows how many people live in KwaNdebele today. Unofficial estimates range up to half a million. Most of these people moved 'voluntarily' to KwaNdebele, in the sense that they were not forcibly relocated in government trucks, apparently because the KwaNdebele slums afford the nearest legal home base from which the industrial region of Pretoria–Rosslyn–Brits is accessible and where families can live together albeit under very difficult and exhausting

245

conditions. The fragment of Bantustan that is physically closest to this industrial region is in fact the Moretele-Odi block of Bophuthatswana, but many of the refugees in KwaNdebele have been directly or indirectly expelled from there, as non-Tswana without legal rights, by a policy of aggressive Tswana nationalism in respect of the allocation of jobs, housing and services.

It was the formal incorporation of Moutse into KwaNdebele on 31 December 1985 that provoked a determined campaign of popular resistance throughout the first seven months of 1986. The Moutse districts have a population of roughly 120,000 predominantly Pedi (North Sotho), and their excision from Lebowa and incorporation into KwaNdebele flew in the face of official rhetoric about rationalizing 'ethno-national' identities. More importantly, however, KwaNdebele's well-publicized plans to take 'independence' fuelled opposition from the Moutse people themselves, because 'independence' would mean the loss of South African citizenship. Resistance to incorporation was thus not merely a question of anxiety over the oppression of non-Ndebele people within KwaNdebele. It was a question of refusal to endorse the loss of residual rights as black South Africans which follows the imposition of citizenship of an 'independent' Bantustan.[27]

On 1 January 1986 three attacks were launched by vigilantes armed with pangas and axes on several villages in Moutse 3. More than 380 men were abducted to Siyabuswa in KwaNdebele, where they were stripped and repeatedly sjambokked[f] on the floor of the community hall which was awash with soapy water. Skosana and Ntuli[g] were identified as directly involved in this. The vigilantes were members of an organization called Mbokhoto, officially sponsored by the KwaNdebele government. Moutse people were thereafter repeatedly terrorized by South African police units, including KwaNdebele police, and by the Mbokhoto. At least forty people were killed, hundreds injured, many detained and assaulted. Some forced removals took place of both Sotho and Ndebele from Moutse to KwaNdebele.[28] Violence flared again in May 1986, sparked off by the death of a man from the Kwaggafontein slum. He had gone to the Mbokhoto headquarters to complain about the abduction of a number of schoolchildren including his daughter. His badly beaten body was later dumped outside his home. A riot followed his funeral. On 12 May a mass meeting was held to demand that 'independence' (scheduled for 11 December 1986) be scrapped and the Mbokhoto disbanded. On 14 May large numbers of people gathered to hear the KwaNdebele government response to these demands. The 30,000 crowd was repeatedly teargassed by helicopter and the meeting broke up in confusion. This brought popular resistance to a head and cabinet ministers already protected behind a barbed wire stockade were forced to seek refuge elsewhere.[29]

These incidents also fuelled a power struggle between the commoners Skosana and Ntuli, heading the KwaNdebele government, and the most important 'traditional' political faction, loyal to the head of the Ndzundza royal house Chief David Mabhogo. One of his sons, Prince Cornelius Mahlangu, was Minister of Health in the KwaNdebele government until December 1986. Another, Prince James Mahlangu, was head of the Ndzundza tribal authority which controls 23 appointed seats. out of 72 seats in the legislative assembly. He declared his sympathy with the popular protest and subsequently co-ordinated legal action against Ntuli. This reflects the ambivalent political position of the Ndzundza royal house and the extent to which the excesses of Mbokhoto had promoted an unusual tactical alliance – between traditionally conservative leadership within the Bantustan and youth and community representatives opposed to 'independence'. This alliance also loosely embraced some white farmers in the region who resent the incorporation of their land into the Bantustan proposed in the 1983 consolidation plans.[30]

Following the imposition of a general state of emergency on 12 June 1986, even more stringent security measures were imposed in KwaNdebele, banning reporting and forbidding non-residents from entering the territory. The entire public service went on indefinite strike on 15 July in protest against 'independence' and the arbitrary violence of Mbokhoto. The schools were boycotted from the nominal return date of 14 July. Nine youths who had fled to the Vlaklaagte slum in KwaNdebele from Mamelodi outside Pretoria, where their homes had been petrol-bombed, were massacred by men posing as ANC representatives who were probably Mbokhoto vigilantes.[31] Meanwhile, the 'Comrades' carried out revenge attacks and burned and looted shops and other businesses owned by members of Mbokhoto. Some of the 'necklaces' were inevitably indiscriminate, and violence was also attributed to a hybrid category of 'Comtsotsis' (Comrade + Tsotsi), ordinary criminals posing as political activists. According to a local priest, about 160 people were killed between mid-May and late July: he estimated one-third had been killed by the police and army, a third by the Mbokhoto and a third by the 'Comrades'.[32] On 30 July Piet Ntuli, prime businessman-thug-politician, was killed by a car bomb. News of his death induced a spontaneous public celebration.[33] Chief Minister Skosana was left isolated and vulnerable. The Mbokhoto was immediately disbanded and on 12 August the legislative assembly called off 'independence'.[34]

In retrospect, it is clear that specific opposition to the incorporation of Moutse turned into generalized opposition to 'independence' throughout KwaNdebele as a result of the daily experience of harassment in the slums. It is still unclear whether the rejection of KwaNdebele 'independence' represents, on the one hand, a significant breakthrough in political mobilization within the rural slums, or on the other hand a temporary setback only for the protagonists of the Bantustan strategy. The unfamiliar tactical alliance between conservative 'tribal' leaders committed to the politics of separate development and radical youth committed to a unitary democratic state is obviously marked by strain and tension. By mid-October 1986, the KwaNdebele government had embarked on another 'spree of arrests', and Pretoria had failed to break the political impasse between the ageing patriarch of the Ndzundza royal house and Chief Minister Skosana. The prospect of reviving the question of 'independence' appeared to be vitiated by the death of Skosana himself in November. But he was succeeded by a 'hardliner', George Mahlangu, not by the popular opposition leader Prince James Mahlangu. The threat of 'independence' was renewed in March 1987 through the repeated detention of members of the legislative assembly who had opposed it, and through a 'unanimous' vote in favour in May.[35]

Meanwhile, political tensions in KwaNdebele have been concentrated on the issue of the incorporation of the Moutse districts into KwaNdebele and the incorporation of a block of land adjoining Moutse 1 – the farms Bloedfontein and Geweerfontein – into Bophuthatswana. A major legal challenge to the excision of Moutse from Lebowa and its incorporation into KwaNdebele was heard at the end of November 1986. The court rejected the arguments of the Moutse communities, but the decision remains subject to appeal. The arguments relate to the loss of representation in the Lebowa legislative assembly; the loss of North Sotho as an official language; the loss of the franchise for women (KwaNdebele does not allow women to vote); and the imposition on the majority North Sotho population of Moutse of an ethnic minority status within KwaNdebele which contradicts the official ideology of the Bantustan strategy.[36]

Another focus of bitter conflict is the implications of the passage of recent legislation which allows the central state to extend the borders of the 'independent' Bantustans and thus arbitrarily to incorporate whole communities within them. Several communities in the western and central Transvaal – Leeuwfontein, Braklaagte, Machakaneng – are being incorporated into Bophuthatswana despite vigorous protest.[37] They are 'black spots' in 'white' South Africa with a long history of refusal to be relocated. A community of about 15,000 people within KwaNdebele, who occupy the farms Bloedfontein and Geweerfontein (see Map 10.2), is also to be incorporated into Bophuthatswana. They are predominantly of North Sotho origin and strongly oppose the prospect of direct subordination to the Bophuthatswana state, which has repeatedly harassed and intimidated non-Tswana ethnic minorities within Bophuthatswana. While the land was to be incorporated, the residents were to be moved to the area of the Rust de Winter dam (see Map 10.2). The government appears to have rescinded its threat to remove the people, but still insists that their land will go to Bophuthatswana. The people concerned are determined neither to move from the land which they have occupied for over sixty years, nor to accept administration by Bophuthatswana.[38]

All of these communities face the loss of their South African citizenship on their incorporation into Bophuthatswana. None of them will necessarily by physically removed as a result. This underlines the insidious quality of the new 'solution'. Instead of removing the people to the Bantustan, bring the Bantustan to the people. Eliminate more black South Africans by a stroke of the pen. Not only, then, have some boundaries been 'hardened' to deprive TBVC citizens of rights in 'South Africa'. The 'hardened' boundaries are also being extended to generate more aliens and thence to deprive more people of such rights.

CONCLUSION

These two case studies may be used to illustrate an observation and a question of general importance. The observation is that any assessment of the significance of 'orderly urbanization' and related aspects of 'reform' of the apartheid state must be based mainly on their impact on the lives of the inhabitants of the rural slums. On the one hand, these people depend for their livelihood on access to the metropolitan labour markets. On the other hand, they are most vulnerable to the strategies of exclusion devised by the state relating to the shortage of housing, the competition for jobs and the loss of citizenship.

The question arises out of the observation. How do struggles of the kind that took place in KwaNdebele throughout 1986 relate to the broader struggle for a unitary democratic state in South Africa? To the outsider, life in KwaNdebele is characterized by two images of struggle. One image is the grinding exhaustion of the daily passage on the Putco buses between a string of distant slums in the central Transvaal and places of work in or beyond Pretoria. The other image is of popular resistance spreading like a fire in the veld. On the face of it, the two images are difficult to reconcile. The only way to reconcile them, and indeed to answer the question above, is through a detailed study of community politics which would illuminate the interaction over time of complex strands of experience: those of violent social dislocation, escalating structural unemployment and tightening subordination to repressive Bantustan administrations. The history of organization of women and of the youth must be of prime importance in such analysis.

Another significant variable in such analysis must be the physical and political distance between the black townships in 'white' South Africa and the rural slums of the Bantustans. For the most part, lines of confrontation in Soweto and the townships of the Rand, of the western Cape and around Port Elizabeth appear relatively clearcut. These areas are routinely terrorized by South African and black municipal police, by the army and by assorted vigilantes; and they are irrevocably politicized against the apartheid state. They are not subject in any direct sense to the intermediate distortions of Bantustan politics. By contrast, non-Tswar commuters from the sprawling slums of the Winter-veld in the Moretele-Odi block of Bophuthatswana to the north-west of Pretoria have experienced brutal harassment by the Bophuthatswana authorities for many years. Likewise, ugly and protracted conflict on the edges of KwaZulu around Durban, between Chief Buthelezi's Inkatha movement, on the one hand, and unions and other organizations affiliated to the United Democratic Front, on the other hand, reflects the fact that black townships in 'white' South Africa and rural slums in the Bantustans are here physically contiguous with one another and in close proximity to the metropolitan region of Durban–Pinetown–Pietermaritzburg. There is a major struggle in this region for control of future political directions. The situation in rural slums which are incorporated within Bantustans and physically isolated from the metropolitan areas is different again. Inevitably they are insulated, to some degree, from the volatile currents of immediate confrontation with the central state. They are characterized, rather, by contradictory insecurities, strange alliances and ambivalent commitments.

An example of what I mean by contradictory insecurities is the appalling dilemma of people in parts of Bophuthatswana who, having established their homes within the Bantustan as refugees from municipal harassment in 'white' South Africa, now face the prospect of losing their jobs because they are treated as foreigners in the country of their birth. Alternatively, they face losing the right to live in Bophuthatswana. An example of a strange alliance is the highly tenuous coalition thrown up in KwaNdebele which embraces white farmers threatened with expropriation of their land, youth and community leaders closely in touch with the politics of resistance at a national level, and local forces of populist and traditionalist opposition within the Bantustan. How far was the successful surge of revolt in KwaNdebele in 1986 an expression merely of immediate and widespread popular revulsion against the vigilante organization Mbokhoto? How far was it an expression of a more fundamental antagonism to a form of political 'independence' which would inevitably intensify people's material insecurities? An example of ambivalent commitments, or of the 'ambiguities of dependence' in Shula Marks' telling phrase,[39] may be found in the same set of particular circumstances. To what extent is the populist opposition leader Prince James Mahlangu facing 'inwards', so to speak, with his eye on 'independence' for KwaNdebele under his leadership as opposed to that of Skosana or George Mahlangu? At

251

what point will he alienate sections of his local constituency which are committed to the destruction of the political framework within which he worked until recently?

EDITORS' NOTES

a   KwaNdebele: one of the smallest and least viable of the so-called self-governing 'homelands' situated north-east of Pretoria and designated as the self-governing territory of the 'South Ndebele'.
b   Alcoholic drinking session.
c   QwaQwa: the smallest of the so-called self-governing 'homelands', situated on the eastern borders of the Orange Free State and designated as the self-governing territory of 'South Sotho'.
d   Mangope: President of Bophuthatswana until his overthrow in 1994 and the reincorporation of Bophuthatswana into South Africa.
e   Lebowa: so-called self-governing territory of the 'Pedi' or 'North Sotho' and situated in the northern Transvaal.
f   *Sjambok*: whip made from animal hide; often associated with beatings administered by white farmers to their black servants and labourers.
g   Political leaders of KwaNdebele.

NOTES

*   I am grateful to William Cobbett for helpful comments on an earlier draft of this article. Various versions were presented to the ASAUK [African Studies Association of the United Kingdom] meeting in Canterbury in September 1986, at seminars in London and Oxford and in a public lecture in Cambridge, October and November 1986. This version was completed on 31 March 1987 and takes no account of events subsequent to that date.
1   For valuable critical analysis of 'orderly urbanization', see D. Hindson, 'Urbanization and Influx Control' and 'Creating New Controls', *Work in Progress*, nos. 40 (January, 1986) and 41 (April, 1986); and the Special Edition on Influx Control Policy, *South African Labour Bulletin* 11, 8 (September/October, 1986), especially V. Watson, 'South African Urbanisation Policy: Past and Present', 77–90, and W. Cobbett, '"Orderly Urbanisation": Continuity and Change in Influx Control', 106–21. For a summary review of experience since July 1986, see *Weekly Mail*, 20 March 1987.
2   In 1979 and for some years afterwards it was known as Onverwacht to its inhabitants, after one of the farms in a block compulsorily purchased from white owners by the government. Its official name of Botshabelo is intended to reflect its initial function as a place of refuge (*botshabelo*) for 'illegal squatters' in the Thaba'Nchu district of Bophuthatswana. The official name has only recently been generally adoₓted by the people who live there. Accordingly, I use both names in the text.

3 For critique of regional development, see W. Cobbett, D. Glaser, D. Hindson and M. Swilling, 'South Africa's Regional Political Economy: A Critical Analysis of Reform Strategy in the 1980s', *South African Review III*, South African Research Service (Johannesburg: Ravan Press, 1986), 137–68.

4 See, particularly, a series of articles by P. van Zeyl, Manager, Research and Corporate Planning, South African Development Trust Corporation (STK): 'An Evolving Development Axis', *Growth* (Autumn, 1985); 'IDPs on the Development Axis', *Growth* (Winter, 1985); 'Botshabelo: Increasing Emphasis on Regional Co-operation Set to Bolster Development Impetus Further', *Growth* (Summer, 1986).

5 W. Cobbett, 'A Test Case for "Planned Urbanization"', *Work in Progress*, no. 42 (May, 1986), 25–30.

6 Figures adapted from C. Simkins, *Four Essays on the Past, Present and Possible Future of the Distribution of the Black Population of South Africa* (Cape Town: Southern Africa Labour and Development Research Unit, 1983), 53–7.

7 J. Graaf, cited in Cobbett, '"Orderly Urbanisation"', 121.

8 For details and analysis, see L. Platzky and C. Walker for the Surplus People Project, *The Surplus People* (Johannesburg: Ravan Press, 1985).

9 F. de Clerq, 'Some Recent Trends in Bophuthatswana: Commuters and Restructuring in Education', *South African Review II*, South African Research Service (Johannesburg: Ravan Press, 1984), 272.

10 South African Institute of Race Relations (SAIRR), *Survey of Race Relations in South Africa 1984* (Johannesburg, 1985), 374; L. Platzky on behalf of the National Committee Against Removals, 'Reprieves and Repression: Relocation in South Africa', *South African Review III*, 396, fn.5.

11 For a review of state housing policy, see P. Hendler, A. Mabin and S. Parnell, 'Rethinking Housing Questions in South Africa', *South African Review III* (19—), 195–207.

12 SAIRR, *Survey 1984* (1985), 258, 259.

13 J. Lelyveld, *Move Your Shadow: South Africa, Black and White* (London: Michael Joseph, 1986), 122. The desperate half-life of KwaNdebele's commuters on the Putco buses is movingly described by the journalist Joe Lelyveld, 127–31, and by the photographer, David Goldblatt in O. Badsha and F. Wilson (eds), *South Africa: The Cordoned Heart* (Cape Town: Gallery Press, 1986).

14 For analysis of industrial decentralization as one element of the strategy of regional development, see Cobbett and others, 'South Africa's Reform Strategy'.

15 Cobbett, 'A Test Case', 27.

16 The history of forced relocation in the Orange Free State is reviewed in detail in vol. 3 of *Forced Removals in South Africa* (Cape Town: The Surplus People Project, 1983). See also C. Murray, 'Struggle from the Margins: Rural Slums in the Orange Free State', in F. Cooper (ed.), *Struggle for the City: Migrant Labour, Capital and the State in Urban Africa* (London: Sage, 1983).

17 Cobbett, 'A Test Case', 26.
18 Cobbett, 'A Test Case', 27.
19 A detailed case study of this household is presented in C. Murray, 'The Political Economy of Forced Relocation: A Study of Two Households Through Time', in P. Spray and J. Suckling (eds), *After Apartheid – Renewing the South African Economy* (London: James Currey, 1987).
20 Van Zeyl, 'IDPs on the Development Axis'. For a damning indictment of employment practices at the Botshabelo IDP, see W. Cobbett, 'Industrialization and Exploitation: The Case of Botshabelo', *South African Labour Bulletin* 12, 3 (April, 1987) 95–109.
21 *Weekly Mail*, 6 February 1987, 20 March 1987.
22 The account of KwaNdebele presented below is drawn from the following sources: the annual *Survey* of the South African Institute of Race Relations, Johannesburg (SAIRR); vol. 5 of *Forced Removals in South Africa*; N. Haysom, *Apartheid's Private Army: The Rise of Right-Wing Vigilantes in South Africa* (London: Catholic Institute for International Relations, 1986), 61–79; *Occasional Newsletters of the Transvaal Rural Action Committee*, Johannesburg (TRAC); I. Obery for TRAC, 'Unusual Alliance Blocks KwaNdebele Independence', *Work in Progress*, no. 44 (September–October, 1986), 3–11; two papers presented at the conference of *The Review of African Political Economy* at the University of Liverpool, 26–28 September 1986: J. Yawitch for TRAC, 'The Anti-Independence Struggle in KwaNdebele', and TRAC, 'Resistance to Forced Removals in the Transvaal 1983–1986', TRAC, *KwaNdebele – the Struggle against 'Independence'* (Johannesburg, 1987); and various press reports (*Weekly Mail, Guardian*, etc.) of 1986. I am indebted to all these sources. I have no experience of fieldwork in KwaNdebele.
23 This section is drawn mainly from the annual SAIRR *Surveys*. See also *Forced Removals in South Africa*, vol. 5, 47–59.
24 T. Malan and P.S. Hattingh, *Black Homelands in South Africa* (Pretoria: Africa Institute of South Africa, 1976), 28.
25 SAIRR, *Survey 1983* (1984), 324–6.
26 *Forced Removals in South Africa*, vol. 5, 54, 205; SAIRR, *Survey 1983* (1984), 334–5.
27 TRAC Newsletter no. 10, Moutse (April, 1986).
28 TRAC Newsletter no. 10, Moutse (April, 1986); Haysom, *Apartheid's Private Army*, 71–9.
29 *Weekly Mail*, 16 May 1986.
30 For details see Yawitch, 'The Anti-Independence Struggle', and Obery, 'Unusual Alliance'.
31 *Weekly Mail*, 18 July 1986.
32 *Weekly Mail*, 25 July 1986; *Guardian*, 28 July 1986.
33 *Observer*, 3 August 1986.
34 *Guardian*, 4 August 1986, 13 August 1986; *Weekly Mail*, 8 August 1986, 15 August 1986.
35 *Weekly Mail*, 9 October 1986, 17 October 1986, 21 November 1986, 28 November 1986, 20 March 1987, 7 May 1987; *Guardian*, 7 May 1987.

36 *Weekly Mail*, 28 November 1986, 5 December 1986.
37 *Weekly Mail*, 12 September 1986; *Guardian*, 27 October 1986.
38 TRAC Newsletter no. 12, Bloedfontein and Geweerfontein (February, 1987).
39 S. Marks, *The Ambiguities of Dependence in South Africa: Class, Nationalism and the State in Twentieth-Century Natal* (Johannesburg: Ravan Press, 1986).

11

ETHNICITY AND PSEUDO-ETHNICITY IN THE CISKEI

J.B. Peires

Jeff Peires, an authority on the history of the Xhosa-speaking peoples, worked at Rhodes University in the eastern Cape before becoming head of department at the black University of the Transkei. An activist as well as a scholar, he has recently been elected an ANC member of parliament. Peires's article represents a critique of state attempts to create tribalism in the homelands, and of the African politicians who sought to take advantage of this strategy. Here, he argues that ethnicity in the Ciskei was imposed from above, as the South African government sought to replace 'puppet' rulers in an area with a long tradition of nationalist political activity. He illustrates the moral uncertainty of the Ciskei's rulers, the material corruption surrounding them (large sums of money were channelled through the homeland governments), and the politics of patronage that grew up around the homeland system. Unsuccessful attempts were made to bolster a Ciskeian identity through newly invented ceremonies and rituals. Jeff Peires's article (originally published anonymously because of its political sensitivity) reflects a powerful element in South African history and social sciences which sees ethnicity as a divisive and undesirable force – in this case a mechanistic and corrupt affair.

* * *

INTRODUCTION: THE CISKEI'S LAND AND PEOPLE

The Ciskei is unique among the South African Bantustan 'homelands' in that it has absolutely no basis in any ethnic, cultural or linguistic fact whatsoever.[1] Unlike Bophuthatswana, KwaZulu, Venda and other territories which are the designated homelands of speakers of the Tswana, Zulu, Venda and other languages, there is no distinctive Ciskeian language and there is no distinctive Ciskeian nationality. The inhabitants of the Ciskei speak Xhosa, as do the inhabitants of the Transkei homeland, but whereas the Transkei leadership rejects the concept of a specifically Transkeian identity and calls for a single greater Xhosaland, the Ciskei government of President Lennox Sebe tries to legitimize itself through the creation of a wholly artificial Ciskeian ethnicity. It is the aim of this article to trace the origins and progress of this vain attempt.

The Ciskei, as its name implies, is a block of territory situated on the side of the Kei River closest to the old Cape Colony of which it once formed part.[2] It is separated from the Transkei by a wedge of European-owned land running from South Africa's tenth-largest city, East London, through King Williams Town and up to Queenstown. This strip, usually referred to as 'the white corridor', was carved out of Xhosa territory during the frontier wars of the nineteenth century. If current proposals are duly implemented, the Ciskei will eventually consist of some 8,300 square kilometres. This area contained in 1980 a resident population of some 650,000, a population density of 126 to the square kilometre – the highest of any South African homeland except for QwaQwa.[3] Over one-third of this population is urban, concentrated around the centres of Mdantsane and Zwelitsha which are nothing but dormitory suburbs for the white corridor cities of East London and King Williams Town respectively.

Over 1,400,000 people classified by the South African government as Ciskeian reside beyond the borders of the Ciskei.[4] It is the policy of the apartheid regime to dump as many as possible of these 'surplus people' into the Ciskei. At least 160,000 of the Ciskei's population has been there for less than ten years, an average influx of about 15,000 a year.[5] Most of these are housed in huge resettlement complexes around Hewu and King Williams Town districts, and new resettlement camps are still springing up. The Surplus People Project Survey of 1980 revealed high unemployment rates of over 30 per cent in most Ciskeian centres, with most people eking out a bare subsistence on poor, starchy diets.[6] The state has attempted to alleviate the situation by encouraging industrial development in the Ciskei, but its system of incentives has done more for the capitalist entrepreneurs involved than for the mass of the Ciskeian poor.

The Ciskei/white corridor area was the scene of intense black–

white contact in schoolhouse and marketplace, and on the battle-field, throughout South Africa's frontier period. The dogged resistance of the Rharhabe Xhosa held the line against colonial invaders for more than a century, longer than any other southern African anti-colonial resistance.[7] At the same time, the region also experienced extensive missionary activity. Mission schools such as Lovedale and Healdtown paved the way for the college at Fort Hare, founded in 1915, which became the subcontinent's premier institution for African higher education until its seizure by the South African government in 1959. Rural districts such as Peddie and Keiskammahoek nurtured an independent commer-cial peasantry, which still flourished at the turn of the century.[8] Elected headmen and literate spokesmen replaced old-style hereditary chiefs as the true representatives of this new class. Newspaper editors and politicians such as J.T. Jabavu and W.B. Rubusana were prominent in Cape politics during the days of the African franchise, and they laid the foundations for twentieth-century progressive political movements in South Africa.[9]

The emergence of the revived African National Congress (ANC) in the 1940s effectively fused the resistance and the edu-cational traditions in the Eastern Cape region. East London has been a stronghold of the ANC since the Defiance Campaign of 1952, and ANC leaders Nelson Mandela, Oliver Tambo and Govan Mbeki are all Xhosa-speakers, as was Robert Sobukwe, the founder of the Pan-Africanist Congress.[10] King Williams Town was the home of Steve Biko and the spiritual centre of the black consciousness movement during the 1960s and 1970s. More recently, the workers of East London have given strong support to the South African Allied Workers Union (SAAWU), which began to organize in the city in the late 1970s.[11] The significance of this is that the region which now forms part of the Ciskei has a deep-rooted historical tradition of fierce resistance to colonial domination which transcends ethnic boundaries and pre-colonial political structures and is now closely linked with a broad South African nationalism. Moreover, as a recent commentator remarked, 'The East Cape's unique combination of a high level of education and a low level of subsistence has always made it one of the most inflammable regions of South Africa.'[12]

THE CISKEI VERSUS THE TRANSKEI IN HISTORICAL PERSPECTIVE

It is impossible to say with any certainty why the Xhosa-speaking people have been divided between the two rival Bantustans of Ciskei and Transkei. The most common popular explanation is that this is an example of 'divide and rule', and that its main purpose is the preservation of East London and the white corridor. I do not agree. The division of Bophuthatswana into six pieces has never posed any problems for its white neighbours, and the South African government has stated with apparent truth that it would not oppose a merger. The separation of the Ciskei from the Transkei is more probably the result of the sort of political accident which can occur in even the best-regulated of societies.

After the Promotion of Bantu Self-Government Act in 1959, Dr Verwoerd, the arch-proponent of the grand apartheid design, was keen to present the world with a practical demonstration of the wisdom of his policies in the form of an independent homeland. The Transkei was almost perfect for his purposes. It was a large contiguous territory, ethnically homogeneous and largely rural, governed by hard-line pro-government chiefs such as Kaiser D. Matanzima and possessing in the Transkeian Territories General Council a vaguely representative body which could, when suitably adjusted, serve as a fig-leaf for autocratic control. The Ciskei was totally different. It consisted at the time of a number of distinct black 'reserves' interspersed in patchwork style with pockets of white-owned farms and towns. Even in the rural areas, elected headmen had largely replaced hereditary chiefs, and the most visible and articulate spokesmen of black interests lived in towns and wanted nothing to do with the so-called Bantu Authorities. Whereas the Transkei was virtually tailor-made for apartheid-style independence as early as 1963, the Ciskei obviously still had a long way to go. In the urgency which surrounded the launching of the Transkei – Self-Government in 1963 and 'Independence' in 1976 – the problem of the Xhosa communities of the Ciskei was temporarily shelved, and when it finally recalled itself to official attention, it did so as a separate problem.

The Ciskeian government grew out of the old Ciskeian General Council established in 1934.[13] In 1961, this was reconstituted as the Ciskei Territorial Authority under the Bantu Authorities policy, and Proclamation R143 of 1968 created an Executive Committee of six ministers and the basis of an autonomous civil service. The first Chief Councillor was Justice Mabandla, chief of the Bhele Mfengu people. In 1972 Lennox Sebe, a member of the cabinet, broke with Mabandla and started his own political party, the Ciskei National Independence Party (CNIP). This was victorious in the 1973 elections, largely due to the connivance of the South African electoral officers. Mabandla's party, the Ciskei National Party, crumbled away in the face of Sebe's impregnable position. Two other opposition parties were started, but neither got off the ground. In 1978 the remaining opposition members, including Mabandla himself, crossed the floor and the Ciskei officially became a one-party state. After a rigged referendum in December 1980, the Ciskei accepted South Africa's version of independence in December 1982.[14] Prophetically, the new Ciskeian flag collapsed the first time it was raised. Mounting opposition in schools, streets and factories led the President to confer increasingly arbitrary powers on his half-brother, Charles Sebe, the commander of the dreaded Ciskei Central Intelligence Service. Charles's power grew steadily for about eighteen months until his vaulting ambition, in the form of an assassination plot, brought his downfall in June 1983. Shortly thereafter, the violent attempts of the Ciskeian authorities to suppress a bus boycott in Mdantsane precipitated a bloody conflict between government and people.[15]

Ever since the fall of Charles Sebe, President Lennox Sebe has ruled alone.[a] Rumours concerning the poor state of his health and the unusual medication he is said to require are fuelled by the fact that, alone in the entire Ciskeian cabinet, the Minister of Health is usually a white. The dissolution in 1985 of a Committee of Four, which screened development proposals before they reached the President's eyes, opened the way for a number of highly dubious entrepreneurs, many of them Israelis, who milked the Ciskeian government for two straight years.[16]

The meteoric promotion to the rank of Major-General of Sebe's only son, Khwane, leads one to suppose that the President is grooming him for the succession. His last rival, Lent Maqoma, was dismissed from the cabinet in January 1985. After the effective suppression of his Ciskei People's Rights Protection Party, Maqoma fled to the Transkei where he plotted the overthrow of the Sebe dynasty with the help of the Matanzima brothers. A spectacular double coup in September 1986, which effected the kidnapping of Khwane Sebe to the Transkei and freed Charles Sebe from his maximum security prison, was nullified in February 1987 when a daring attack on Sebe's presidential palace was foiled by his guards. The South African government intervened to end the squabbles of its vassals. The Transkei was warned off, and Lennox Sebe's position in the Ciskei now seems stronger than ever.[17]

These are the bare bones of the Ciskei's political history. We now turn to the role of ethnicity in shaping the course of these events.

MFENGU–RHARHABE RIVALRY AND THE RISE OF LENNOX SEBE

Conventionally, one distinguishes between two ethnic groups in the Ciskei: the Rharhabe Xhosa, who are descended from the first Bantu-speaking people to inhabit the area, and the Mfengu, a generic name for several distinct groupings of associated clans who fled from Zululand during the time of King Shaka (1818–28) and settled in the eastern Cape.[18] It is important to emphasize that members of both these groups are to be found in the Transkei as well as the Ciskei: they cannot be characterized as distinctly Ciskeian peoples. Initial cultural differences between Rharhabe and Mfengu – for example, that the Mfengu pierced the ears and the Xhosa did not – have long since faded into insignificance. They have been overshadowed by the cataclysmic events of the year 1835, when the Mfengu were persuaded by the missionary Ayliff to desert their Xhosa patrons and seek colonial protection.

On 14 May 1835, the Mfengu gathered under an old milkwood tree in Peddie district and swore a great oath to obey the Queen, to accept Christianity and to educate their children. This oath was to have momentous consequences. The Mfengu fought alongside the colonial forces in all the frontier wars and were rewarded by extensive tracts of Rharhabe land. As the better-educated and more European-oriented group, they naturally secured the bulk of élite positions as clerks, teachers, peasants and petty traders that were available to blacks in an elective system based on merit and achievement, as opposed to the pre-colonial Xhosa pattern of strong hereditary chiefs. They viewed

261

themselves as the bearers of a great universal Christian Civilization, and tended to regard the Rharbabe and other Xhosa as backward and uncivilized. Every 14 May since 1907 has been celebrated as Fingo Emancipation Day, with a ceremony held under the old milkwood tree where the Mfengu oath was sworn.

The Rharhabe, for their part, resented Mfengu predominance in the professions and salaried posts, their hold on the headmanships and other organs of local political authority, and their control of land which had formerly belonged to the Xhosa. S.E.K. Mqhayi, the Xhosa national poet, accused the Mfengu of celebrating Fingo Emancipation on the anniversary of the very day that the revered Xhosa king Hintsa was murdered and mutilated by colonial forces in 1835. In 1909, the Xhosa responded with a memorial celebration dedicated to Ntsikana (d. 1821), the first local prophet of Christianity, who was a Rharhabe Xhosa. The rivalry between Rharhabe and Mfengu, originating in frontier wars and sustained by economic and social competition ever since, thus found institutional expression as far back as the turn of this century.

The National Party's policy of retribalization, first expressed in the Bantu Authorities Act of 1951, aimed at pulling down the remnants of the old Cape liberal tradition and its concept of universal equality grounded in common Christian and democratic ideals and replacing it with a tamed and deformed version of pre-colonial political discipline hinging on chieftainship. This development obviously threatened the Mfengu, who had been the main beneficiaries of the Cape tradition, and offered opportunities to the Rharhabe whose ancient rights and long discarded chieftainships had been fully recorded in the old books and documents that government ethnologists now rediscovered. A new spirit of self-assertiveness entered the Rharhabe ranks, and the return of the Rharhabe paramountcy from eighty years of exile beyond the Kei became the occasion of deliberate public insults directed against the Mfengu.

Ironically, it was the Mfengu attempt to pre-empt their Rharhabe rivals which precipitated their downfall. Justice Mabandla, who was both a Mfengu hereditary chief and an educated man, seemed to accommodate both government and Mfengu aspirations. Uncomfortably aware that the new dispensation played into Rharhabe hands, in 1968 Mbandla and his associates issued a 'Fingo Manifesto', in which they requested that the Mfengu be regarded as entirely independent of the Rharhabe, and that representation in the coming 'New Deal' arrangements outlined by the Proclamation R143 of 1968 should be structured along ethnic lines. The South African government was not averse to stirring up ethnic hatreds and the Commissioner General made a public attack on the Xhosa during the Fingo Emancipation celebration of 1969. The New Deal Executive was explicitly made up of two Mfengu, two Rharhabe, one Sotho and one Thembu. With the excision of Herschel and Glen Grey districts, which became part of the Transkei in 1976, the latter groups lost their political significance.

Mabandla was Chief Executive. Sebe, the leading Rharhabe, was Minister of Education. They did not work well together. Mabandla accused Sebe of holding secret meetings and plotting against his government. Sebe accused Mabandla of ethnic favouritism and of blocking the applications of Rharhabe chiefs for government recognition. When Sebe was dropped to the less glamorous Agriculture portfolio, he began to organize his own political party, the Ciskei National Independence Party (CNIP), for the upcoming 1973 elections. The CNIP was backed by almost all those Rharhabe who were prepared to accept Bantu Authorities. The other Xhosa member of the Executive Council, L.S. Mtoba, stayed with Mabandla, as did the Rharhabe Paramount Chief, Bazindhlovu Sandile. But the presence of such prominent Rharhabe in his ranks did not help Mabandla. 'Why should we be ruled by a Fingo?' the CNIP asked, and by persistently beating on the ethnic drum, they awakened the historical and material grievances of the Rharhabe and rallied them to Sebe's cause.

RESETTLEMENT AND ETHNICITY

The CNIP victory in the 1973 elections was almost certainly the result of a South African governmental decision, as is shown by the role of South African officials in committing electoral irregularities on Sebe's behalf.[19] One can only speculate as to why South Africa preferred Sebe. Mabandla was docile enough, though his performance as Chief Executive had been weak and unimpressive. On the other hand, certain long-term factors were working in Sebe's favour. These were intimately connected with South Africa's policies of retribalization and resettlement and it is appropriate to discuss them in some detail.

We have already seen that the frontier wars of the nineteenth century resulted in the wholesale destruction of the old Rharhabe chiefdoms and the confiscation of their lands. Some of these were given to the Colony's Mfengu allies and the rest were distributed to white settlers. In order to confer some sort of geopolitical unity on the Ciskei, the South African government was forced to embark on a massive programme of reallocating territory, officially termed the 'consolidation of the Ciskei'. Briefly the idea is to join up most of the scattered patches of black-owned land by purchasing some 300,000 hectares of adjacent white farmland, while knocking out eleven 'awkwardly situated Bantu areas' in the white corridor. Even though much of this land has been earmarked for the accommodation of people resettled from the white corridor it nevertheless represents a significant increase in the extent of land nominally allocated to blacks in the region. The better part of these lands will be farmed on a commercial basis by Ciskei parastatals, and the rest will probably degenerate into resettlement camps.[20]

One cannot even begin to discuss the horrifying implications of mass relocation in an article on ethnicity. Here it is only pertinent to remark that relatively few persons are thrown into resettlement camps by direct government action: bulldozers, armed policemen, people carted away by the truckload. The majority of resettled persons are rendered homeless by the apparently impersonal application of regulations: no work permit, no residence rights, papers not in order and so forth. In particular, tens of thousands of displaced agricultural labourers, forced from the white-owned farms on which their families had resided for generations, have no legal place of residence outside their designated homeland, and no family links even there. For people in such desperate straits, even a resettlement camp appears to be something of a refuge.[21]

The purchase of white farmland and the influx of displaced persons from the white rural areas created the necessary opportunity for the resuscitation of several old Rharhabe chieftainships which had been in abeyance since the Ninth, and last, Frontier War of 1877–8.[22] Government ethnologist A.O. Jackson has indicated that aspirant chiefs need to fulfil the following practical requirements:

> The claimant's right to be regarded as a chief must be demonstrated genealogically. He must have a sufficiently

large following and his following must have its own territory in which it lives.[23]

Genealogical demonstration was never a problem. Among the Xhosa, all sons of chiefs became chiefs. An important chief like Ngqika (d. 1829) might generate five chiefly lineages which are still recognized today. Every one of the literally thousands of members of the royal Tshawe clan is entitled to chieftainship somewhere along the line – if only he can find a territory and a following. Once South Africa started adding land and people to the Ciskei, this problem was easily solved. New chieftainships were established in one of three possible ways.

First the population of a given location could reject the authority of their officially recognized chief and invite in a new chief. The Rharhabe of Gqumahashe, Victoria East, for example, had long campaigned for the return of the old Tyhali chieftainship to supersede the authority of their recognized chief, the Mfengu Justice Mabandla. Second, where white farmlands were allocated for black resettlement, aspirant chiefs with enough influence could claim the newly released land as their ancestral home, and thus acquire both territory and following in one fell swoop. Thus after the South African authorities had decided to turn the farm vacated by a Mr Fetter into Ndevana resettlement camp, President Sebe himself was able to recognize the farm as his long lost ancestral land and its people as his own personal chiefdom, the amaKhambashe.[24] Third, when individuals settled in a rural area as tenants or squatters without permanent land rights, these newcomers might band together under an ethnic banner and claim to be a single 'tribe', having historical rights. This occurred in Nyaniso, Peddie district (always a Mfengu area), where the newcomers were incited by an aspirant chief with a fake pedigree to declare themselves members of the Gwali chiefdom and thus claim historical rights from their unfortunate Mfengu hosts.[25]

Altogether, eight new Rharhabe chieftainships and one new Mfengu chieftainship were created. All went to Sebe supporters. Some of these (Gqunukhwebe, Ngcangathelo, imiNgxalase) were the products of long-pressed claims which had considerable historical justification, but question marks hang over some of the others. Chief Lent Maqoma, for instance, descends from his illustrious ancestor through a female. Yet he was preferred to other members of his family with stronger claims. Claims from Transkei chiefs too closely associated with the anti-Sebe Rharhabe Paramount Chief (Anta, for instance, or the amaMbalu) were overlooked. S.M. Burns-Ncamashe, a highly educated man with an outstanding knowledge of history, wrote up most of the chieftainship applications and slipped in one for himself as well. Initially he tried to pass himself off as a chief of the old, but small and obscure Hleke lineage, but the existing amaHleke would not have him. He then successfully prevailed on the head of the almost defunct Gwali lineage, a timid and illiterate village sub-headman in the Transkei, to recognize him as the head of the amaGwali in the Ciskei. This claim is regarded with some cynicism by those who remember the young Ncamashe as a member of the non-royal Kwayi clan.[26]

The most noteworthy case of contrived chieftainship is that of President Sebe himself. Sebe was regarded by his schoolfellows at Lovedale as a member of the royal Tshawe clan, but not as a chief. Indeed Paramount Chief Sandile once taunted Sebe with being a commoner, and this may have decided him to seek a title of his own. In March 1977, he declared that his great-grandfather had been awarded chieftainship by Chief Phatho because of his heroism in 1847 in the War of the Axe. This is historically possible, but it would give Sebe a rank infinitely junior to the many biological descendants of Chief Phatho who remain without chieftainships. Later during the year, Sebe came up with a better idea. This time he claimed descent from a certain Chief Tyarha, who probably lived in the middle of the eighteenth century, but concerning whom literally nothing is known.[27] This second claim is almost certainly fictitious. Indeed, the President's own brother, Charles Sebe, declared after his disgrace that Lennox's father was not a Sebe after all but a Dhlamini (that is, a common Mfengu clan name). The traditional territory of the hitherto unknown Khambashe chiefdom turned out, by wonderful coincidence, to be Fetter's farm, later Ndevana resettlement camp. By 1984 there were at least 50,000 people living in appalling conditions at Ndevana, but this was unlikely to have distressed the President for he had only visited the place once during his first three years as its chief. He has never visited the resettlement camp at Tsweletswele, also within his tribal area, whose 8,000 inhabitants were attracted by the unfulfilled promises of his agents.[28] The benign view of resettlement taken by Sebe and other Ciskeian chiefs may not be unconnected with the fact that their salary is directly linked to the number of their adherents. They therefore have a real financial stake in forced resettlements.[29]

The appointment of nine pro-Sebe chiefs turned Sebe's razor-thin majority of between 24 and 26 in the Ciskei Legislative Assembly into a comfortable margin. This doomed Mabandla's party to eternal opposition, and caused the hasty defection of its members into the government ranks. The early Sebe had done extremely well out of his espousal of a narrow, Mfengu-bashing, Rharhabe ethnicity. It had secured him his parliamentary major-ity and his own personal chieftainship as well.

LENNOX SEBE CHANGES HiS TUNE

One of the first things that Lennox Sebe did after attaining a position of unquestionable power was to attempt to heal the ugly breach between Rharhabe and Mfengu which he himself had done so much to inflame. Sebe had always had some Mfengu supporters, notably the Zizi chief, Njokweni, whose support – said to have been purchased by a bribe – gave him his first narrow majority. Sebe sought to extend this support by placing pro-Sebe candidates into vacant Mfengu headmanships and regencies, and he eventually welcomed the whole opposition party, including the wretched Mabandla, into the CNIP. The annual Fingo Emancipation and Ntsikana Day ceremonies were suppressed because they 'divided the Ciskei nation along ethnic lines'.[30] President Sebe now aimed to build a new and united nation owing allegiance to neither Rharhabe nor Mfengu ethnic loyalties, but united in a single Ciskeian nationalism. It is possi-ble, of course, that the President was motivated exclusively by a desire to promote peace and harmony, and that he perceived the dangerous possibilities of uncontrolled ethnic hatreds. But there were other factors as well, and these must be considered in turn.

One major anomaly in Sebe's role as champion of the Rharhabe cause was the uncompromising hostility of the Rharhabe Para-mount Chief, Bazindhlovu Sandile. This is not as strange as it might seem. The Sandile family was exiled to the Transkei after the frontier war of 1877–8, and it only returned in 1961, thanks to the apartheid policy of boosting traditional authorities. Though acknowledged as Paramounts of all the Rharhabe, the Sandile family nevertheless possessed no territory or subjects under their direct control and were regarded as possibly dangerous interlopers by the Ciskei Rharhabe chiefs. Bazindhlovu Sandile, who ascended the Rharhabe throne in 1969, was a weak, colourless man who drank too much and lacked the stature of his late father.

His youth had been passed among the Transkei Rharhabe chiefs, and he recognized the seniority of the Transkei-based Gcaleka branch of the Tshawe royal clan. The political insignificance of the Transkei Rharhabe exiles had, moreover, led them to exalt hereditary rank and faithful adherence to the old customs above the sort of power games and backstairs intrigue endemic in homeland politics. Bazindhlovu rejected Sebe as an upstart commoner, and somewhat naively called on his people to follow their Paramount Chief. His view of *ubuRharhabe* (Rharhabe-hood) thus far transcended the Ciskei in both space and time. It could even be argued that the Sandile family represented an authentic historical tradition of Rharhabe ethnicity, which was incompatible with the bogus pseudo-tradition inherent in any South African-sponsored ethnic homeland.

Bazindhlovu Sandile died suddenly and prematurely in April 1976.[31] Whereas Bazindhlovu alive was an acute embarrassment to the Ciskeian authorities, Bazindhlovu dead might well have proved an asset. The noble chief Sandile (d. 1878) was precisely the sort of folk-hero whom Sebe and his friends professed to respect, and they wished to co-opt his name into the emerging Ciskei pantheon through the support of his descendants. The Sandile family wished to give Bazindhlovu a traditional funeral at which his Transkei Rharhabe relatives and the Gcaleka Paramount Xolilizwe Sigcawu would all be present. The Ciskei government wanted a Ciskei state funeral at which no 'outsiders' (that is, Transkeians) would be present. A strong CNIP delegation travelled up to the mourning Great Place and demanded the body. Fortunately, the family had already deposited it with a firm of white undertakers. The CNIP men then demanded the body from the undertakers who, forewarned by the Sandile family, refused to give it up. Unable to stop the funeral, the Ciskei government obstructed it as far as possible by refusing to assign earth-moving equipment and by initially refusing to contribute a state subsidy.

Xolilizwe Sigcawu, the Transkei-based king of all the Xhosa, was present at the funeral. So were Sebe and the CNIP. But when Xolilizwe announced that Bazindhlovu's widow would carry on as Regent for her minor son according to Xhosa custom, Chief L.W. Maqoma rose on the government side. This was something for the 'Rharhabe Tribunal', a pro-CNIP body, he said, not a matter for the family or outsiders to decide. Chief Maqoma himself was, in fact, the CNIP's man for the job. The family nominated Bazindhlovu's widow. To no one's surprise, the government ethnologist supported Maqoma who remained Regent until he fell from Sebe's favour in 1978. In 1987 there is still no sign of the installation of Bazindhlovu's son, Maxhoba, although he is past 30. This suggests that, for all his vaunted traditionalism, Sebe still sees the Rharhabe paramountcy as a wild card and a potential threat to his exclusive monopoly of legitimacy.

The tragic farce of Bazindhlovu's funeral was repeated at that of his Chief Councillor, Isaac Sangotsha. Sangotsha had been an active figure in opposition politics until the collapse of the Mabandla party when, an old man, he retired to his country home. A fervent Catholic, Sangotsha refused to attend Easter services at Ntaba kaNdoda (see p. 271) and, almost alone in his village, he went to church on Good Friday. He must have been somewhat indiscreet in his opinions because he was picked up by the police. He returned, broken in health and spirit, and died soon thereafter in July 1982. The Ciskei government offered to pay for the funeral and arrange the programme. The Master of Ceremonies was the then Ciskei Vice-President, the Reverend Wilson Xaba, who delivered a sermon on the theme, 'He made some mistakes, but he was one of us'. Isaac Sangotsha was buried in a beautiful coffin by the very men he most hated and struggled against. In the Ciskei one cannot even call one's body one's own.

Returning to our main theme, there was yet another reason for Sebe to abandon a Rharhabe ethnic posture. In as much as the CNIP was an ethnic party expressing pro-Rharhabe, anti-Mfengu sentiments, it was truly a party of like-minded individuals working for common goals. Sebe was the leader, but the party had a *raison d'être* independent of his personal will and ambition. Men such as S.M. Burns-Ncamashe, L.F. Siyo, A.Z. Lamani and L.W. Maqoma gave their loyalty to the CNIP rather than to L.L.W. Sebe, and they regarded themselves as potential leaders of that party. They saw the election victory of 1973 as a triumph for the CNIP rather than a vote of confidence in Sebe personally. Sebe, however, wished to rule alone. He disliked the corporate nature of his party and wanted to turn it into a patronage machine dependent entirely on himself. First Burns-Ncamashe, in 1975, and then Siyo, in 1977, were pushed out of the CNIP. Prominent hereditary chiefs Maqoma and Jongilanga were shuffled around the ministries so as to remind them of their utter dependence on the word of Sebe. Political nonentities such as A.M. Tapa and Sebe's brother-in-law, Simon Hebe, whose only conceivable qualification for office was their loyalty to the President, were elevated to positions of power. The promotion of selected Mfengu, including arch-rival Mabandla, to the cabinet was an integral part of Sebe's strategy of replacing government by party with government by patronage. Sebe knew that he could count on the absolute loyalty of his Mfengu recruits, who depended entirely on him for support against their Rharhabe rivals and their own betrayed followers. Dropping his anti-Mfengu rhetoric was a small price to pay for the broadening of his support.

THE THREAT FROM TRANSKEI

Long before Transkei 'independence' in 1976, Transkei President Matanzima demanded the amalgamation of the Transkei and the Ciskei into a single greater Xhosa homeland.[32] It was generally agreed on both sides of the Kei River that the Transkei, being much the larger, wealthier and more populous, would swallow up the Ciskei in any merger which might take place. Matanzima was openly willing to sponsor any Ciskei politician who supported amalgamation, and it is rumoured that Mabandla, Sebe and L.F. Siyo all received Transkeian aid while they were in opposition. The Transkei assembly passed a motion unilaterally annexing the Ciskei, and Transkei paid the costs of two Supreme Court legal battles against the establishment of a second Xhosa homeland.

Although Matanzima is not a popular figure in the Ciskei, many people are well-disposed towards unification. 'We are all one people', they tend to say, if the subject of unification is broached, and they regard the creation of two separate Xhosa states as a device to ensure the safety of the white corridor. Ciskei government spokesmen struggle to answer the case for unification. Clearly they cannot state publicly that they fear for their power and their positions. Vice-President Willie Xaba, using the Afrikaans word 'suiwer', argued that the Ciskeians were 'pure' Xhosa, whereas the Transkei consisted of mixed Xhosa-speaking tribes.[33] In the Supreme Court, Ciskei counsel stated that Ciskeian ethnic groups were 'independent' of Transkeian ethnic groups. These arguments collapse in the face of the existence of the Transkei Rharhabe and the traditional subordination of the Rharhabe to the Transkei-based Gcaleka royal house. As for the Mfengu, there are four Mfengu magisterial districts in the Transkei, which together constitute a Regional Authority known as Fingoland. Clearly the Ciskei government urgently required a national identity for the Ciskei which sharply differentiated it from the Transkei.

The years since the Soweto Uprising of 1976 have seen an upsurge in public opposition to the Ciskei authorities. School boycotts in 1976, 1977, 1980 and 1983; riots at Fort Hare, including an attack on Sebe's motorcade; trade union organization; clandestine ANC paramilitary activity; and the bloody Mdantsane bus boycott of 1983 – all indicate the growing disaffection of the mass of the so-called 'Ciskeian' population who never accepted ethnicity or homelands in the first place. Sebe was forced to close down his own *alma mater* at Lovedale and the old mission institution of Healdtown. He is clearly perturbed by his lack of appeal to the rising generation, and his calls to 'the youth' are not without a touch of pathos:

> We need our youth in our nation-building ... they must stop their revolt now as the bright day of justice emerges. ... When the clarion calls to defend our great South Africa against the ever-increasing Communism threat, the great Ciskeians will be the first to defend the temples of our fathers, the shrines of this country.[34]

Ciskei clearly faced a crisis of legitimacy. It lacked any basis in historical reality, popular support or educated opinion, and it had been forced to suppress whatever genuine ethnic feeling had once existed. The Ciskei nation had to be created from scratch.

PSEUDO-ETHNICITY: THE 'MAKING' OF A 'NATION'

The central feature of Sebe's new Ciskeian nationalist ideology is the 'Temple' or 'national shrine' at Ntaba kaNdoda ('Mountain of Man'), a somewhat overgrown foothill of the Amatole range about 30 kilometres from King Williams Town. The national shrine is the personal brainchild of the President, conceived during a visit to Mount Massada in Israel in 1977.[35] Every self-respecting nation had something to worship:

> In Egypt, it's the Nile; in Kenya, it's Mount Kenya; in India, it's the cow; in America, it's the national flag.[36]

In the Ciskei, it was Ntaba kaNdoda.

The place for the national shrine was probably suggested by S.E.K. Mqhayi's well-known poem, studied by every Xhosa schoolchild, which says that the old chiefs and diviners used to point to Ntaba kaNdoda and that it was a place where the Xhosa High God Qamata heard his people:

> You should bless this Ntaba kaNdoda!
> You should wish good grace to Ntaba kaNdoda!
> I speak to you, nations of the Xhosa,
> You are the great nations of the Creation.[37]

So far, so good. But Mqhayi nowhere mentions the word 'Ciskei'. The poet (d. 1945) was a leading figure in the Ntsikana Day celebrations, and his 'Intaba kaNdoda' is above all a Rharhabe poem. Nor is it true, as Sebe often claims, that Ntaba kaNdoda was the scene of the last stand by the bold Ciskeian warriors against the colonial invaders. That honour belongs more correctly to the isiDenge forests, which are not even within the boundaries of the modern Ciskei, and which are, in any case, too closely associated with the descendants of Chief Sandile, who lies buried there. On the whole, however, one cannot dispute that, if one is determined to have a national shrine in the Ciskei, Ntaba kaNdoda is as good a place as any other.

It is when we come to the shrine itself and the ceremonies associated with it, that the equivocation really starts. Unlike the centralized Zulu kingdom, the Xhosa lacked any great capital or politico-religious centre. Each of the many chiefs had his own Great Place, but even this was barely distinguishable from the common man's homestead.[38] The Xhosa did not build in stone, and had no great annual ceremonies such as the first-fruits celebrations further north. Even prayers for rain, the only occasion on which the Xhosa normally invoked the High God, were usually held on a chiefly rather than an ethnic basis. Despite, or perhaps because of, this singular lack of precedent, President Sebe decided that a massive complex costing at least R860,000 and built by LTA (Ciskei)[39] – a company in which several Ciskei cabinet ministers enjoy directorships – was the most appropriate expression of the Ciskeian spirit.

The National Shrine consists of an auditorium for conferences and party congresses and an 18,000-seat arena for public events centred on a huge symbolic structure of uncertain import, which vaguely resembles a pair of up-ended half-open pliers. There is also a Heroes' Acre, a graveyard where the future heroes of the nation will be buried, including all the chiefs. Not all the chiefs are equally enthusiastic about this honour, and at least one prominent pro-Sebe Mfengu chief refused outright.[40] Ntaba kaNdoda is further garnished with a beautiful full-size statue of President Sebe himself.[41] Part of the bill was presumably underwritten by the South African government, the rest being funded by compulsory deductions from the salaries of public servants and endless extortions from private citizens.

The public ceremonies certainly seem to owe more to biblical references than to Xhosa religion. The new buildings are freely referred to as the Temple, often in a pseudo-biblical context.[42] Goats, not cattle, are the preferred sacrificial animal. Easter weekend is the chosen time for national services.

Until the building of a new capital at Bisho (see p. 27), most official ceremonies, such as party congresses and passing-out parades, were held at Ntaba kaNdoda. Even a nurses' ceremony, held to commemorate the registration of the first black nurse, was formally transferred from the hospital where she had qualified to the holy Temple.[43]

A wise person says, 'If you are proud of your nation you should make your presence visible on Ntaba kaNdoda.'[44]

This comment appeared in the Ciskei government's propaganda organ, *Umthombo*, and is true in more ways than one. Attendance at Ntaba kaNdoda functions is obligatory for all civil servants, teachers, headmen, people holding Ciskei or parastatal business licences, and all aspirants to such positions. Those who do not make their presence visible are sure to be reported by rival associates and patronage seekers. When the people of Zwelitsha threatened to boycott the Independence Celebrations in 1985, Sebe personally threatened to cut off the town's electricity and water.[45]

Despite all the emphasis on the warrior chiefs of old, only three of Sebe's leading followers had any ancestry worth boasting about. Of these, Chief Lent Whyte Maqoma was the most ambitious.[46] He was descended, albeit somewhat circuitously, from indubitably the greatest of the nineteenth-century fighting chiefs. The original Maqoma (d. 1873) had perished alone on Robben Island, the only man that the Imperial government never dared to release. Lent Maqoma had substantial personal support in Port Elizabeth and the Fort Beaufort/Adelaide areas. He was appointed Acting Chief of the Rharhabe after Bazindhlovu's death. When Siyo and his friends were expelled from the CNIP in 1977, Lent became the obvious Number Two to Sebe in the CNIP hierarchy. Indeed, he was a little too obvious. Sebe did not like any authority not stemming directly from himself.

Lent Maqoma seems to have been genuinely interested in the ancestor to whom he owed his high position. Acting on his own initiative, he launched a campaign to bring back old Maqoma's bones from Robben Island. After all efforts by officials and historians to locate Maqoma's remains had failed, Lent engaged an albino seer named Charity Sonandi who allegedly discovered a few manacled bones on Robben Island to the accompaniment of rainfall, thunder and lightning. These supposed remains were loaded on a South African warship and carried off to Ntaba kaNdoda for a hero's burial in August 1978. Sebe gave the keynote address, but, in retrospect, it is clear that he hated every minute of it. Admittedly the occasion was a copybook example of everything he had ever said about the link between the old chiefs and Ciskei nationhood, but clearly the hero of the hour was L.W. Maqoma and not L.L.W. Sebe. The reinternment simply highlighted the contrast between Maqoma's noble birth and Sebe's own extremely suspect ancestry. Maqoma had stolen Sebe's thunder on the President's very own mountain.

After a decent pause, Sebe reasserted his authority. An officially approved public demonstration – the only one of its kind ever held in Zwelitsha – of homeless people was organized to protest against Lent's performance as Minister responsible for Housing. Maqoma was demoted to a less important portfolio, and his closest cabinet colleague, W. Ximiya, was removed altogether. His son-in-law and other clients were relieved of their jobs. The clairvoyant Ms Sonandi was banished from the Ciskei because, as she put it, 'I am giving immense spiritual power to Chief Lent Whyte Maqoma'. Maqoma was eventually dismissed from the cabinet, stripped of his chieftainship, and exiled from the Ciskei. His very name was obliterated from the public buildings.[47] The lesson of Maqoma's bones is clear enough: even Ciskei nationhood cannot be allowed to take precedence over the President's personal political interests.

The administrative headquarters of the Ciskei government were temporarily housed in Zwelitsha, outside King Williams Town, for several years. The Sebe cabinet pondered a move to the town of Alice, certainly the cultural centre of the eastern Cape missionary tradition, but also a stone's throw away from the militantly anti-Sebe students at the University of Fort Hare. Then, in 1979, a South African commission publicly recommended that the whole of King Williams Town be incorporated into the Ciskei, which virtually surrounds the city. Fierce opposition from the white residents, led by a local gun dealer, severely embarrassed the South African government, and shortly before the 1981 elections it announced that the city would remain white after all. Sebe, who had done a fair amount of sabre-rattling on the issue, was discomfited and, to save his face among his own supporters, the South African government indulged him with a new capital. He chose a site called Yellowwoods about seven kilometres from King Williams Town, and soon entered into the spirit of the South African *carte-blanche*, informing the contractors that:

Ciskeians regarded the establishment of the capital as sacred activity and there can be no talk of this or that costing too much, or cutting down on this or that item to bring cost within budget. ... It is your duty when interpreting these documents to place the life and spirit of the Ciskei people into them.[48]

The contractors appear to have taken the President at his word, and with a budget of some R158 million they have not needed to be overly concerned with the problem of minimizing costs. From the results of their efforts, it would appear that the life and spirit of the Ciskeian people were best expressed in terms of another huge stadium; a new Legislative Assembly building adorned with a bust of President Sebe to match his statue at Ntaba kaNdoda; vast rectangular office block buildings for the extortionate Ciskei civil service; new headquarters for the Ciskei Security Police; and, last but not least, a presidential palace. Bisho will get a new university, since Fort Hare is insufficiently patriotic. It will also get an élite school 'modelled on English public school principles', a curious nursery for the Ciskeian spirit.

Naturally President Sebe could not admit that the new capital, dubbed Bisho, was just a poor substitute for King Williams Town. So he was forced to claim that 'Bisho' was in fact the 'original name of antiquity of the whole of the King Williams Town municipal area'. In fact, the original Xhosa name for the district was Qonce (Buffalo River), which Sebe cannot appropriate because it is always used by the Xhosa to refer specifically to that very city of King Williams Town which had been definitively excluded from the Ciskei. Bisho is a perfectly legitimate synonym, popularized moreover in a well-known Xhosa song, 'Bisho, My Home', but it is false to assert, as Sebe has done, that it is a more ancient and therefore more valid name than Qonce.[49]

Not wanted on the site are the old villages of Tyutyu, Bhalasi and Skobeni, long established as eyesores and anachronisms by Ciskeian planners. In March 1987, South Africa gave President Sebe a 'free gift' of R6.1 million to remove the three communities so as to permit expansion of Bisho's élite housing projects. Within six months more than 1,000 Tyutyu residents had been removed with very little in the way of compensation. They told the press that 'their forebears were buried at Tyutyu and they would like to be buried next to them according to the Xhosa custom'.[50] Clearly, however, such unreasonable customs cannot form part of the 'traditional' heritage of the new Ciskei.

'Nation' (*isizwe*) and 'nationhood' (*ubuzwe*) are the most overworked words in the Ciskeian political vocabulary, as exemplified in the following example of Presidential rhetoric:

> The spirit of nationalism which does not waver among Ciskeians was created by the bravery and hardships experienced by the heroes of the wars which were fought to keep the Ciskei a free country, where all people would share equally in the pride of their nationhood.[51]

The fallen heroes were often invoked to give Ciskei nationhood some sort of time-depth, although, as we have seen, they belong to the Rharhabe rather than to the Ciskeian past. Ciskeian military bases have been named after Sandile and Jongumsobomvu (Maqoma). The word 'nation' figures in the title Ikrwela leSizwe (Sword of the Nation), a 'crack Ciskeian anti-terrorist squad' presented with their wings at Ntaba kaNdoda, comprising men of whom President Sebe remarked, 'one man was capable of facing 500 men without wasting bullets'.[52] The Intsika yeSizwe (Pillar of the Nation) is a youth movement modelled on the Malawi Young Pioneers movement and trained with Israeli and South African Defence Force assistance. Its aim is to:

bring the cultural and historic heritage of the Ciskei to the notice of Ciskeian youth, provide useful and profitable employment to school leavers, serve the territory and the community, and stimulate in youth a sense of discipline, patriotism, nationalism, and a love of the soil.[53]

Its director, Reverend Matabese, said that his movement would be 'run on military lines' with the emphasis on drawing urban youth into a rural environment. The urban youth, who hate the Ciskei government, found the idea completely unattractive, however, and a completely new youth scheme, with higher rates of pay, is now envisaged.[54] The symbolism of national consciousness has found further expression on the bus fleets of the monopolistic parastatal Ciskeian Transport Corporation, which sports the logo 'Zezama-Ciskei Amahle', officially translated as 'We belong to the beautiful Ciskeians', which sentiment the Managing Director assured the public represented the philosophy of the bus company.[55] The bloody bus boycotts of late 1983 adequately demonstrated the feelings of the beautiful Ciskeians towards their patriotic bus company.

Napoleon is reputed to have said that men are led by toys. President Sebe is both an ardent exponent and an eminent example of this dictum. The President bought himself a R2 million Westwind 2 jet which no airfield in his statelet could handle and no Ciskeian could fly. Soon afterwards the President signed a R25 million contract with a Panamanian-registered company to build a new 'international airport' for Bisho. This airport is now complete. It can take a Boeing 747, which makes it larger than the South African airport in nearby East London, but by the end of 1987 nothing larger than light planes and helicopters had used its 2.5 kilometre runway. Although it costs R2.5 million a year to maintain this white elephant, one cannot travel from the Ciskei's capital to the airport without crossing South African territory.[56]

While the commuters of Mdantsane lost lives trying to stop a 10 cent increase in bus fares, the President negotiated the sale of a R75,000 Daimler and ordered 13 new BMWs for his cabinet, the existing ones being 'nearly three years old'. In addition to his official palace, the President possesses as personal property a R1 million private home at Bisho. This was paid for by compulsory contributions of between R5 and R10 from every Ciskeian citizen. He also owns a seaside cottage and a farm. Apart from the two hundred or so agricultural labourers who receive 'training' on this farm, the full-time farm labourers' salaries are also paid by the Ciskeian government. When some of these excesses were exposed by the disgruntled Lent Maqoma, the National Assembly immediately passed legislation validating all government expenditure on Sebe's private residences.[57] On the more spiritual plane, the erstwhile commoner Sebe awarded himself a chieftainship, while the erstwhile non-matriculant (Sebe never finished school) also had himself awarded an LlD (Doctorate in Law) from the University of Fort Hare.[58] Thus plain 'Mr Sebe' has become 'the Honourable Chief Dr Sebe'.

What is good for Sebe must of course be good for the Ciskei. So now there is the Order of Ntaba kaNdoda, 'awarded only to those general officers and brigadiers of the Ciskei Department of State Security and other armed forces for exceptional meritorious services of major military importance'.[59] First recipient was L.L.W. Sebe, who, incidentally, is also a full general and commands the Ciskei Defence Force.[60] For deeds of lesser merit, there is the Sandile medal. L.L.W. Sebe has one of those as well. For 'loyal and dedicated employees of the Ciskei Government' there is the Order of the Blue Crane. This too adorns the President's lapel.[61] All these decorations and medals are awarded at special ceremonies held on Ntaba kaNdoda.

The quest for a 'Ciskeian' culture extends even to feminine apparel. Beads and bare breasts have official approval as never before. A 'Miss Traditional Ciskei' beauty contest forms part of the annual Independence Celebrations.[62] Although the Ciskei is arguably the most successfully missionized of all South Africa's homelands, its President took a bevy of bare-breasted dancers to represent its 'culture' at an Israeli trade exhibition in 1983.[63] Still to come is the 50,000 hectare, R12 million Lennox Sebe Game Reserve and a R4 million cultural museum at Ntaba kaNdoda, complete with an 'outdoor kraal museum' and a craft centre at which such obsolete trades as beadwork, stick-carving and the manufacture of beer-strainers will be encouraged. Last but not least, the Ciskei has acquired its own hangman, who will execute his duties at the Ciskei's new, fully equipped central prison.[64]

CONCLUSION

This article recognizes the existence of ethnic consciousness as a real phenomenon which cannot be denied or otherwise wished away. Where there is competition for power or for material resources, and where competing factions are able to stake out their claims in ethnic terms, such rival factions might seize on almost any aspect of language, history, culture or physical type and turn it into the criterion of ethnic difference. In the region now known as the Ciskei, the historical conflict between the Rharhabe and the Mfengu had created an ethnic consciousness which was reinforced by the material advantages which the Mfengu had achieved and enjoyed. When South Africa's new apartheid policy created the opportunity for the Rharhabe to challenge the material dominance of the Mfengu, they mobilized under the leadership of Lennox Sebe and were able to gain political power by the manipulation of 'homeland' structures.

Once in power, however, it suited Sebe to defuse the ethnic situation. This turned out to be easy. Once loyalty to Lennox Sebe replaced loyalty to one's ethnic group as the main avenue to power and wealth, ethnic association became less important and ethnic feeling correspondingly less bitter. But once he had abandoned his ethnic stance, Sebe faced a crisis of legitimacy. He required a hegemonic ideology which would win the support of Ciskeian subjects against the rival claims of older ethnicities, such as that of the Rharhabe royal house, the pan-Xhosa nationalism as proposed by K.D. Matanzima of the Transkei, and the broader South African revolutionary nationalism embraced, for example, by students, workers, bus boycotters and the ANC. Sebe chose an ideology of 'Ciskeian nationalism' thus committing himself to the invention of a wholly novel and therefore wholly bogus ethnicity.

How effective has this programme of pseudo-ethnicity been? There are those who argue that, given time, these admittedly artificial signs and symbols will acquire an aura of tradition. Others argue that whereas, for example, Chief Gatsha Buthelezi in KwaZulu can call on a potent feeling of national pride and military achievement, Sebe's appeals to a Ciskeian national consciousness will not take root because they refer to something which is simply not there. I tend to the second conclusion. It has been the failure of the concept of Ciskeian nationhood to capture, to even the slightest extent, the imagination and support of the ordinary person which drove the Ciskeian regime to an ever increasing dependence on brute repression in the form of Charles Sebe and the Ciskei Central Intelligence Service.

Between 1985 and 1988, however, we have seen a decreasing emphasis on Ciskeian ethnicity and a greater emphasis on an all-out espousal of consumerism and self-indulgence thinly disguised as a commitment to Free Enterprise.[65] New tax laws, abolishing company tax and limiting personal tax to a mere 15 per cent, have turned the Ciskei into a self-proclaimed tax-haven for the rich. Good agricultural land has been given away at R26 per hectare to Sebe's favourites.[66] The Ciskei People's Development Bank has given sweetheart loans to the same favourites of Sebe for the acquisition of hotels, garages and trading-stores.[67] And the government's declared intention of 'privatizing' the Ciskei's many parastatals can only add more honey to the honey-pot.

The *nouveau riche* city of Bisho is at least a faithful reflection of the society which gave it birth. Inside its rapidly expanding shopping arcades the Ciskeian élite contemplate the purchase of jacuzzis and three-piece suits. Outside, prestigious housing developments have already over-run the village of Tyutyu and stand poised to attack the next target, Bhalasi. Across the road, hundreds of glassy-eyed civil servants pop coils of one Rand coins into flashing slot machines at the Amatola Sun casino.

But some things never change. Lennox Sebe has used the Transkei's 1987 attack on his palace to whip up a little pro-Ciskei sentiment. Sick Transkeians were expelled from Ciskeian hospital beds.[68] A new 'Ciskei Development and Security Fund' was started for purposes which have never been specified. 'Voluntary donations' of between R10 and R20 per Ciskeian and R500 per business have been levied, and those foolish enough not to volunteer have lost their pensions or their cattle or their business licences.[69] Through this patriotic exercise R200,000 was amassed. In March 1987, President Sebe mounted yet another customary ceremony at the Bisho Independence Stadium. The time had come for the sixteen government departments to present their contributions to the new fund. As each delegation stepped forward to hand over its cheque, dancers ululated and sang traditional songs.[70]

EDITORS' NOTE

a   This article was written when L. Sebe was still incumbent ruler of the Ciskei. He was toppled by a 'coup' in 1990, out of which Brigadier O. Gqozo emerged as ruler for a brief and bloody period. The Ciskei is now being reincorporated into South Africa.

NOTES

1   It cannot be expected that an article of this nature dealing with a territory such as the Ciskei can be too explicit about stating its sources. I hope, however, that by supplying sources for the statistical material and supporting documentation for some of the more surprising data I have managed to give credibility to the whole.

2   There is no compact or trustworthy account of the Ciskei today. A great deal of unevenly presented raw material is to be found in the following very different books: University of Fort Hare, *The Ciskei – A Bantu Homeland* (Fort Hare, 1971); N. Charton (ed.), *Ciskei* (London, 1980); Surplus People Project, *Forced Removals in South Africa*, vol. II, *The Eastern Cape* (Cape Town and Pietermaritzburg, 1983); G. Quail *et al.*, *Report of the Ciskei Commission* (Pretoria, 1980). For a useful and incisive journalistic portrait of the Ciskei, see J. Lelyveld, *Move Your Shadow: South Africa, Black and White* (New York, 1985), 155–84.

3   Quail, *Report*, 19; Surplus People Project, *Forced Removals*, 19.

4   Quail, *Report*, 15.

5   Surplus People Project, *Forced Removals*, 41, 67.

6   Surplus People Project, *Forced Removals*, 336–8.

7   J.B. Peires, *The House of Phalo* (Johannesburg, 1981), ch. 9.

8   C. Bundy, *The Rise and Fall of the South African Peasantry* (London, 1979).

9   P. Walshe, *The Rise of African Nationalism in South Africa* (Berkeley, CA, 1971), ch. 1.

10   T. Lodge, *Black Politics in South Africa since 1945* (London, 1983), 27, 55–8, 348–9.

11   'Flashpoint: East London', *South African Labour Bulletin*, 7, special issue (February, 1982), 1–92.

12   Surplus People Project, *Forced Removals*, 3.

13   For the early constitutional development of the Ciskei, see C.C.S. Holdt, 'Constitutional Development', in University of Fort Hare, *The Ciskei – A Bantu Homeland*. For the later period, N. Charton and G.R. kaTywakadi, 'Ciskeian Political Parties', in Charton, *Ciskei*.

14   On the referendum, see especially *Work in Progress* (Johannesburg), 18 June 1981.

15   For the most recent events in the Ciskei–East London area, see

N. Haysom, 'Ruling with the Whip', Occasional Paper 5, Centre for Applied Legal Studies, University of the Witwatersrand, Johannesburg (1983).

16 *Eastern Province Herald*, 5 December 1985. It is impossible to give further details of these fascinating events here, but see for example *Sunday Star*, 18 August 1985, and the *Weekly Mail*, 16 July 1987.

17 These events were covered in detail in the local press. See for example *Daily Dispatch*, 30 September 1986, 20 February and 11 April 1987.

18 This section and the next are based on R.A. Moyer, 'Some Current Manifestations of Early Mfengu History', Institute of Commonwealth Studies, Collected Seminar Papers on the Societies of Southern Africa, vol. 3 (1971–2), and C.W. Manona, 'Ethnic Relations in the Ciskei', in Charton, *Ciskei*.

19 Charton and kaTywakadi, 'Ciskeian Political Parties', 130.

20 This paragraph is based on Surplus People Project, *Forced Removals*, 33–8, 110–11, 118–19.

21 On the causes of forced relocation in the Ciskei, see Surplus People Project, *Forced Removals*, 99–111.

22 On the resuscitation of the Rharhabe chieftainships, see J.B. Peires, 'Continuity and Change in Ciskei Chieftainship', Institute of Commonwealth Studies, Collected Seminar Papers on the Societies of Southern Africa, vol. 8 (1976–7).

23 Quoted in Peires, 'Continuity', 137.

24 Surplus People Project, *Forced Removals*, 72.

25 Manona, 'Ethnic Relations', 117.

26 Information on the Maqoma and Burns-Ncamashe chieftainships derived from private sources.

27 On Sebe's initial claims see Peires, 'Continuity', 138–9. Sebe's allegedly illegitimate birth was common gossip throughout the Ciskei after Charles Sebe was detained.

28 S. Bekker *et al.*, 'Tsweletswele', Institute of Social and Economic Research Development Studies Working Papers, no. 13 (Grahamstown, 1983), 11–12.

29 Surplus People Project, *Forced Removals*, 119; 89–90 for attitude of Chief Njokweni of Peddie towards resettlement.

30 *Eastern Province Herald*, 6 October 1978.

31 Information on the Rharhabe Paramountcy from a former Ciskeian now resident in the Transkei. There is a brief and incomplete account in Peires, 'Continuity', 139.

32 Matanzima's wish to amalgamate the Ciskei with the Transkei has often been expressed. See for example *Daily Dispatch*, 28 October 1976; *Star*, 24 March 1977. For the Transkei-sponsored court cases against Ciskei independence, see *Star*, 29 September 1981.

33 *The Mercury* (King Williams Town), 22 April 1982.

34 *Rand Daily Mail*, 29 December 1980.

35 *The Mercury*, 15 April 1982.

36 *Umthombo* (Zwelitsha), June 1978. *Umthombo* is published by the Ciskei Department of Information.

37 S.E.K. Mqhayi, 'Intaba kaNdoda', in Mqhayi, *Ityala lama Wele* (1914; 7th edn, Lovedale, 1931), 87.

38 Peires, *House of Phalo*, 39–40.

39 For the building and the costs at Ntaba kaNdoda, see *Rand Daily Mail*, 17 August 1981; *Daily Dispatch*, 14 January 1981.

40 Institute of Race Relations, *Annual Survey of Race Relations*, vol. 33 (Johannesburg, 1979), 326.

41 *Daily Dispatch*, 4 April 1983.

42 Speech by L. Sebe, *Imvo zaBantsundu* (King Williams Town), 16 April 1982, for example noted that: 'The holy Temple of the Nation erected at Ntaba kaNdoda is visible and conclusive witness of the faith and pride of the Ciskeian nation.'

43 *Golden City Press*, 27 February 1983.

44 *Umthombo*, June 1978.

45 *Eastern Province Herald*, 5 December 1985.

46 D. Mickleburgh, 'Maqoma Goes Home', *Flying Springbok* (SA Airways magazine), August 1983, is a vivid if silly description. See also M.G. Whisson and C.W. Manona, 'Maqoma and Ciskeian Politics Today' in Charton, *Ciskei*.

47 *Sunday Times* (Johannesburg), 17 June 1979: *Eastern Province Herald*, 4 August 1987.

48 *Daily Dispatch*, 28 May 1981. For Bisho, see also Institute of Race Relations, *Annual Survey of Race Relations*, vol. 35 (Johannesburg, 1981), 302.

49 For the debate on the meaning of 'Bisho', see *Evening Post* (Port Elizabeth), 21 May 1981; *Daily Dispatch*, 11 June 1981.

50 *Daily Dispatch*, 21 March and 9 May 1987.

51 L. Sebe, quoted in *Imvo* (King Williams Town), 16 April 1982.

52 *Daily Dispatch*, 12 and 25 May 1982.

53 Institute of Race Relations, *Annual Survey of Race Relations*, vol. 34 (Johannesburg, 1980), 402. See also *Daily Dispatch*, 25 February 1980.

54 *Pretoria News*, 28 September 1983.

55 *Daily Dispatch*, 3 December 1982.

56 *Eastern Province Herald*, 30 November 1983, 17 May and 22 June 1984, 21 January 1987. *Weekly Mail*, 16 July 1987.

57 *Daily Dispatch*, 9 May 1984 and 28 July 1987; *Eastern Province Herald*, 4 December 1985 and 4 August 1987.

58 *Eastern Province Herald*, 30 April 1979. Sebe has what is called in South Africa 'JC plus three', that is, a Junior Certificate (two years short of final year) and a three-year course at a teacher training college. The Transkei's former Prime Minister George Matanzima once accused Sebe of having failed his final examinations.

59 *Daily Dispatch*, 26 November 1981.

60 *Daily Dispatch*, 23 February 1982.

62 *Daily Dispatch*, 3 December 1983.

63 *Eastern Province Herald*, 30 November 1983.

64 *Weekend Post* (Port Elizabeth), 20 and 27 June 1986.

65 Much of the information in this paragraph is derived from the eulogistic pages of T. Bates's glossy brochure, 'The Republic of Ciskei'

(Durban and Bisho, 1987), subtitled '*The* Tax Paradise of Southern Africa'.

66 The land in question was originally purchased by the South African government for between R350 and R1,000 per hectare. *Daily Dispatch*, 6 June 1987.

67 *Daily Dispatch*, 20 June and 8 September 1987.

68 *Daily Dispatch*, 29 January, 3 February and 28 March 1987.

69 *City Press*, 26 April 1987.

70 *Daily Dispatch*, 13 March 1987.

GLOSSARY

African: term usually applied to describe Bantu-speaking indigenous peoples of Southern Africa.

Afrikaner: 'white' speakers of Afrikaans (a language derived principally from Dutch), many of whom are – or claim to be – the descendants of early settlers at the Cape.

ANC: the African National Congress, founded in 1912, is the oldest and most influential of the liberation movements. Under the leadership of Nelson Mandela, the ANC came to power in South Africa in 1994.

articulation: theoretical concept developed particularly in Marxist anthropology. Refers to the interlocking relationships that exist when 'pre capitalist' and 'capitalist' forms of production meet.

Asian/Indian: term used to describe the descendants of immigrants from the Indian subcontinent, many of whom were originally recruited in the 1860s as indentured labourers for the sugar plantations of Natal.

Bambatha: the Bambatha rebellion of 1906 arose out of resistance in Zululand to the imposition by the colonial authorities of a poll tax. This act of defiance has been seen as perhaps the last expression of armed 'primary resistance' to white colonial rule in South Africa. The revolt was ruthlessly crushed by the government forces; as many as 4,000 Africans were killed during its suppression, along with Chief Bambatha himself.

Bantustan: the term applied in the 1950s to areas reserved for African occupation (hence 'reserves'). Many of these had existed since the nineteenth century and included the heartlands of some old African chiefdoms. The Nationalist government intended to extend and consolidate them into ten units, pushing the total area to over 13 per cent of the total land surface. They were given a form of self-rule which was later intended to become political independence. 'Bantustan', initially used by H.F. Verwoerd, was taken up by the opposition critical of the balkanization of the country, as a disparaging term for these mini- and micro-states or 'homelands'.

GLOSSARY

betterment planning: refers to policies pursued by the government from the 1930s to control patterns of land usage in the African reserves and improve the productivity of agriculture in the reserves.

'black spots': pertains to pockets of land occupied by blacks (often with freehold tenure) and surrounded by officially designated 'white' land.

Broederbond: the Afrikaner Broederbond ('League of Brothers'), founded shortly after the First World War, was a secretive society devoted to the cultural and political welfare of the Afrikaner people. The Broederbond was a major influence on government policy, especially during the apartheid era.

chief/chiefdom: hereditary or nominated individuals who exercise political and social jurisdiction over their 'tribal' subjects.

colour bar: term used to describe discriminatory legislative mechanisms (especially in connection with employment) designed to secure privileges for one or more statutorily defined racial groups.

'coloured': a highly unspecific (and controversial) ethnic category used to describe the 'mixed race' descendants of white settlers, slaves and the indigenous peoples of Southern Africa.

'comrades': term used to describe militant young supporters of the African National Congress.

Dutch Reformed Church (DRC): refers collectively to the umbrella church (embracing three separate churches) to which the majority of Afrikaners have historically belonged. The DRC is Calvinist in orientation and has played a leading role in the formulation of apartheid ideology.

'Ethiopianism': term used to describe African churches which separated from white-controlled mission churches in the nineteenth century. More broadly, Ethiopianism refers to political and spiritual traditions of African pride and independence.

Fusion: term used to describe the political merger in 1933–4 between the governing National Party under J.B.M. Hertzog and the opposition South African Party under J.C. Smuts.

Glen Grey: district of the Eastern Cape. Also refers to a legislative act (1894) named after the district which many interpret as a precursor of segregationist policies in regard to land and labour.

hegemony/hegemonic: theoretical term (associated particularly with the writings of Antonio Gramsci) denoting the overwhelming political and/or ideological dominance of one social class or political group over society as a whole.

Herenigde Nasionale Party: Reunited National Party. The official name of the party that came to power in 1948 under the leadership of Dr D.F. Malan. The HNP later became known simply as the NP or National Party.

Het Volk: political party (meaning 'The People') formed in the Transvaal in 1905 under the leadership of General Louis Botha. The party was committed to reconciliation between Boers and Britons in the aftermath of the South African War and played an important role in bringing about Union in 1910.

homelands: see Bantustan.

ICU: the Industrial and Commercial Workers' Union, founded in Cape Town in 1919 by Clements Kadalie, gathered many adherents among African workers, farm labourers and peasants. Reached the height of its influence in the mid- to late 1920s.

influx control: bureaucratic and legal mechanisms designed to restrict and control processes of African urbanization as well as access to the labour market.

Inkatha: political and cultural movement, re-established in 1975 by Chief Mangosuthu Buthelezi, and dedicated to the promotion of Zulu nationalism.

'insiders': describes those Africans possessing (qualified) residential rights in officially designated 'white' cities.

Khoisan: refers both to 'Bushmen' and 'Hottentots'. The term is preferred by many anthropologists and historians because of its non-derogatory connotations.

KwaNdebele: one of the smallest and least viable of the so-called self-governing 'homelands' situated north-east of Pretoria and designated as the self governing territory of the 'South Ndebele'.

labour-tenancy: system whereby farm labourers work for fixed periods (typically 90 or 180 days) for landowners; for the remainder of the year they are permitted to farm land which they occupy but do not own.

Lebowa: so-called self-governing territory of the 'Pedi' or 'North Sotho' and situated in the eastern Transvaal.

location: term describing urban (and sometimes rural) residential area officially designated for African occupation.

Lovedale: mission station founded in the eastern Cape in 1824. Lovedale School, established in 1841, was responsible for the formal education of several generations of African leaders.

merchant capital: theoretical term pertaining to phase of capitalist development in which profits are generated through processes of exchange rather than production.

Mfecane: term used to describe the massive upheaval and dispersion of African peoples throughout Southern Africa in the 1820s and 1830s, principally as a result of the rise and consolidation of the Zulu kingdom in Natal.

mode(s) of production: theoretical term, now seldom used, which was

287

coined to express the concept of a production system and its associated form of social organization.

pass laws: network of legislation designed to control and restrict the movement of African labour into towns and cities.

patriarchy: system whereby men attain and preserve positions of social, cultural and economic power over women and junior males.

pre-capitalist: theoretical term pertaining to societies in which non-capitalist forms of production predominate.

proletarianization: theoretical term describing the process whereby men and women are left with nothing to sell but their labour power. This social division of labour relates specifically to the rise of factory production under conditions of capitalism.

QwaQwa: the smallest of the so-called self-governing 'homelands', situated on the eastern borders of the Orange Free State and designated as the self-governing territory of the 'South Sotho'.

rehabilitation: see 'betterment'.

reserves: see Bantustan.

separate development: an ideological euphemism for apartheid.

sjambok: whip made from animal hide. Often associated with beatings administered by white farmers to their black servants and labourers.

social Darwinism: term used to describe philosophies of political and/or racial hierarchy based on the application of (especially) Darwinian theories of evolutionary struggle to conditions of human social existence.

South African Party (SAP): established on a countrywide basis after Union in 1910, it was the ruling party in the all-white South African parliament until 1924 under Generals L. Botha and J.C. Smuts. It was a vehicle for moderate Afrikaner opinion, as well as many English-speakers, anxious to establish conciliation and white unity.

Union: following the Act of Union in 1909, the ex-British colonies of the Cape and Natal merged with the defeated Afrikaner republics of Transvaal and the Orange Free State to form the self-governing Union of South Africa.

United Democratic Front: mass political organization formed in 1983. The UDF was generally supportive of the policies of the then-banned African National Congress and did much to popularize opposition to apartheid in the 1980s.

Volk: Afrikaans (and German) word approximating to 'people' or 'nation'.

Witwatersrand: region centring on Johannesburg around which much of the mining and industrial capacity of South Africa is concentrated.